Set a study plan
and a goal!

_____'s study plan for Grammar Gateway Basic

Write your goal and what you hope to accomplish.

I'll finish this book by _____ / _____ / _____.

My goal is to _____.

Choose a study plan.

☐ within a month : 4 units a day

☐ within two months : 2 units a day

☐ within _____ : _____units a day

Cross out units when you finish them. Review units that were difficult for you.

	2	3	4	5	6	7	8	9	10	11	12	13	14	15	16	17	18	19	20
21	22	23	24	25	26	27	28	29	30	31	32	33	34	35	36	37	38	39	40
41	42	43	44	45	46	47	48	49	50	51	52	53	54	55	56	57	58	59	60
61	62	63	64	65	66	67	68	69	70	71	72	73	74	75	76	77	78	79	80
81	82	83	84	85	86	87	88	89	90	91	92	93	94	95	96	97	98	99	100

|H|A|C|K|E|R|S|

Grammar Gateway
Basic

Hackers Language
Research Institute

GRAMMAR GATEWAY
BASIC

PREFACE

Grammar Gateway Basic is . . .

a basic grammar book for beginners that will help strengthen your English skills.

The book has 100 units covering essential grammar points. The units are based on the observation and analysis of the way native English speakers write and speak. Each unit is made up of two pages. On the left is an easy grammar lesson, and on the right are activities to practice the grammar points you just learned. For beginners of English, the book provides easy explanations and a variety of illustrations to make learning more fun. Most important of all, the examples and various practice questions contain sentences that are used in real life. This allows you not only to learn basic grammar but to also improve your speaking and writing skills.

Grammar Gateway Basic will make English less difficult and more accessible than ever before. We hope that this book will become a stepping stone on the path that leads to your success.

CONTENTS

Modal Verbs

Passive

Questions

-ing and to . . .

Nouns and Pronouns

CONTENTS

Quantity

Adjectives and Adverbs

Prepositions and Phrasal Verbs

Conjunctions and Clauses

THE FEATURES OF THE BOOK

01.
An easy-to-understand grammar book!

- Simple terms and clear explanations
- Charts and graphs that explain grammar points

02.
A fun way to learn grammar!

- Lively illustrations that make learning more enjoyable and more effective
- A variety of practice questions to keep you interested

03.
An effective tool for self-study!

- One unit comprised of two pages to help you absorb and complete each unit easily
- A study schedule that allows you to check your progress and finish the book on your own

04.
A grammar book to improve speaking and writing!

- Examples from real life that you can apply in everyday conversation and writing
- Practice activities where you complete sentences and conversations to help you develop your speaking and writing skills

THE STRUCTURE OF THE BOOK

MP3 file notes

You can listen to and follow along the example sentences and practice questions with the MP3 files provided at HackersIngang.com.

Illustrations

The fun and lively illustrations help you learn each unit more effectively.

Grammar lessons + Charts/Graphs

The grammar lessons are explained with easy terms, and the charts/graphs help you understand the lessons at a glance.

Example sentences

The example sentences help you understand how grammar points are used.

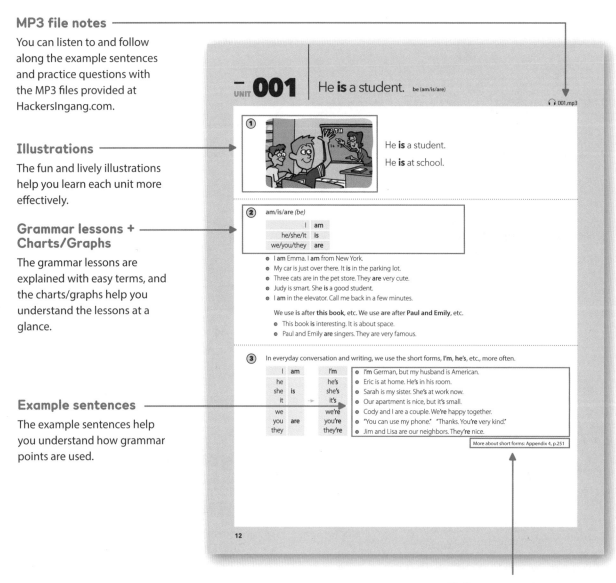

Reference notes

The notes guide you to the pages that give you further understanding of what you learned.

PRACTICE

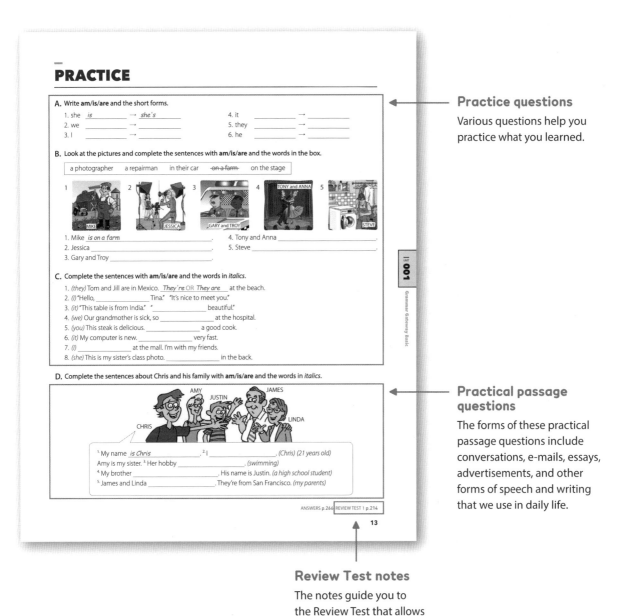

A. Write **am/is/are** and the short forms.

1. she _is_ → _she's_
2. we _____ → _____
3. I _____ → _____
4. it _____ → _____
5. they _____ → _____
6. he _____ → _____

B. Look at the pictures and complete the sentences with **am/is/are** and the words in the box.

| a photographer   a repairman   in their car   ~~on a farm~~   on the stage |

1 MIKE 2 JESSICA 3 GARY and TROY 4 TONY and ANNA 5 STEVE

1. Mike _is on a farm_ .
2. Jessica _____ .
3. Gary and Troy _____ .
4. Tony and Anna _____ .
5. Steve _____ .

C. Complete the sentences with **am/is/are** and the words in *italics*.

1. *(they)* Tom and Jill are in Mexico. _They're_ OR _They are_ at the beach.
2. *(I)* "Hello, _____ Tina." "It's nice to meet you."
3. *(it)* "This table is from India." " _____ beautiful."
4. *(we)* Our grandmother is sick, so _____ at the hospital.
5. *(you)* This steak is delicious. _____ a good cook.
6. *(it)* My computer is new. _____ very fast.
7. *(I)* _____ at the mall. I'm with my friends.
8. *(she)* This is my sister's class photo. _____ in the back.

D. Complete the sentences about Chris and his family with **am/is/are** and the words in *italics*.

AMY JUSTIN JAMES CHRIS LINDA

[1] My name _is Chris_ . [2] I _____ . *(Chris) (21 years old)*
Amy is my sister. [3] Her hobby _____ . *(swimming)*
[4] My brother _____ . His name is Justin. *(a high school student)*
[5] James and Linda _____ . They're from San Francisco. *(my parents)*

ANSWERS p.266 REVIEW TEST 1 p.214

13

Practice questions

Various questions help you practice what you learned.

Practical passage questions

The forms of these practical passage questions include conversations, e-mails, essays, advertisements, and other forms of speech and writing that we use in daily life.

Review Test notes

The notes guide you to the Review Test that allows you to review the units comprehensively.

UNIT 001
Grammar Gateway Basic

①

He **is** a student.

He **is** at school.

---

② **am/is/are** *(be)*

I	am
he/she/it	is
we/you/they	are

- I **am** Emma. I **am** from New York.
- My car is just over there. It **is** in the parking lot.
- Three cats are in the pet store. They **are** very cute.
- Judy is smart. She **is** a good student.
- I **am** in the elevator. Call me back in a few minutes.

We use **is** after **this book**, etc. We use **are** after **Paul and Emily**, etc.

- This book **is** interesting. It is about space.
- Paul and Emily **are** singers. They are very famous.

---

③ In everyday conversation and writing, we use the short forms, **I'm**, **he's**, etc., more often.

I	am		I'm
he			he's
she	is		she's
it		→	it's
we			we're
you	are		you're
they			they're

- I'm German, but my husband is American.
- Eric is at home. He's in his room.
- Sarah is my sister. She's at work now.
- Our apartment is nice, but it's small.
- Cody and I are a couple. We're happy together.
- "You can use my phone." "Thanks. You're very kind."
- Jim and Lisa are our neighbors. They're nice.

More about short forms: Appendix 4, p.251

12

PRACTICE

A. Write **am/is/are** and the short forms.

1. she _is_ → _she's_
2. we _____ → _____
3. I _____ → _____

4. it _____ → _____
5. they _____ → _____
6. he _____ → _____

B. Look at the pictures and complete the sentences with **am/is/are** and the words in the box.

| a photographer | a repairman | in their car | ~~on a farm~~ | on the stage |

1. Mike _is on a farm_ .
2. Jessica _____ .
3. Gary and Troy _____ .
4. Tony and Anna _____ .
5. Steve _____ .

C. Complete the sentences with **am/is/are** and the words in *italics*.

1. *(they)* Tom and Jill are in Mexico. _They're OR They are_ at the beach.
2. *(I)* "Hello, _____ Tina." "It's nice to meet you."
3. *(it)* "This table is from India." "_____ beautiful."
4. *(we)* Our grandmother is sick, so _____ at the hospital.
5. *(you)* This steak is delicious. _____ a good cook.
6. *(it)* My computer is new. _____ very fast.
7. *(I)* _____ at the mall. I'm with my friends.
8. *(she)* This is my sister's class photo. _____ in the back.

D. Complete the sentences about Chris and his family with **am/is/are** and the words in *italics*.

1. My name _is Chris_ . 2. I _____ . *(Chris) (21 years old)*
Amy is my sister. 3. Her hobby _____ . *(swimming)*
4. My brother _____ . His name is Justin. *(a high school student)*
5. James and Linda _____ . They're from San Francisco. *(my parents)*

ANSWERS p.266, REVIEW TEST 1 p.214

He **is not** hungry.

be *negative* (**am/is/are not**)

🎧 002.mp3

①

I'm full.

He **is** full.

NEGATIVE He **is not** hungry.

---

② **am/is/are** + **not** *(be negative)*

			NEGATIVE			
I	**am**	→	I	**am**	
he/she/it	**is**		he/she/it	**is**	**not**
we/you/they	**are**		we/you/they	**are**	

- I **am not** from Japan. I'm Korean.
- "The dress **is not** in the closet." "Oh, it's in the washing machine."
- We **are not** busy. Let's watch a movie together.
- I **am not** at school now. Come and see me at the station.
- Carla **is not** in her office. She's out for lunch.
- "These apples **are not** expensive." "Good! Let's get some."

---

③ In everyday conversation and writing, we use the short forms, **I'm not**, **he's not**, etc., more often.

I	**am not**		**I'm not**
he			he**'s not** / he **isn't**
she	**is not**	→	she**'s not** / she **isn't**
it			it**'s not** / it **isn't**
we			we**'re not** / we **aren't**
you	**are not**		you**'re not** / you **aren't**
they			they**'re not** / they **aren't**

- I**'m not** tall, but I'm good at basketball.
- "Where is John?" "He**'s not** here."
- We**'re not** brothers. We're cousins.
- Today **isn't** Saturday. It's Sunday.
- Don't worry. You**'re not** late.
- "Those boxes are big." "Yes, but they **aren't** heavy."

Note that **I'm not** is the only short form of **I am not**.

- **I'm not** sleepy. I'm just bored.

14

PRACTICE

A. Complete the sentences with **am/is/are not** and the words in *italics*.

1. *(I)* _I'm not OR I am not_ an adult. I'm only 15 years old.
2. *(this water)* _____ cold. It's warm.
3. *(you)* It's already 8 a.m. and _____ ready for school. Hurry up!
4. *(Mark)* _____ at the restaurant. He's at the bank.
5. *(we)* It's lunch time, but _____ hungry.
6. *(I)* "Are you OK?" "Don't worry. _____ sick anymore."
7. *(Sharon)* _____ my best friend. We're not close.
8. *(my books)* _____ in my room. I can't find them.

B. Clara is giving you the wrong information. Give her the correct information with **am/is/are not**.

CLARA

1. Her name is Diane.	_Her name isn't Diane_ OR _Her name is not Diane_ . It's Kate.
2. Richard is 23 years old.	_____ . He's 25 years old.
3. Sally and Alex are from Brazil.	_____ . They're from Cuba.
4. You are a nurse.	_____ . I'm a doctor.
5. Tomorrow is Thursday.	_____ . It's Friday.

C. Write the short forms of **am/is/are** or **am/is/are not**.

1. Tara is in France, but she _'s not OR isn't_ in Paris.
2. Cindy and Luke aren't here. They _____ at the lake.
3. We're not at the airport. We _____ still in the taxi.
4. I _____ sorry I'm late. Let's start the meeting.
5. Moscow isn't a country. It _____ a city.
6. "Do you want some juice?" "No, thanks. I _____ thirsty."
7. My office _____ far from home. It's only three blocks away.
8. I _____ a professional musician, but I can play the guitar well.

D. The following information is about Hawaii. Complete the sentences with **am/is/are** or **am/is/are not**.

Welcome to Hawaii

1. Hawaii _is_ a beautiful island.
The weather is usually warm all year.
2. It _____ cold, even in December.
3. Beautiful beaches _____ in Hawaii too.
4. They _____ close to the airport, but they are popular.
Please enjoy your stay here.

ANSWERS p.266, REVIEW TEST 1 p.214

🎧 003.mp3

① Are you from China?

Yes, I am.

She is from China.

QUESTION **Is she** from China?

---

② **Am/Is/Are ...?** *(be questions)*

We use **am/is/are** before **I/he/we**/etc. *(subjects)* in questions.

			QUESTIONS	
I	am		Am	I ...?
he/she/it	is	→	Is	he/she/it ...?
we/you/they	are		Are	we/you/they ...?

- Excuse me. **Am I** near Main Street?
- "**Is he** your father?" "No, he's my uncle."
- "**Are we** in the same class?" "Yes. I'm Danny."
- "**Is Diana** in her room?" "No, she's out."
- Your eyes are red. **Are you** tired?
- "**Is it** warm outside?" "Yes. The weather is great."
- "**Are those cookies** good?" "Yes, they're delicious."

---

③ We can give short answers to questions.

Yes,	I	am.		No,	I	'm not.
	he/she/it	is.			he/she/it	's not. / isn't.
	we/you/they	are.			we/you/they	're not. / aren't.

- "**Are you** Pamela?" "**Yes, I am.**" (= Yes, I am Pamela.)
- "**Is the radio** loud?" "**No,** it's **not.**" (= No, it's not loud.)
- "**Is Mom** in the kitchen?" "**Yes,** she **is.**"
- "**Are the guests** here?" "**No,** they **aren't.**"

In this case, we do not use short forms, **I'm**, **he's**, etc., after **Yes**.

- "Are you a musician?" "Yes, I **am.**" (*NOT* Yes, I'm.)
- "It's 7 a.m. Is Jason awake?" "Yes, he **is.**" (*NOT* Yes, he's.)

PRACTICE

A. Write **am/is/are**.

1. "_Are_ you in the bathroom?" "Yes, I am."
2. "_____ your cat white?" "No. It's black."
3. "I'm cold." "I am too. _____ the windows closed?"
4. "Excuse me. _____ I at Gate 6?" "No. Gate 6 is not in this terminal."
5. "_____ our car at the repair shop?" "No. It's in the parking garage."
6. "Are you 33 years old?" "Yes. _____ we the same age?"
7. "_____ you an artist?" "Yes. I'm a painter."

B. Complete the questions with **am/is/are** and the subjects in *italics*.

1. *(Jackie)* "_Is Jackie_ in Europe?" "Yes, she is."
2. *(it)* "_____ cloudy today?" "No. There's not a cloud in the sky."
3. *(I)* I'm here to see Mr. Smith. _____ in the right building?
4. *(you)* I can't hear you well. _____ on the subway?
5. *(today)* "_____ your birthday?" "Yes, it is."
6. *(Joel and Mary)* "_____ at the theater?" "I think so, but I'm not sure."
7. *(she)* "My sister is an actress." "Really? _____ famous?"
8. *(we)* "_____ ready for the meeting?" "Yes. Let's begin."

C. Read the questions and write short answers.

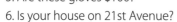

1. Are you and Estevan Mexican?   _Yes, we are_. We're from Mexico City.
2. Are you busy?   _____. I'm free right now.
3. Is Brandon a banker?   _____. He's a doctor.
4. Are you at the train station?   _____. I'm at Dale Station.
5. Are these gloves $100?   _____. They're $80.
6. Is your house on 21st Avenue?   _____. It's on 22nd Street.
7. Is Angela 17 years old?   _____. She's a high school student.

D. Complete the conversation with **am/is/are** and the words in *italics*.

CHRIS: Hi. ¹· _I'm Chris_ OR _I am Chris_. *(I, Chris)*
CHUN: Hi, Chris. ²· _____. *(My name, Chun)*
CHRIS: ³· _____? *(you, from China)*
CHUN: ⁴· Yes, _____. *(I, Chinese)*
       ⁵· _____? *(you, in this class)*
CHRIS: ⁶· Yes, I think _____. *(we, in the same class)*
       It's nice to meet you.

CHRIS

CHUN

ANSWERS p.266, REVIEW TEST 1 p.214

UNIT 004 | She **is making** a cake. *Present progressive (am/is/are + -ing)*

🎧 004.mp3

①

She **is making** a cake.

"is making" is the *present progressive*.

---

② We use **am/is/are + -ing** *(present progressive)* to talk about actions in progress now.

I	am (= 'm)	cooking
he she it	is (= 's)	visiting enjoying looking
we you they	are (= 're)	

- Come home soon. I **am cooking** dinner now.
- Ralph isn't here. He **is visiting** his grandparents in Thailand.
- Thank you for inviting us. We **are enjoying** the party.
- "I**'m looking** for my glasses." "They're on your desk."
- Rebecca **is cleaning** her room right now.
- Jonathan is late for school, but he**'s** still **sleeping**.
- "Look! It**'s snowing**." "Let's go outside."
- Frank and Brenda are in the library. They**'re studying** for an exam.

---

③ The **-ing** spelling is different for **come**, **run**, **lie**, etc.

come → com**ing** take → tak**ing** have → hav**ing**	run → ru**nning** sit → si**tting** shop → sho**pping**	lie → l**ying** tie → t**ying** die → d**ying**

More about **-ing** spelling: Appendix 3, p.248

- Hurry up! The train is **coming**.
- Daniel, you're **running** too fast. Wait for me!
- A couple is **sitting** on the grass, and their dogs are **lying** beside them.
- "Who is in the bathroom?" "Sophie. She's **taking** a shower."

PRACTICE

A. Write the **-ing** form of each verb.

1. ask → *asking*
2. sit → _____
3. write → _____
4. have → _____

5. come → _____
6. shop → _____
7. wait → _____
8. die → _____

B. Look at the pictures and complete the sentences with the words in *italics*.

1  2  3

1. *(listen to music)* He *'s listening to music* OR *is listening to music* _____.
   (play with a ball) The dog *is playing with a ball* _____.
2. *(eat popcorn)* They _____.
   (cry) They _____.
3. *(drive)* She _____.
   (ring) The phone _____.

C. Look at the picture and complete the sentences with the words in the box.

| ~~cross the street~~ | enter the bank | fly in the sky | play the violin | stand at the bus stop |

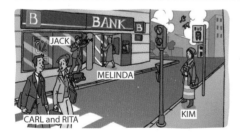

1. Carl and Rita *are crossing the street* _____.
2. Jack _____.
3. Melinda _____.
4. Two birds _____.
5. Kim _____.

D. Complete the sentences with the words in *italics*.

1. *(I, pack)* **I'm packing** OR **I am packing** ____ for my trip. I'm very excited.
2. *(he, have)* "Where's Tim?" "_____ lunch at the cafeteria."
3. *(the children, help)* _____ their dad in the garden. They're planting flowers.
4. *(Mitchell, prepare)* _____ for a meeting. He's busy.
5. *(they, jog)* "Where are Alex and Ed?" "_____ in the park."
6. *(I, tie)* Please stop for a minute. _____ my shoes.
7. *(we, sell)* _____ tickets for the opera. They are $80 each.
8. *(she, get)* Maggie is at the hair salon. _____ a haircut.

ANSWERS p.266, REVIEW TEST 1 p.214

He **is not driving.** *Present progressive negative and questions*

He **is eating** lunch.

NEGATIVE He **is not driving**.

am/is/are not + -ing *(present progressive negative)*

I	**am not** (= 'm not)	**doing** **using** **traveling** **listening**
he she it	**is not** (= 's not / isn't)	
we you they	**are not** (= 're not / aren't)	

- I **am not doing** anything. Let's go out.
- I'm **not using** the chair. You can use it.
- Tom is in Seattle with Ann. He **is not traveling** alone.
- "Jane! I'm talking to you." "I think she **isn't listening**."
- It's cloudy, but it**'s not snowing**.
- We **are not working** today. We're on vacation.
- What's wrong? You**'re not looking** well.
- Where are the children? They **aren't playing** in the garden.

Is it raining?

Yes, it is.

It **is raining**.

QUESTION **Is** it **raining**?

Am/Is/Are + subject + -ing . . .? *(present progressive questions)*

Am	I	
Is	he she it	**speaking ...?** **coming ...?** **taking ...?** **working ...?**
Are	we you they	

- **Am** I **speaking** too quickly?
- Where's Bob? **Is** he **coming** home now?
- "Sarah's not in her room. **Is** she **taking** a walk?" "Yes, she is."
- "**Is** the printer **working**?" "No, it's broken."
- "**Are** we **winning** the game?" "Yes, we are."
- "It smells good! **Are** you **baking** bread?" "Yes. Are you hungry?"
- "**Are** the subways still **running**?" "No. It's already 1 a.m."

We can give short answers to questions.

- "**Is** Stacy **studying** now?" "**Yes, she is.**" (= Yes, she's studying now.)
- "**Are** you **sleeping**?" "**No, I'm not.**" (= No, I'm not sleeping.)

PRACTICE

A. Complete the sentences with the verbs in the box. Write negative sentences if necessary.

enjoy	move	swim	teach	~~watch~~	wear

1. "Can I change the channel?" "Sorry, but I *'m watching* OR *am watching*____ this show."
2. The bus _____ because of the traffic.
3. "Is that board game fun?" "Yes. We _____ it a lot."
4. You _____ your seat belt. That's dangerous.
5. Mr. Taylor _____ Russian. It's not German.
6. I _____ because the water is too deep.

B. Complete the sentences with the words in *italics*.

1. *(Glen, look)* " *Is Glen looking*_____ for me?" "Yes. He's waiting at your office."
2. *(my sister, listen)* I can't study because _____ to the radio in my room.
3. *(you, cry)* "_____? What's wrong?" "Don't worry. I'm OK now."
4. *(I, sing)* "_____ too loudly?" "No. I'm not sleeping anymore, so it's fine."
5. *(you and Vicky, bake)* "_____ something?" "Yes. We're making a blueberry pie."
6. *(the wind, blow)* _____ a lot today. Bring your coat.
7. *(your brothers, ride)* "_____ their bicycles?" "Yes. They're at the park."
8. *(Kyle, wear)* _____ a new suit. He looks great!

C. Read the questions and write short answers.

1. Is Helen exercising at the gym?	*No, she's not* OR *No, she isn't*__. She's at the bookstore.
2. Are you doing your homework?	_____. I'm doing the last question.
3. Are you drawing a picture?	_____. I'm writing a report.
4. Is David taking a shower?	_____. He's cleaning the bathroom.
5. Are the children having breakfast?	_____. They're eating cereal.
6. Is it snowing outside?	_____. Let's make a snowman.

D. Complete the conversation with the words in *italics*. Write negative sentences if necessary.

Waitress: 1. *Are you enjoying*_____ your meal? *(you, enjoy)*

JOE: 2. Yes, _____ pancakes, and they're delicious! *(I, have)*

Waitress: Good. 3. _____ anything. *(you, drink)*
How about some coffee?

JOE: Yes, please. The restaurant is crowded today.

Waitress: 4. Yes, _____ all pies at half price. *(we, sell)*

JOE: That's great! Can I have some apple pie, then?

Waitress

JOE

ANSWERS p.267, REVIEW TEST 1 p.214

They **like** holidays. *Present simple (1)*

①

They **like** holidays.

"**like**" is the *present simple*.

---

② I **visit**, he **sells** . . . *(present simple)*

I/we/you/they	visit live exercise
he/she/it	sells sits snows

- I **visit** my aunt in Miami every year.
- "What is Kevin's job?" "He **sells** cars."
- We **live** in an apartment downtown.
- Sue **sits** next to me in my math class.
- Tom and Ben are at the gym. They **exercise** in the morning.
- It often **snows** here in January.

We add **-s** to the *verb* after **he/she/it**.

- Emily **wants** a computer for her birthday.
- My son usually **eats** toast for breakfast.

---

③ We add **-es** to **teach**, **go**, **study**, etc.

teach → teach**es**	go → go**es**	miss → miss**es**	study → stud**ies**
finish → finish**es**	do → do**es**	pass → pass**es**	fly → fl**ies**

More about **-s/-es** spelling: Appendix 3, p.248

- Professor Kim **teaches** American history.
- This train **goes** to Washington, DC.
- Alice **misses** her friend Alex. He lives in a different city now.
- Larry **studies** fashion design at college.

We use **have** after **I/we/you/they**, and **has** after **he/she/it**.

- I have a dog, and Brian **has** a cat.

PRACTICE

A. Choose the correct one.

1. I ((drive)/ drives) to work every day.
2. The sun is up today. It (shine / shines) in the sky.
3. Kyle and Gary live close to school. They (walk / walks) to school together.
4. We (ride / rides) our bikes on weekends.
5. My cousin likes me a lot. She often (call / calls) me.
6. "My office is in that building." "Oh, you (work / works) for a big company."
7. This jacket is on sale today. It (cost / costs) $30.
8. Scott has short hair. He (get / gets) a haircut every month.

B. Complete the sentences with the verbs in *italics*. Use the *present simple*.

1. *(finish)* Tate _finishes_ work at 7 p.m. and arrives home at 8 p.m.
2. *(carry)* My mom _____ a photo of my family in her wallet.
3. *(do)* Sharon _____ yoga every weekend.
4. *(fly)* My uncle takes many business trips. He often _____ to Dubai.
5. *(have)* Jeremy _____ a new hat. It's a gift from his friend.
6. *(reach)* That plant is very tall. It _____ to the ceiling.
7. *(go)* Ryan watches a lot of movies. He _____ to the theater every Friday.
8. *(pass)* "Look at the subway map. This train _____ Cooper station." "Oh, no! We're on the wrong train."

C. Complete the sentences with the verbs in the box. Use the *present simple*.

| buy | cry | do | have | play | speak | ~~take~~ |

1. William _takes_ a shower every morning.
2. Mark _____ his laundry every Saturday.
3. New York _____ many tall buildings. It's a big city.
4. My parents are from Germany, so I _____ German at home.
5. "Peggy _____ the drums well." "Yes. She's amazing."
6. Babies _____ when they are hungry.
7. Phil and Marco usually _____ bread from a bakery on Larch Street.

D. Complete the conversation with the words in *italics*. Use the *present simple*.

JUSTIN: 1. _I love_ _____ holidays. Especially Christmas! *(I, love)*

LINDA: Yes, you do. 2. _____ it too, but I don't. *(your father, like)*

JUSTIN: Why not, Mom?

LINDA: 3. Well, _____ a party every Christmas. *(we, have)*
4. _____ everything for the party. *(I, prepare)*

JUSTIN: I can help. 5. Dad! _____ our help! *(Mom, want)*

LINDA: Thanks, Justin.

JUSTIN

LINDA

ANSWERS p.267, REVIEW TEST 1 p.214

①

He **drives** to work every morning.

② We use the *present simple* to talk about things that happen regularly.

- I often **meet** my friends on Fridays.
- We **go** to the movies every weekend.
- Jessica **travels** a lot in the summer.
- Mom usually **exercises** at night.
- Naomi **writes** e-mails to her customers sometimes.
- My friend and I **play** golf every day after work.

③ We use the *present simple* to talk about things that are true for a long time.

- Mexicans **speak** Spanish.
- Edward is a lawyer. He **works** for a big company.
- That store **sells** fresh fruit. Let's go there.
- Peter and Nicole are my neighbors. They **live** next door.
- Some students **wear** uniforms at school.
- Ms. White is a professor. She **teaches** science.

④ We use the *present simple* to talk about scientific facts.

- The sun **rises** in the east.
- Leaves **fall** from trees in autumn.
- Rain **comes** from clouds.
- All birds **have** feathers.
- Owls **hunt** at night.

PRACTICE

A. Look at Karen's schedule and complete the sentences.

WEEKDAY SCHEDULE

07:00	wake up
08:00	leave home
09:00	start work
NOON	go to lunch
06:00	finish work

1. Karen _wakes up_____ at 7 o'clock.
2. She _____ at 8 o'clock.
3. She _____ at 9 o'clock.
4. She _____ at noon.
5. She _____ at 6 o'clock.

B. Complete the sentences with the words in *italics*. Use the *present simple*.

1. *(I, walk)* _I walk_____ to my office sometimes.
2. *(Hannah, wash)* _____ her car on weekends.
3. *(the post office, open)* _____ at 9 a.m. every day.
4. *(pandas, eat)* _____ for 12 hours a day.
5. *(my husband and I, make)* _____ dinner together on Fridays.
6. *(water, cover)* _____ about 75 percent of Earth.

C. Complete the sentences with the verbs in the box. Use the *present simple*.

bake	close	collect	~~give~~	jog	like	need

1. Many people _give_____ presents on Christmas.
2. Patrick _____ stamps. It's his hobby.
3. Carl _____ the winter. He hates hot weather.
4. My sister often _____ cookies at home. They taste great.
5. Plants _____ water and sunlight to live.
6. National museums _____ on holidays.
7. Steve is very healthy. He _____ every morning.

D. The following information is about the Amazon rainforest. Complete the sentences with the verbs in the box using the *present simple*.

cut	have	hunt	live	need	~~rain~~

The Amazon rainforest

The Amazon rainforest is in South America.
1. It _rains_____ a lot there in the summer.
2. The Amazon rainforest _____ millions of trees.
3. Also, many animals _____ in the rainforest.
They are all important to the global environment.
4. However, some people _____ down the trees.
5. They _____ the animals too.
6. So the rainforest _____ our protection.

ANSWERS p.267, REVIEW TEST 1 p.214

🎧 008.mp3

①

> I don't like fish.

She **likes** fish.

NEGATIVE He **does not like** fish.

② **do/does not** + **work/play**/etc. *(present simple negative)*

I we you they	do not (= don't)	work play need swim
he she it	does not (= doesn't)	

- "I **do not work** on weekends." "That's good."
- Ray has a guitar, but he **does not play** it much.
- You **don't need** a jacket. It's warm today.
- Dina **doesn't swim**. She's afraid of the water.
- We **don't know** this city well. We're visitors.

In everyday conversation and writing, we use the short forms, **don't** and **doesn't**, more often.

- My parents **don't travel** a lot. They usually stay at home.
- "The store **doesn't open** early in the morning."
  "Let's go to another store, then."

③ We use **doesn't** after **he/she/it**. We do not use **don't**.

- "Is that Anita?" "No, she **doesn't wear** glasses." (*NOT* she don't wear)
- Charlie **doesn't eat** meat. He's a vegetarian. (*NOT* Charlie don't eat)
- "I like this hotel. The room **doesn't cost** a lot of money." "It has a nice view too."

Note that we do not add **-s/-es** to the *verb* after **doesn't**.

- Martin **doesn't cook** at home. He usually eats out. (*NOT* Martin doesn't cooks)
- This sofa is very big. It **doesn't fit** here. (*NOT* It doesn't fits)

PRACTICE

A. Complete the negative sentences with the words in *italics*. Use the *present simple*.

1. *(have a watch)* "What time is it?" "Sorry. I _don't have a watch_ OR _do not have a watch_."
2. *(understand Chinese)* Scott has many Chinese friends, but he _____.
3. *(look well)* "You _____." "I think I have a cold."
4. *(have a lot of homework)* "I usually _____." "Wow, you're lucky!"
5. *(watch TV)* Judy _____. She prefers to read.
6. *(make any noise)* My apartment is quiet. My neighbors _____.
7. *(clean)* Clark _____ his room often. It's usually dirty.

B. Look at the pictures and complete the sentences with the verbs in *italics*. Write negative sentences if necessary.

1	2	3	4	5

This is our car.   You're Ted, right?   Yes, I am.   I hate the rain.

1. *(have)* They _have_ a car.
2. *(know)* He _____ the answer.
3. *(remember)* She _____ his name.
4. *(want)* They _____ any more food.
5. *(like)* She _____ rainy days.

C. Complete the sentences with the verbs in the box using the *present simple*. Write negative sentences if necessary.

bite	buy	show	snow	~~talk~~	work

1. Bernie _doesn't talk_ OR _does not talk_ much. He's really shy.
2. My brother and I are doctors. We _____ at a hospital.
3. The theater _____ a new play every first week of the month.
4. Don't worry. My dog _____ people.
5. I _____ shoes online. I always try them on at a store.
6. It _____ a lot in Alaska. It's very cold.

D. Complete the conversation with the verbs in *italics*. Write negative sentences if necessary.

JAMES: What's for dinner, Linda?
LINDA: Fish and salad.
JAMES: Really? ¹·I _don't like_ OR _do not like_ fish. *(like)*
LINDA: I know. ²·You _____ seafood, James. *(eat)*
But please try some this time.
JAMES: ³·But it _____ good! *(smell)*
⁴·And I _____ the taste. *(hate)*
LINDA: ⁵·Oh, James. It _____ fine. Try a little. *(taste)*

ANSWERS p.267, REVIEW TEST 1 p.214

UNIT 008

Grammar Gateway Basic

27

| # **Do** you **speak** English? *Present simple questions (Do/Does ...?)*

🎧 009.mp3

①

> Do you **speak** English?

> Yes, I do.

You **speak** English.

QUESTION **Do** you **speak** English?

---

② **Do/Does** + *subject* + **look/work**/etc. ...? *(present simple questions)*

Do	I we you they	**look** ...? **work** ...? **like** ...? **have** ...?
Does	he she it	

- **Do** I **look** OK in this dress?
- "Andrew is not in his office." "**Does** he **work** from home today?"
- **Do** you **like** Italian food? I know a good restaurant.
- "**Do** we **have** any milk?" "Look in the fridge."
- "My sister lives in a two-bedroom apartment alone." "**Does** she **need** a roommate?"
- "**Do** your parents **visit** you often?" "Yes. Every week."
- "The new café has several kinds of coffee." "**Does** it **sell** coffee beans too?"

  Note that we do not add **-s/-es** to the *verb* after **Does** + *subject*.

  - "**Does Matthew wear** a uniform at school?" (*NOT* Does Matthew wears)
    "No. His school doesn't have a uniform."
  - "Jane is fixing the fence." "**Does she want** any help?" (*NOT* Does she wants)

---

③ We can give short answers to questions.

Yes,	I/we/you/they	**do.**		No,	I/we/you/they	**don't.**
	he/she/it	**does.**			he/she/it	**doesn't.**

- "**Do** you **know** Susie?" "**Yes, I do.**" (= Yes, I know Susie.)
- "**Does** Harry **play** the cello?" "**No, he doesn't.**" (= No, he doesn't play the cello.)
- "**Do** we **have** any plans for Friday this week?" "**No, we don't.**"
- "**Does** the new bed **feel** comfortable?" "**Yes, it does.**"

PRACTICE

A. Complete the questions with the words in *italics*.

1. *(you, remember me)* <u>Do you remember me</u> _____ ?
2. *(Rosa, have a boyfriend)* _____ ?
3. *(Mr. Gill, need more time)* _____ on the report?
4. *(we, know your phone number)* _____ ?
5. *(you, own a bicycle)* _____ ?
6. *(the bus, usually arrive)* _____ on time?
7. *(your kids, like dogs)* _____ ?

Of course! Hi, Cathy.
Yes. His name is Mike.
Yes. He's very busy.
Probably not.
No, but I want one.
No, it doesn't.
Yes. They love them.

B. Complete the questions with the given words.

drive	go	know	~~live~~	play	talk	work

1. *(Anna)* " <u>Does Anna live</u> _____ on 3rd Avenue?" "No. Her house is on 4th Street."
2. *(we)* " _____ that girl?" "Yes. She's in our art class."
3. *(your children)* " _____ to bed early?" "Yes. They usually sleep before 9 p.m."
4. *(Janet)* " _____ a blue car?" "No. She has a black van."
5. *(Ted)* " _____ baseball?" "No. He only watches it on TV."
6. *(George)* " _____ at a clothing store now?" "Yes, he enjoys his new job."
7. *(you)* " _____ in French with your French friends?" "No, in English."

C. Read the questions and write short answers.

1. A: Do I need a haircut?
   B: <u>No, you don't</u> . Your hair is fine.

2. A: Do you often read magazines?
   B: _____ . It's my favorite hobby.

3. A: Does Steve usually eat out for lunch?
   B: _____ . He always brings his lunch.

4. A: Do you use the Internet a lot?
   B: _____ . I can't work without it.

5. A: Does your daughter go to college?
   B: _____ . She's in high school.

6. A: Do you and Hannah meet often?
   B: _____ . We're very close.

D. Chris is traveling in Vietnam. Complete the conversation with the words in *italics*. Write negative sentences if necessary.

CHRIS: Excuse me. 1. <u>Do you speak English</u> ? *(you, speak, English)*
Clerk: Yes. Can I help you?
CHRIS: 2. _____ . *(I, want, some mangoes)*
Clerk: 3. Sorry, _____ . *(we, have, mangoes)*
       How about oranges?
CHRIS: OK. I'll take one. 4. _____ ? *(it, taste, good)*
Clerk: Sure. Here, you can try it.

CHRIS

Clerk

ANSWERS p.267, REVIEW TEST 1 p.214

UNIT
009

Grammar Gateway Basic

I am doing vs. **I do** *Present progressive vs. Present simple*

🎧 010.mp3

(1)

Present progressive   He **is playing** a game now.

Present simple   He **plays** soccer often,
but he's not playing soccer now.

---

(2) ***Present progressive*** (I am doing . . .)

We use the *present progressive* to talk about actions in progress now.

- I'm **jogging** now.
- Jeff **isn't wearing** a suit today.
- Is it **snowing** a lot outside?
- Look! Lena and Nancy **are dancing**.
- Louis **is cooking** Thai food. It smells good.
- My sisters **aren't watching** TV. They're talking.

Present simple (I do . . .)

We use the *present simple* to talk about things that happen regularly or are true for a long time.

- I **jog** every morning.
- Jeff **doesn't** usually **wear** suits.
- **Does** it **snow** a lot here in December?
- Lena and Nancy **dance** very well.
- Louis **cooks** Thai food often.
- My sisters **don't watch** TV much.

---

(3) We usually do not use the *present progressive* with the following *verbs*:

want	love	prefer	know	agree	remember
need	like	hate	believe	understand	forget

- Marie **loves** tea. She drinks it every morning.
- Margaret and I are very different. She never **agrees** with me.
- "**Do** you **need** some help?" "Yes. I **don't understand** this question."
- "I sometimes **forget** people's names." "Me too."

---

(4) **have/has**

We do not use the *present progressive* with **have/has.**

- Steven **has** a big house. It's beautiful. *(NOT Steven is having)*

But we can use the *present progressive* when **have/has** means "to eat."

- I usually **have** dinner with my wife, but now I'm **having** dinner alone.

PRACTICE

A. Look at the pictures and complete the sentences with the verbs in *italics*.

1
Name: ANTON
Job: car mechanic

2
Name: LIZ
Job: sales clerk

3
Name: GINO
Job: fashion designer

4
Name: GEORGE
Job: painter

1. *(fix, eat)* Anton <u>fixes</u> cars. He <u>'s eating OR is eating</u> a sandwich.
2. *(ride, work)* Liz _____ a horse. She _____ at a shop.
3. *(play, design)* Gino _____ soccer. He _____ clothes.
4. *(paint, sleep)* George _____ pictures. He _____ right now.

B. Complete the sentences with the words in *italics*. Use the *present progressive* or *present simple*.

1. *(he, wash)* "Is Dad in the garage?" "Yes, <u>He's washing OR He is washing</u> the car."
2. *(Angela, go)* _____ to the dentist every six months.
3. *(I, look)* "_____ for my cell phone." "Oh, it's on the kitchen table."
4. *(the post office, not deliver)* _____ mail on Sundays.
5. *(we, buy)* _____ our groceries at that supermarket every week.
6. *(Jason and Fred, not study)* _____ now. They're at the gym.
7. *(Mr. Smith's phone, ring)* _____, but he isn't answering it.

C. Complete the sentences with the verbs in the box. Use the *present progressive* or *present simple*.

attend	hate	~~play~~	remember	spend	swim

1. "Do you have any hobbies?" "I sometimes <u>play</u> the drums on weekends."
2. Look! There are some ducks in the water. They _____.
3. My brother loves reading. He usually _____ a lot of time at the library.
4. "_____ you _____ Harry's address?" "No, I don't."
5. Nicole is at a church now. She _____ a wedding.
6. Michelle _____ snakes. She's afraid of them.

D. Find and change any mistakes in each sentence. Put ✓ if the sentence is correct.

1. Howard is knowing my brother. They go to the same school.   *is knowing → knows*
2. Are Matt and Tammy having lunch together now?   _____
3. Tom and Sally are at the mall. They shop.   _____
4. "I'm not lying. It's not my fault." "I believe you."   _____
5. Brian isn't having a car. He takes the bus to work.   _____
6. I don't do anything right now. Let's go for a walk.   _____

ANSWERS p.268, REVIEW TEST 1 p.214

🎧 011.mp3

①

Yesterday   Now

She **is** at home now.

Yesterday, she **was** in the hospital.

② **was/were** (past of **am/is/are**)

I	
he/she/it	**was**
we/you/they	**were**

- I **was** really happy yesterday. It **was** my birthday.
- "We **were** in Houston last month." "Oh, I like that city."
- "My father **was** a taxi driver many years ago." "What does he do now?"
- You **were** at the theater last night. How was the movie?
- Patricia **was** single last year, but now she's married.
- We **were** at home all day yesterday. We **were** very bored.

   We do not use short forms with **was/were**.

   - "When I **was** young, I **was** interested in airplanes." "Me too." (NOT I's)
   - Our children were at the zoo yesterday. **They were** so excited. (NOT They're)

③ The past of **am/is** is **was**, and the past of **are** is **were**.

- I **was** a student five years ago. Now I**'m** a teacher.
- Melisa and Dan **were** in Bangkok last week. Now they**'re** back.
- "It **was** cloudy yesterday, but it**'s** sunny today." "Yes. The sky is very clear."
- Fred and I **are** very close because we **were** roommates for three years.

PRACTICE

A. At 1 p.m. yesterday, each person was at a different place. Complete the sentences with the words in the box.

| ~~at home~~ at school at a restaurant at a store |

1. I _was at home_____.

2. I _____.

3. We _____.

4. I _____.

B. Complete the sentences with **was/were** and the subjects in *italics*.

1. *(I)* _I was_____ in Italy three weeks ago.
2. *(the stars)* _____ beautiful last night.
3. *(he)* "Do you know Mr. Williams?" "Yes. _____ my boss two years ago."
4. *(these gloves)* "_____ in my car." "Oh, those are mine."
5. *(my friends and I)* _____ at a concert last weekend.
6. *(it)* _____ very hot on Sunday, so we were at the pool all day.

C. Write **am/is/are** or **was/were**.

1. I can't find my keys. They _were_____ here a minute ago.
2. I _____ short in middle school. Now I _____ tall.
3. "You _____ in a hurry this morning." "Yes. I _____ late for an appointment."
4. "Jenny _____ sick yesterday." "_____ she OK now?"
5. "Look! These cups _____ $10 each." "Really? They _____ on sale last week."
6. Patrick _____ in London last month. He _____ in Paris now. He _____ very busy these days.

D. Complete the sentences about Michael Kim with **am/is/are** or **was/were**.

1. Michael Kim _is_____ a famous pop singer today.
2. He _____ a pilot 10 years ago, but he made a band with his friends.
3. Their albums _____ successful, so the band was very popular.
Last year, Michael left the band. 4. It _____ sad news for his fans.
5. Michael _____ now a solo singer.
6. But he and his friends _____ still close.

ANSWERS p.268, REVIEW TEST 2 p.216

| He **was not** cold. was/were *negative* and *questions*

(1)

Yesterday

She **was** cold.

NEGATIVE He **was not** cold.

---

(2) **was/were not** *(negative)*

I	**was not**
he/she/it	**(= wasn't)**
we/you/they	**were not** **(= weren't)**

- I **was not** good at math in high school.
- Melanie and I **were not** friends a year ago. Now we're best friends.
- My vacation was great, but it **wasn't** very long.
- "You **weren't** in the office last week." "I was on a business trip."
- Michelle usually has lunch at the cafeteria, but she **wasn't** there yesterday.

In everyday conversation and writing, we use the short forms, **wasn't** and **weren't**, more often.

- The museum **wasn't** open last Wednesday. It was a holiday.
- "I like your shoes." "Thanks. They **weren't** expensive, but I think they're nice."

---

(3) **Was/Were . . . ?** *(questions)*

Was	I ...?
	he/she/it ...?
Were	we/you/they ...?

- I can't remember the end of the movie. **Was I** asleep?
- "**Were you** busy yesterday?" "Not really."
- "**Was Tom** at the park this morning?" "No, he was at home."
- "I was late for a meeting with my clients." "**Were they** upset?"
- "I was at Wendy's birthday party." "**Was it** fun?"

We can give short answers to questions.

Yes,	I/he/she/it	**was.**
	we/you/they	**were.**

No,	I/he/she/it	**wasn't.**
	we/you/they	**weren't.**

- "**Were you** at the mall last Sunday?" "**Yes, I was.**" (= Yes, I was at the mall.)
- "**Was the restaurant** OK?" "**No, it wasn't.**" (= No, it wasn't OK.)
- "**Were your parents** with you at your graduation?" "**Yes,** they **were.**"

PRACTICE

A. Look at the pictures and complete the sentences with **was/wasn't** and the words in *italics*.

1. *(tired)* Philip _was tired_____.
2. *(asleep)* He _____ on the bus.
3. *(on time)* He _____.

4. *(angry)* His boss _____ with him.
5. *(happy)* He _____.

B. Write **was/were** or **wasn't/weren't**.

1. "How was your date last Friday?"   "Good. It _was_____ nice."
2. Cory and I were at the same school, but we _____ in the same class.
3. The exam _____ easy. My grade isn't very good.
4. The boxes weren't heavy. They _____ empty.
5. The sky _____ clear last night. There wasn't a cloud in the sky.
6. "I can't find the keys. They _____ in the bag."   "Here they are!"

C. Complete the sentences with **was/were** and the words in *italics*.

1. *(we, on the same flight)* " _Were we on the same flight_____?"   "Yes, we were."
2. *(Howard, at the meeting)* " _____ yesterday?"   "No, he wasn't."
3. *(you, with Jessica)* " _____ on Saturday?"   "No. I was with Rob."
4. *(Kim and Lucy, there)* I was at the picnic last weekend. _____ too.
5. *(the baseball game, exciting)* " _____."   "Yes. It was fun."
6. *(your mom, a cook)* " _____?"   "Yes, she was."
7. *(I, in Lisbon)* "You were in Portugal last week, right?"   "Yes. _____."
8. *(you, at the gym)* " _____ this morning?"   "No. I was at home. Why?"

D. Complete the conversation with **was/were** and the words in *italics*.

CHRIS: ¹· _Were you in class_____ this morning? *(you, in class)*
AMY: ²· No. _____. I'm sick. *(I, not, at school)*
CHRIS: ³· But you were with me yesterday, and _____.
    (you, fine)
AMY: I think I have a cold. ⁴· _____ when we were driving
    home together. *(the window, open)*
CHRIS: ⁵· _____? *(you, cold)*
AMY: Yes, I was.
CHRIS: Oh, I wasn't. Sorry, that was my fault.

CHRIS

AMY

ANSWERS p.268, REVIEW TEST 2 p.216

| He **walked** to school yesterday. *Past simple*

🎧 013.mp3

①

Yesterday

He **walks** to school every day.

He **walked** to school yesterday.

"**walked**" is the *past simple*.

---

② **clean/finish/etc. + -ed** *(past simple)*

We use the *past simple* to talk about finished actions.

	clean	finish	watch	laugh	wait
Past simple	**cleaned**	**finished**	**watched**	**laughed**	**waited**

- "Your house is very clean." "I **cleaned** it last Friday."
- The soccer game **finished** at 5 o'clock yesterday.
- Eric was bored, so he **watched** TV.
- "Everyone **laughed** at Ken's joke." "Yes. It was very funny."
- "Was the restaurant crowded?" "Yes. We **waited** for an hour."

---

③ We add **-d/-ied**/etc. to **live**, **die**, etc.

| live → lived   die → died   study → studied   plan → planned | More about -(e)d spelling: Appendix 3, p.249 |

- "I **lived** in New Jersey last year." "Where do you live now?"
- Vincent van Gogh **died** in 1890.
- Jenny **studied** medicine for six years. Now, she works at a pharmacy.
- We're so excited. We **planned** our vacation a month ago.

Some *verbs* are irregular.

| have → **had**   get → **got**   buy → **bought**   go → **went** | More about irregular verbs: Appendix 2, p.246 |

- Emily **had** bacon and eggs for breakfast this morning.
- Mr. Roland **got** a call from his boss.
- "I **bought** a new sofa last week." "Was it expensive?"
- "Noel and Cory are at the café together. Are they friends?" "Yes. They **went** to the same school."

---

④ We usually use the *past simple* with **yesterday**, **last week**, **in 1789**, etc.

- The bus **arrived** 20 minutes late **yesterday**.
- I **had** a great time at the festival **last week**.
- George Washington **became** the first president of the United States **in 1789**.

PRACTICE

A. Complete the sentences with the verbs in the box. Use the *past simple*.

cry	~~freeze~~	go	invite	play	work

1. The lake _froze_____ last winter, so I went skating a lot.
2. I _____ tennis in high school.
3. My neighbors _____ me for dinner last Friday.
4. The baby was sick yesterday. She _____ all night.
5. Joe _____ to the store this morning for some milk.
6. Jessica _____ at a bookstore when she was in college.

B. Complete the sentences with the words in *italics*. Use the *present simple* or *past simple*.

1. *(the company, hire)* _The company hired_____ new employees three weeks ago.
2. *(it, close)* "Is the mall still open?" "Yes. _____ at 10 p.m. every day."
3. *(Laura and Nick, get)* _____ married last year.
4. *(Earth, travel)* _____ around the Sun.
5. *(we, laugh)* "Evan has a new costume for Halloween. It looks funny." "I know! _____ a lot."
6. *(I, forget)* "I'm sorry. _____ your book." "That's OK."
7. *(Jeff, fly)* _____ to Singapore on business every month.
8. *(I, need)* It's cold out here! _____ a scarf.

UNIT 013

C. Find and change any mistakes in each sentence. Put ✓ if the sentence is correct.

1. I live in New York a year ago.   _live → lived_
2. We paint our rooms every year.   _____
3. My mom meets my father in 2000.   _____
4. Clara took a trip last summer.   _____
5. It rains a lot yesterday.   _____
6. That actor wins many awards last year.   _____
7. Holly and her brother ate cereal this morning.   _____

D. Complete the conversation with the words in *italics*.

JUSTIN

JUSTIN: 1. I _walked to school_____ alone this morning. Where were you?
(walk to school)

SANDY: 2. I _____ because I woke up late this morning.
(take the bus)

JUSTIN: Oh. Why?

SANDY: 3. I _____ last night. *(go to bed late)*
4. I _____ . *(study for our test)*

JUSTIN: What? Do we have a test today?

SANDY

ANSWERS p.268, REVIEW TEST 2 p.216

🎧 014.mp3

① **did not** + **enjoy/know**/etc. *(past simple negative)*

I/he/she/it we/you/they	did not (= didn't)	enjoy know sleep answer

How was the movie?

I did not enjoy it.

- A: How was the movie?
  B: I **did not enjoy** it.
- Bob **didn't know** Janice in high school. They met in college.
- We **didn't sleep** much last night because of the storm.
- Mr. Williams called Rose, but she **didn't answer** the phone.

In everyday conversation and writing, we use **didn't** more often.

- "Where is the stapler?" "I don't know. I **didn't take** it."
- "Oh, I dropped my phone!" "Don't worry. It **didn't break**."

Note that we do not add **-(e)d** to the *verb* after **didn't**.

- I **didn't stay** at home last weekend. I went out with my friends. (*NOT* I didn't stayed)
- Danny **didn't fix** the printer. I did. (*NOT* Danny didn't fixed)

② **Did** + *subject* + **like/tell**/etc. . . .? *(past simple questions)*

Did	I/he/she/it we/you/they	like ...? tell ...? leave ...? rain ...?

MOVIE

Did you **like** the movie?

- A: **Did** you **like** the movie?
  B: It was boring. I fell asleep.
- **Did** Susie **tell** you about her wedding?
- "**Did** I **leave** my coat here?" "Yes. Here you go."
- The streets are wet. **Did** it **rain**?

Note that we do not add **-(e)d** to the *verb* after **Did** + *subject*.

- There was a fire alarm. **Did you hear** it? (*NOT* Did you heard)
- "**Did Mr. Green send** you an e-mail?" "No, not yet." (*NOT* Did Mr. Green sent)

We can give short answers to questions.

Yes,	I/he/she/it we/you/they	did.		No,	I/he/she/it we/you/they	didn't.

- "**Did** you **take** these pictures?" "**Yes, I did.**" (= Yes, I took these pictures.)
- "**Did** Mark **get** a haircut?" "**No, he didn't.**" (= No, he didn't get a haircut.)

PRACTICE

A. Look at Miranda's schedule for yesterday. Write sentences about the things she did and didn't do.

1. do the laundry	☐	1. _She didn't do the laundry_ OR _She did not do the laundry_ .
2. read the newspaper	☐	2. _____ .
3. go to the gym	☑	3. _____ .
4. wash the car	☐	4. _____ .
5. attend a cooking class	☑	5. _____ .
6. have lunch with Jackie	☑	6. _____ .

B. Complete the questions with the words in *italics*. Use the *past simple*.

1. *(you, lose)* _Did you lose_ _____ some weight? Yes. I lost five pounds.
2. *(Sarah, pass)* _____ her math exam? Yes. She's so happy.
3. *(you, read)* _____ this book? Yes. It was very good.
4. *(someone, knock)* _____ on the door? No. I don't think so.
5. *(you, get)* _____ my invitation? I sent it yesterday. Yes, I did.
6. *(we, miss)* _____ the train? No. We're on time.
7. *(Dave, grow up)* _____ in France? No. He's from Italy.
8. *(the Smiths, buy)* _____ a house? Yes. It's very nice.

UNIT 014

Grammar Gateway Basic

C. Complete the sentences with the given words using the *past simple*. Write negative sentences if necessary.

buy   c̶o̶o̶k̶   find   lock   meet   visit

1. *(I)* _I didn't cook_ OR _I did not cook_ _____ dinner tonight. I ordered a pizza instead.
2. *(you)* " _____ these earrings?" "No. I made them."
3. *(my friends and I)* _____ the Eiffel Tower because we had no time.
4. *(Elena)* " _____ Tom Cruise on the street!" "She's so lucky!"
5. *(we)* Oh, _____ the front door. Let's go back home right away!
6. *(Jake)* " _____ a job." "That's great! I'm happy for him."

D. Complete the conversation with the words in *italics* using the *past simple*. Write negative sentences if necessary.

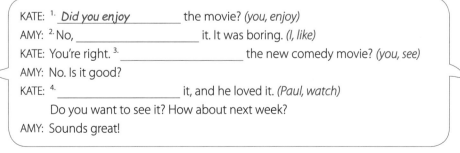

KATE: 1. _Did you enjoy_ _____ the movie? *(you, enjoy)*
AMY: 2. No, _____ it. It was boring. *(I, like)*
KATE: You're right. 3. _____ the new comedy movie? *(you, see)*
AMY: No. Is it good?
KATE: 4. _____ it, and he loved it. *(Paul, watch)*
    Do you want to see it? How about next week?
AMY: Sounds great!

KATE

AMY

ANSWERS p.268, REVIEW TEST 2 p.216

🎧 015.mp3

①

Yesterday at 7 o'clock

At 7 o'clock, he was at school.

He **was playing** the guitar.

"**was playing**" is the *past progressive*.

---

② We use **was/were** + **-ing** *(past progressive)* to talk about actions in progress at a certain time in the past.

I/he/she/it	was	taking studying
we/you/they	were	having cleaning

- I **was taking** a shower when Lisa called.
- Ted **was studying** in London in 2015.
- At 1 o'clock today, we **were having** coffee at a café.
- Benny and Simon **were cleaning** the kitchen this morning.
- "Did you see Joe and Rita?"   "They **were talking** with the boss."

---

③ The past of **am/is** + **-ing** is **was** + **-ing**, and the past of **are** + **-ing** is **were** + **-ing**.

- Vanessa **was sleeping** at 6 a.m. Now, she **is making** breakfast.
- Some kids **were swimming** in the pool a few minutes ago. They **are leaving** now.
- It **was snowing** when I got on the bus. I am home now, and the sun **is shining**.

---

④ We use the *present progressive* to talk about actions in progress now.

I'm watching a movie now.

PAST   NOW   FUTURE

- I'm **watching** a movie now. I'll call you back.
- "Jen **is looking** for you. She's waiting in your office."   "Oh, I see."
- My classmates and I **are working** on a project right now.

We use the *past progressive* to talk about actions in progress at a certain time in the past.

I was watching a movie.

2:00   3:00   4:30
movie began   movie finished

- I **was watching** a movie at 3 o'clock yesterday.
- "Jen **was looking** for you an hour ago."   "I just met with her."
- My classmates and I **were working** on a project last night.

PRACTICE

A. Yesterday, Jay arrived at a party at 8 p.m. and met his friends. Complete the sentences with the verbs in the box using the *past progressive*.

carry	dance	eat	~~sing~~	wave

 1 ANN
 2 MIKE EMMA
 3 JENNY
 4 JACK BILL
5 RYAN

When Jay arrived at the party...

1. Ann _was singing_____ a song.
2. Mike and Emma _____ together.
3. Jenny _____ a gift.
4. Jack and Bill _____ cake.
5. Ryan _____ his hand.

B. Complete the sentences with the verbs in the box. Use the *past progressive*.

attend	cross	listen	play	~~wait~~

1. "Why are you late?" "Many people _were waiting_____ at the taxi stand this morning."
2. Dad _____ to loud music, so he didn't hear the doorbell.
3. Tara and I _____ a swimming class an hour ago.
4. I saw John and Fred at the park. They _____ basketball.
5. "I _____ the street when someone called my name." "Who was it?"

C. Complete the sentences with the words in *italics*. Use the *present progressive* or *past progressive*.

1. *(Jim and Monica, drink)* _Jim and Monica were drinking_____ wine together at a bar last night.
2. *(they, watch)* "Why are there so many people on that hill?" "_____ the sunrise."
3. *(Alice, lie)* _____ in bed when someone knocked on the door.
4. *(I, visit)* "Were you in town on Christmas?" "No. _____ my family in Texas."
5. *(we, stand)* _____ at the bus stop when the accident happened.
6. *(he, hold)* "Excuse me. I'm looking for Mr. Bell."
   "He's right there. _____ an umbrella in his hand."

D. Complete the conversation with the words in *italics*. Use the *past progressive*.

 LINDA

LINDA: Justin, you're home late.
JUSTIN: 1. _I was playing_____ the guitar with my friends. *(I, play)*
LINDA: I called you a lot, but you didn't answer.
JUSTIN: 2. _____ for a concert. *(we, practice)*
LINDA: 3. Well, _____ about you. *(I, worry)*
JUSTIN: Sorry, Mom. 4. _____ loudly, so I didn't hear my phone.
   (we, perform)

JUSTIN

ANSWERS p.269, REVIEW TEST 2 p.216

① was/were not + -ing *(past progressive negative)*

I/he/she/it	**was not** (= wasn't)	**practicing** waiting
we/you/they	**were not** (= weren't)	listening jogging

Yesterday at 10 o'clock

- He **was not practicing**. He was sleeping.
- "Sorry I'm late."
  "Don't worry. We **were not waiting** long."
- "Can I turn off the radio?" "Sure. I **wasn't listening** to it."
- Dylan **wasn't jogging** at 8 p.m. He was at home.
- Sean and Max **weren't eating**. They were still looking at the menu.
- "Did you see Hilary? Was she with Kyle?" "I saw her, but she **wasn't meeting** him."

② Was/Were + *subject* + -ing . . .? *(past progressive questions)*

Was	I/he/she/it	**talking** ...? **working** ...?
Were	we/you/they	**driving** ...? **attending** ...?

- **Was** I **talking** too loudly?
- "**Were** you **working** in Florida in 2017?" "No. I was in Seattle."
- "**Was** Lucy **driving**?" "No. I was driving."
- **Were** you and Todd **attending** a wedding when I called on Sunday?
- "**Was** it **raining** when you arrived?" "No. The weather was nice."

We can give short answers to questions.

Yes,	I/he/she/it	**was.**	No,	I/he/she/it	**wasn't.**
	we/you/they	**were.**		we/you/they	**weren't.**

- "**Was** Diane **washing** her car when you saw her?"
  "**Yes**, she **was**." (= Yes, she was washing her car.)
- "**Were** you and your roommate **watching** the soccer game at noon?"
  "**No,** we **weren't**." (= No, we weren't watching the soccer game.)
- "**Were** you **fighting** with your friend outside last night?" "No, I wasn't."

PRACTICE

A. At 7 p.m. yesterday, a man saw a thief. The police officer is asking the man some questions. Complete the conversation with the words in *italics*.

Was the thief wearing a cap?

1. *(he, wear, a red cap)* Yes. _He was wearing a red cap_ .

Was a woman sitting on this bench?

2. *(a woman, not sit, here)* No. _____.

Were you meeting your friends on the street?

3. *(I, meet, them, outside)* Yes. _____.

Was the thief carrying a backpack?

4. *(he, not carry, a bag)* No. _____.

B. Complete the sentences with the words in *italics*. Use the *past progressive*.

1. *(you, read, it)* "Where is my book? Did you take it?" "Oh, _were you reading it_____?"
2. *(Joe and I, enjoy, the party)* _____, so we didn't sleep much that night.
3. *(Evan, write, an e-mail)* _____ when I visited him.
4. *(we, wait, for the bus)* _____ when we saw the accident.
5. *(it, snow, there)* "_____ when I called you?" "Yes, but it just stopped."
6. *(Sally, go, to the bank)* "_____ when you saw her?"
   "No. She was going to the hospital."

C. Complete the sentences with the given words using the *past progressive*. Write negative sentences if necessary.

buy	practice	~~ride~~	walk	work

1. *(Nick)* _Nick wasn't riding_ OR _Nick was not riding_____ his bicycle. He was on his skateboard.
2. *(Victor)* "I heard the piano. _____?" "Yes, he was."
3. *(Eric and I)* _____ in the office at noon. We were out for lunch.
4. *(I)* "I saw you at the mall. Were you shopping?" "Yes. _____ a new tie."
5. *(you)* You are all wet! _____ home from school when the rain started?

cook	sit	swim	talk	visit

6. *(we)* _____ the food when the guests arrived. It was ready a few minutes later.
7. *(I)* "Did you ask me something?" "No. _____ to you."
8. *(Clara)* "_____ this morning?" "No. She was jogging with me."
9. *(I)* "Why did you move to a different seat?" "_____ in the wrong seat."
10. *(you and Pete)* _____ your parents last weekend? When I visited your
    house, no one was there.

ANSWERS p.269, REVIEW TEST 2 p.216

He **used to** be a football player. used to

🎧 017.mp3

①

I **used to be** a football player.

Past   Now

He is a golfer now.

He **used to be** a football player.
(= He was a football player, but now he's not a football player.)

---

② We use **used to** + **be/work**/etc. to talk about things that were true in the past but are not true now.

I/we/you/they he/she/it	used to	be work cry climb

- I'm a music teacher, but I **used to be** a singer. (= I was a singer, but now I'm not a singer.)
- "Do you know Sandra?" "Yes. We **used to work** together." (= We worked together, but now we don't work together.)
- When Henry was young, he **used to cry** a lot.
- My sister and I **used to climb** that mountain on weekends. Now she's too busy.

---

③ **didn't use to . . .** *(negative)*
- I **didn't use to sleep** late. These days, I wake up around 10 o'clock.
- You **didn't use to cook**. When did you start?
- Julia **didn't use to enjoy** rock music, but she listens to it every day now.

did + *subject* + **use to . . .?** *(questions)*
- "**Did you use to ride** a bicycle to school?" "Yes. I lived close to school."
- "What **did that company use to make** before phones?" "Computers."
- "**Did people use to write** letters often?" "Yes. That was the only form of communication."

---

④ We use **used to** to talk about habits and situations that existed in the past but not now.
- My father **used to smoke** every day, but he doesn't smoke anymore. (= My father smoked, but now he doesn't smoke.)
- I **used to live** alone, but now I have a roommate. (= I lived alone, but now I don't live alone.)

Note that we use the *present simple* to talk about the present.
- Cindy **used to study** French. She **studies** Italian these days.
- "Do you play video games?" "I **used to**, but I **don't play** them anymore."

PRACTICE

A. Look at the pictures and complete the sentences with **used to**.

1 *I don't play basketball.* / *I play basketball.*
2 *I love dogs.* / *I'm afraid of dogs.*
3 *I like my car.* / *I want a new car.*
4 *We live in New York.* / *We live in San Francisco.*

1. He _used to play_ basketball.
2. He _____ afraid of dogs.

3. He _____ his car.
4. They _____ in San Francisco.

B. Complete the sentences with **used to** and the verbs in *italics*. Write negative sentences if necessary.

1. *(sleep)* My daughter _used to sleep_ with her doll when she was young.
2. *(drink)* "Does Tim drink coffee?" "Sometimes. He _____ it at all before."
3. *(eat)* I _____ a lot of spicy food, but it wasn't good for my stomach.
4. *(own)* "Mike _____ a large van." "Why did he sell it?"
5. *(sell)* "That shop _____ delicious cookies." "Right. I miss those cookies."
6. *(speak)* "Maria _____ English well." "I didn't know that. Her English is good."
7. *(be)* That place _____ a pharmacy. Now it's a bank.

C. Complete the sentences with the verbs in the box. Use **used to** or the *present simple*.

~~believe~~	exercise	go	listen	remember	take

1. I _used to believe_ in Santa Claus, but I don't anymore.
2. Jennifer _____ every day. She wants to lose some weight.
3. Eddie _____ to hip-hop music. Now he prefers jazz.
4. "Do you know that woman's name?" "Yes. I _____ her name. It's Marsha."
5. The Smiths _____ fishing a lot. They don't have much time these days.
6. "We _____ that bus to the station." "Right. It was always crowded."

D. Complete the conversation with **used to** and the verbs in the box.

be	come	have	~~play~~

CHRIS

JAMES

CHRIS: Dad, is this you in the picture?
JAMES: 1. Yes. I _used to play_ football.
CHRIS: Wow. You looked different.
JAMES: I know. 2. I _____ a lot of hair.
  3. And your mom _____ to every game.
CHRIS: Really?
JAMES: Oh, yes. 4. She _____ a cheerleader!

ANSWERS p.269, REVIEW TEST 2 p.216

UNIT 018 | She **has washed** the dishes. *Present perfect (1)*

🎧 018.mp3

①

30 minutes ago   Now

> I **have washed** the dishes.

She **has washed** the dishes.
(She washed the dishes, and they are clean now.)

"has washed" is the *present perfect*.

---

② **have/has + learned/worked/etc. *(present perfect)***

We use *past participles* (learned, worked, etc.) after **have/has**.

I/we/you/they	have (= 've)	learned
he/she/it	has (= 's)	worked waited

- My children **have learned** English for six years. They're very good at it.
- Ann **has worked** for Mr. Lee for a long time, so she knows him well.
- "When did my client get here?" "He**'s waited** for 10 minutes."

Past participles are **live/ask/**etc. + **-(e)d**.

live-lived-**lived** ask-asked-**asked** talk-talked-**talked**	More about -**(e)d** spelling: Appendix 3, p.249

Some *past participles* are irregular.

have-had-**had** give-gave-**given** come-came-**come**	More about irregular verbs: Appendix 2, p.246

---

③ We use the *present perfect* in negative sentences and questions in the following ways:

NEGATIVE

I/we/you/they	have not (= haven't)	done
he/she/it	has not (= hasn't)	played

QUESTIONS

Have	I/we/you/they	finished ...?
Has	he/she/it	stopped ...?

- I **have not done** my homework, so I can't go to bed now.
- Your train to Ottawa is at 8 p.m. today. **Have** you **finished** packing?
- Tiffany used to play the piano, but she **hasn't played** it for 10 years.
- "**Has** the rain **stopped**?" "No, it's still raining."

---

④ We use the *present perfect* to talk about past actions that have a connection with the present.

- I **have lived** in LA since 2013. (= I moved to LA in 2013, and I live in LA now.)
- "Where's Brian?" "I don't know. He **hasn't answered** my call."
  (= He didn't answer my call in the past, and I don't know where he is now.)
- "**Have you been** to Egypt before?" "Yes. It's a beautiful place."

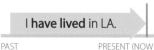

I **have lived** in LA.

PAST   PRESENT (NOW)

46

PRACTICE

A. Look at the pictures and complete the sentences with the verbs in the box. Use the *present perfect*.

break	eat	~~leave~~	make	paint	take

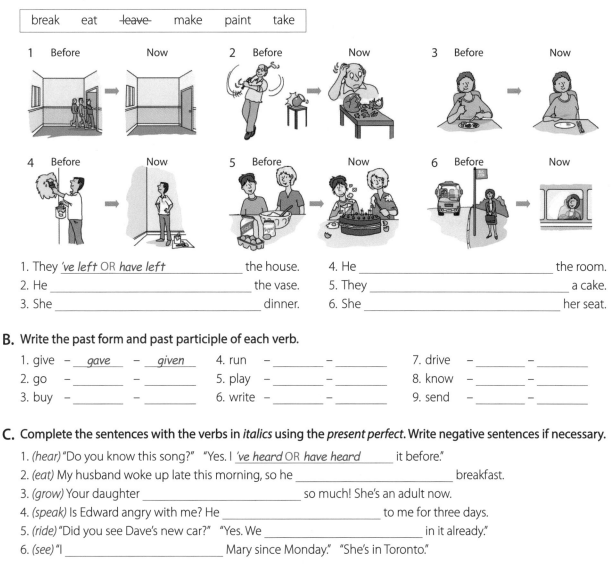

1 Before Now
2 Before Now
3 Before Now
4 Before Now
5 Before Now
6 Before Now

1. They *'ve left* OR *have left* _____ the house.
2. He _____ the vase.
3. She _____ dinner.

4. He _____ the room.
5. They _____ a cake.
6. She _____ her seat.

B. Write the past form and past participle of each verb.

1. give – *gave* – *given*   4. run – _____ – _____   7. drive – _____ – _____
2. go – _____ – _____   5. play – _____ – _____   8. know – _____ – _____
3. buy – _____ – _____   6. write – _____ – _____   9. send – _____ – _____

C. Complete the sentences with the verbs in *italics* using the *present perfect*. Write negative sentences if necessary.

1. *(hear)* "Do you know this song?" "Yes. I *'ve heard* OR *have heard* _____ it before."
2. *(eat)* My husband woke up late this morning, so he _____ breakfast.
3. *(grow)* Your daughter _____ so much! She's an adult now.
4. *(speak)* Is Edward angry with me? He _____ to me for three days.
5. *(ride)* "Did you see Dave's new car?" "Yes. We _____ in it already."
6. *(see)* "I _____ Mary since Monday." "She's in Toronto."

D. Complete the questions with the words in *italics*. Use the *present perfect*.

1. *(you, see my bag)* Have you seen my bag _____ ?   Yes. It's under the table.
2. *(you, study)* _____ for the test?   No, not yet.
3. *(Ben, finish the report)* _____ ?   No. He's doing it now.
4. *(you, read)* _____ War and Peace?   No. Is it interesting?
5. *(Amanda, call you)* _____ ?   No. Maybe she's busy.
6. *(the guests, arrive)* _____ ?   Yes. They're here.

ANSWERS p.269, REVIEW TEST 3 p.218

UNIT
018

Grammar Gateway Basic

| He **has known** her **for** five years. *Present perfect (2)*
Continuous actions

🎧 019.mp3

①

Hi, I'm Justin.

In 2014 (5 years ago)   Now

Justin met Sandy five years ago.
They're still friends.

He **has known** her **for five years**.

OR He **has known** her **since 2014**.

---

② We use the *present perfect* to talk about actions that started in the past and continue until now. We often use the *present perfect* with **for** or **since**.

have/has . . . for + *period of time* (three months, etc.)

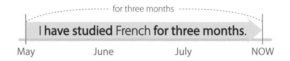

for three months

I **have studied** French **for three months.**

May   June   July   NOW

- I **have studied** French **for three months.** (= I started studying French three months ago, and I still study it now.)
- Lily **has lived** in England **for two years.** (= Lily moved to England two years ago, and she still lives there now.)
- We **haven't seen** Kathy **for a week.** Did she go somewhere?
- "**Has** this store **been** closed **for a few days**?" "Yes. The owners are on vacation."

have/has . . . since + *starting point* (May, etc.)

since May

I **have studied** French **since May.**

May   NOW

- I **have studied** French **since May.** (= I started studying French in May, and I still study it now.)
- Lily **has lived** in England **since 2017.** (= Lily moved to England in 2017, and she still lives there now.)
- We **haven't seen** Kathy **since Thursday.** Is she busy these days?
- "**Has** this store **been** closed **since yesterday**?" "Yes. It'll open again tomorrow."

---

③ We use **How long have you . . .?** to ask about the duration of an action that started in the past and continue until now.

- "**How long have you been** here?" "For three weeks."
- "Steve collects comic books." "**How long has he collected** them?"
- "**How long have you had** your driver's license?" "Since last year."

PRACTICE

A. Look at the pictures and complete the sentences with the verbs in the box. Use the *present perfect*.

catch	drive	grow	live	stay	~~study~~

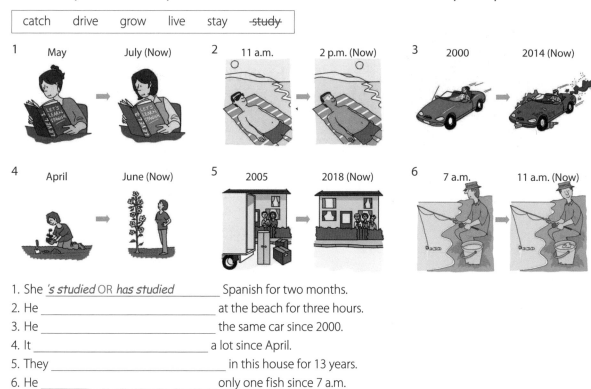

1 May → July (Now)
2 11 a.m. → 2 p.m. (Now)
3 2000 → 2014 (Now)
4 April → June (Now)
5 2005 → 2018 (Now)
6 7 a.m. → 11 a.m. (Now)

1. She *'s studied* OR *has studied* _____ Spanish for two months.
2. He _____ at the beach for three hours.
3. He _____ the same car since 2000.
4. It _____ a lot since April.
5. They _____ in this house for 13 years.
6. He _____ only one fish since 7 a.m.

B. Complete the sentences with **for/since** and the words in *italics*. Use the *present perfect*.

1. *(lose 10 pounds)* "Emily _has lost 10 pounds since_ _____ last month." "Wow. That's amazing!"
2. *(be married)* Stan and Louise _____ eight years. They have two kids.
3. *(not rain)* Farmers are worried because it _____ January.
4. *(drive his car)* Ken _____ nine hours. He's very tired right now.
5. *(not talk to Ben)* I _____ two weeks. I've been so busy lately.
6. *(not eat anything)* What's wrong with Luke? He _____ yesterday.
7. *(know them)* The Jones are our neighbors. We _____ 10 years.

C. Complete the questions with **How long . . .?** Use the *present perfect*.

1. A: I work at a coffee shop.
   B: _How long have you worked_ _____ there?

2. A: Kelly can play the flute very well.
   B: _____ it?

3. A: Alex and Sam attend the same school.
   B: _____ the same school?

4. A: My daughter takes ballet lessons.
   B: _____ them?

5. A: Jimmy is sleeping.
   B: _____ asleep?

6. A: I have a roommate.
   B: _____ a roommate?

ANSWERS p.269, REVIEW TEST 3 p.218

They **haven't seen** the movie. *Present perfect (3) Experiences*

🎧 020.mp3

①

We **haven't seen** the movie.

They **haven't seen** the movie.

---

② We use the *present perfect* to talk about someone's experiences until now.

We **have visited** Europe many times.

PAST   NOW

- We **have visited** Europe many times.
- I **haven't tried** Indian food. Is it good?
- Tony **has met** the president before.
- Mandy **hasn't taken** art lessons, but she draws really well.

---

③ We use **Have you ever . . .?** to ask about someone's experiences in life until now.

- **Have you ever stayed** up all night?
- "**Have you ever made** cookies?" "Yes. How about you?"
- "**Have you ever heard** of Matt Jonas?" "No. Who is he?"

We use **have/has never . . .** when someone has no experience of something in life until now.

- I **have never owned** a pet.
- "Sam always studies very hard." "Right. He**'s never failed** an exam."
- Excuse me. Can we have some forks? We**'ve never used** chopsticks before.

---

④ We use **have/has been (to)** to talk about visiting experiences.

- Mr. Miller **has been to** many countries.
- "Where does Erika live?" "I don't know. I **haven't been to** her house."
- I went to the new restaurant yesterday. **Have** you **been** there?

But we use **have/has gone (to)** when someone went somewhere and is there now.

- "Have you seen Sue this week?" "She **has gone to** LA for vacation." (= She went to LA and she's there now.)
- "Is Travis home? Can I talk to him?" "Sorry, but he**'s gone** out." (= He went out and he's somewhere else now.)

PRACTICE

A. Write sentences about your experiences with **I've** or **I've never** and the words in the box.

1. be to Sweden
2. play chess before
3. live in the country
4. ride a roller coaster
5. see a kangaroo
6. have a pet

1. *I've (never) been to Sweden* .
2. _____ .
3. _____ .
4. _____ .
5. _____ .
6. _____ .

YOU

B. Complete the questions with **Have you ever . . .?** and the words in the box.

be to Paris	~~eat sushi~~	go bungee jumping
run a marathon	swim in the ocean	watch an opera

1. A: *Have you ever eaten sushi* ?
   B: Yes. It's delicious.

2. A: _____ ?
   B: Yes, last year. The music was amazing.

3. A: _____ ?
   B: No. I'm afraid of heights.

4. A: _____ ?
   B: Yes. There are many beaches in my town.

5. A: _____ ?
   B: Yes. It's a beautiful city.

6. A: _____ ?
   B: Yes, but I didn't finish the race.

C. Write **have/has been** or **have/has gone**.

1. "Where's Lucy?" "She *'s gone* OR *has gone* to bed."
2. Martin _____ to the new park three times. He loved it.
3. "Where is Sarah? She didn't come to work today." "She _____ to Europe for a week."
4. "Is Kyle in his office?" "No. He _____ to the gym."
5. "This street looks familiar, doesn't it?" "You're right. We _____ here before."

D. Complete the conversation with the words in *italics*. Use the *present perfect*.

SANDY: 1. I *haven't seen* OR *have not seen* this movie. *(not see)*
2. _____ it? *(you, watch)*

JUSTIN: No, but it looks like a movie about Russia.
3. _____ to Russia? *(you, ever, be)*

SANDY: 4. No, I _____ there. *(not be)*

JUSTIN: I went there last fall.
The culture was interesting, and the food was delicious.
5. _____ Russian food before? *(you, eat)*

SANDY: 6. No, I _____ it, but I want to. *(never, try)*

SANDY

JUSTIN

ANSWERS p.270, REVIEW TEST 3 p.218

UNIT 021 | I **did** VS. I **have done** *Past simple vs. Present perfect*

🎧 021.mp3

①

They **moved** to New York in 2000.
(= They came to New York in 2000.)

How long have you lived in New York?

We**'ve lived** here since 2000.

They **have lived** in New York since 2000.
(= They came to New York in 2000 and still live there now.)

②

Christine **went** to the beach an hour ago.

Christine **has gone** to the beach.

PAST   NOW

We use the *past simple* to talk about finished actions.

- Christine **went** to the beach an hour ago.
  (= Christine left for the beach an hour ago.)
- Mason **changed** his phone number last week.
  (= His phone number changed last week.)
- My boss **didn't attend** yesterday's meeting.
- "Did you **meet** my sister at the mall?"
  "Yes. We had coffee together."

We use the *present perfect* to talk about past actions that have a connection with the present.

- Christine **has gone** to the beach.
  (= Christine went to the beach, and she's there now.)
- Mason **has changed** his phone number.
  (= Mason changed his phone number, and it's different now.)
- My boss **hasn't attended** many meetings.
- "**Have** you **met** my sister before?"
  "Of course. I know her very well."

③ Note that we use the *present perfect* to talk about actions that started in the past and continue until now. We do not use the *past simple*.

- The weather **has been perfect** this week. Let's go for a drive today.
  (*NOT* The weather was perfect)
- Amanda **has been sick** for a few days. She's still in the hospital.
  (*NOT* Amanda was sick)
- "How long **have** you **been here**?" "For an hour. Is Jake here yet?"

④ We only use the *past simple* to talk about a time in the past (last night, two days ago, etc.).

- "I **watched** a football game **last night**." "How was it?"
  (*NOT* I have watched a football game last night.)
- Aaron is on vacation. He **left** for Hawaii **two days ago**.
  (*NOT* He has left for Hawaii two days ago.)

PRACTICE

A. Complete the sentences with the verbs in the box. Use the *present perfect* or *past simple*.

be	~~call~~	grow	invent	see

1. "Did you meet Pam lately?" "No, but she _called_ me."
2. I'm a doctor at this hospital. I _____ here for two years.
3. Alexander Graham Bell _____ the telephone in 1876.
4. I _____ a huge snake at the zoo last weekend.
5. "Your son _____ a lot since last year." "Yes. He's very tall now."

B. Find and change any mistakes in each sentence. Put ✓ if the sentence is correct.

1. Mary hasn't gone to work yesterday.   _____ *hasn't gone → didn't go* _____
2. My brother graduated from college last May.   _____
3. I didn't use my computer since last Friday.   _____
4. Jill knew Ann for 10 years. They are best friends.   _____
5. We've stayed in this hotel for a week. Everything has been perfect.   _____
6. Tony and his wife have visited India in 2006.   _____

C. Complete the sentences with the words in *italics*. Use the *present perfect* or *past simple*.

1. A: (*you, give*) _You gave_ me this book last week, and I finished it.
   B: (*I, not read*) _I haven't read_ OR _I have not read_ that book. Did you enjoy it?
2. A: (*I, not see*) _____ John since last week.
   B: (*Brenna, talk*) Really? I heard _____ to him today.
3. A: (*Ms. Conner, speak*) _____ French very well at the meeting.
   B: (*she, take*) I know. _____ French lessons for a year now.
4. A: (*I, join*) _____ this company last week. How about you?
   B: (*we, work*) _____ here for three months.
5. A: (*my plane, not arrive*) _____ for three hours. Is there a problem?
   B. (*it, depart*) _____ late from Singapore this morning.

D. Complete the conversation with the words in *italics*. Use the *present perfect* or *past simple*.

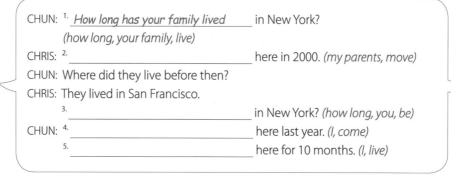

CHUN: 1. _How long has your family lived_ in New York?
(*how long, your family, live*)
CHRIS: 2. _____ here in 2000. (*my parents, move*)
CHUN: Where did they live before then?
CHRIS: They lived in San Francisco.
3. _____ in New York? (*how long, you, be*)
CHUN: 4. _____ here last year. (*I, come*)
5. _____ here for 10 months. (*I, live*)

CHUN

CHRIS

ANSWERS p.270, REVIEW TEST 3 p.218

I've just bought this camera. *just, already, yet*

🎧 022.mp3

① **have/has + just + bought/arrived/etc.**

We can use **just** with the *present perfect*. **just** means "a short time ago."

I've just bought this camera.

- A: I**'ve just bought** this camera.
  B: We don't need it, James!
- The plane from Boston **has just arrived** at the airport.
- "Am I late for the meeting?" "No. We**'ve just started.**"
- "Excuse me. You**'ve just dropped** your wallet." "Oh, thank you."

② **have/has + already + made/baked/etc.**

We can use **already** with the *present perfect*. **already** means "earlier than expected."

I've already made plans for Saturday.

- I**'ve already made** plans for Saturday.
- "We need a cake for Dad's birthday." "Mom **has already baked** one."
- "Jamie was looking for you." "I**'ve already talked** to her."
- "Let's invite Andy to our party." "I**'ve already invited** him."

③ We can use **yet** with the *present perfect* in negative sentences. **yet** means "until now."

haven't/hasn't + arrived/done/etc. . . . yet

Where is Chris?

He hasn't arrived yet.

- A: Where is Chris?
  B: He **hasn't arrived yet.**
- "Did you do the laundry?" "No, I **haven't done** it **yet.**"
- Don't touch the chair. The paint **hasn't dried yet.**
- "Is Dr. Lee in her office?" "She **hasn't come** back from lunch **yet.**"

Have/Has + subject + eaten/sold/etc. . . . yet?

- "**Have** you **eaten** dinner **yet**?" "No. I'm so hungry."
- "**Has** Jake **sold** his car **yet**?" "Not yet."
- "**Has** Anna **returned** from her trip **yet**?" "No. She'll be back next week."

④ We can use **just**, **already**, or **yet** with the *present perfect* and *past simple*.

- I**'ve just finished** cleaning. *OR* I **just finished** cleaning.
- Monica **has already spent** all of her money. *OR* Monica **already spent** all of her money.
- "Did we miss the bus?" "No, it **hasn't come yet.**" *OR* "No, it **didn't come yet.**"
- **Have** Marie and Darcy **moved** to their new apartment **yet**?
  OR **Did** Marie and Darcy **move** to their new apartment **yet**?

PRACTICE

A. Look at the pictures and complete the sentences with **just** and the verbs in the box. Use the *present perfect*.

dive	~~leave~~	meet	open

1. She *'s just left* OR *has just left* _____ the house.
2. He _____ into the pool.
3. The mall _____.
4. They _____ each other.

(Picture 4 speech bubbles: "Are you Tom?" "Yes. Are you Sue?")

B. Complete the conversations with **already** and the words in *italics*. Use the *present perfect*.

1. I don't see Clara's car in the parking lot.
2. Let's go out for some coffee.
3. Does our boss need this report?
4. Let's send Mom a birthday card.

(she, leave) *She's already left* OR *She has already left*.
(we, have) _____ coffee.
(he, read) No. _____ it.
(I, send) _____ her one.

C. Complete the sentences with **yet** and the words in *italics* using the *present perfect*. Write negative sentences if necessary.

1. *(I, take, it)* "Did you take the Spanish class?" "No. *I haven't taken it yet* OR *I have not taken it yet* ."
2. *(you, visit, him)* "My uncle is in the hospital." "_____?"
3. *(he, start, it)* "Is Mr. Collins working on the new project?" "No. _____."
4. *(I, see, him)* "Kevin came back from his vacation." "Really? _____!"
5. *(Lily, call you, back)* "_____?" "Maybe she forgot."

D. Complete the conversation with the words in *italics* using the *present perfect*. Write negative sentences if necessary.

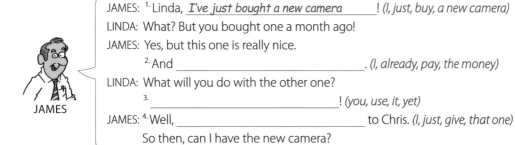

JAMES: [1.] Linda, *I've just bought a new camera* ! *(I, just, buy, a new camera)*
LINDA: What? But you bought one a month ago!
JAMES: Yes, but this one is really nice.
[2.] And _____. *(I, already, pay, the money)*
LINDA: What will you do with the other one?
[3.] _____! *(you, use, it, yet)*
JAMES: [4.] Well, _____ to Chris. *(I, just, give, that one)*
So then, can I have the new camera?

ANSWERS p.270, REVIEW TEST 3 p.218

55

①

She **runs** every day.
She **ran** yesterday.

She **will run** tomorrow.

"**will run**" is a future event.

---

② We use **will** + **be**/**need**/etc. to talk about future events.

I/we/you/they he/she/it	will (= 'll)	be need like

- I **will be** in the office this afternoon.
- It's cold outside. You**'ll need** a coat.
- "I've got some flowers for Jane." "That's sweet. She**'ll like** them a lot."

---

③ We use **will** to talk about things that we know or think about the future.

- Sharon **will be** 18 years old next year.
- "I'm worried about the test on Wednesday." "Don't worry. You**'ll do** fine."

We also use **will** to talk about things that we decide to do in the future.

- "Larry, the music is too loud!" "OK. I**'ll turn** down the volume."
- I think we're lost. I**'ll ask** for directions.

---

④ We use **will** in negative sentences and questions in the following ways:

NEGATIVE

I/we/you/they he/she/it	will not (= won't)	make tell leave

QUESTIONS

Will	I/we/you/they he/she/it	go ...? finish ...? snow ...?

- "The baby is sleeping." "OK. I **will not make** any noise."
- "**Will** you **go** to the library this week?" "Yes. I want to borrow some books."
- "We're planning a surprise party for Patty." "All right. I **won't tell** her about it."
- "**Will** Rob **finish** the report by noon?" "I hope so."
- "I'll be a few minutes late." "Take your time. We **won't leave** without you."
- "**Will** it **snow** tomorrow?" "Maybe."

PRACTICE

A. Complete the sentences with **will** and the words in *italics*.

1. *(the class, begin)* _The class will begin_ soon. Let's sit over here.
2. *(you, find)* "Where is Mr. Gill's office?" "Go to the 7th floor. _____ it next to the elevator."
3. *(they, win)* The Tigers won last year's championship. _____ this year's championship too.
4. *(she, return)* Polly has gone to her swimming class. _____ home in an hour.
5. *(we, need)* Laura's family will join us for dinner. _____ a table for five people.
6. *(it, help)* "This machine is not working." "Check the manual. _____."

B. Complete the sentences with **I'll** and the words in the box.

drive	lend you	~~see you~~	take it

1. Bill, _I'll see you_ _____ later.

Goodbye.

2. You look tired. _____.

3. _____ some money.

I lost my wallet.

4. Yes, I love it! _____.

Do you like the jacket?

C. Complete the sentences with **will** and the verbs in the box. Write negative sentences if necessary.

call	explain	forget	~~love~~	sleep	stop	take

1. "I'm planning a trip to Jeju Island." "It's beautiful there. You _'ll love_ OR _will love_ it."
2. "Is the museum far from here?" "No. We can walk. It _____ long."
3. "Your appointment is next Tuesday at 2:30." "I'll write it down. I _____"
4. "I don't understand this question." "Ask Bob. He _____ it to you."
5. The bus _____ at 24th Avenue next Friday. The road will be closed for a parade.
6. Don't drink too much coffee. You _____ well.
7. "Judy hasn't arrived yet." "OK. I _____ her."

D. Put **will** and the words in *italics* in the correct order.

1. *(to work / tomorrow / you / drive)* "_Will you drive to work tomorrow_ ?" "Probably."
2. *(we / the train / miss)* Hurry up. We don't have enough time. _____!
3. *(you / me / at the airport / meet)* "_____?" "No. At your hotel."
4. *(be / here / she / in a minute)* "Where's Ann?" "She's on the phone. _____"
5. *(the chicken salad / I / have)* "Are you ready to order?" "Yes. _____, please."
6. *(travel / this fall / your family)* "_____?" "Yes. We'll visit Vietnam for a week."
7. *(Jonathan / pass / the exam)* "_____?" "Well, he studied hard for it."
8. *(it / I / change)* "That tie doesn't match your suit." "Really? _____, then."

ANSWERS p.270, REVIEW TEST 4 p.220

| He**'s going to** make dinner. Future (2) **am/is/are going to**

(1)

I'm going to make dinner.

He**'s going to make** dinner.

"is going to make" is a future event.

---

(2) We can also use **am/is/are going to** + **be/meet**/etc. to talk about future events.

I	am		be
he/she/it	is	going to	meet
we/you/they	are		visit
			stay

- It**'s going to be** very hot today.
- I talked to Joe about the picnic. We**'re going to meet** tomorrow at 9:30.
- Lisa **is going to visit** her parents. She**'s going to stay** with them for a week.

---

(3) We use **am/is/are going to** to talk about things that we have decided to do in the future.

- Susan **is going to move** to Chicago. She has a new job there.
- "Roy **is going to get** married!" "I know. He already told me."

We also use **am/is/are going to** to talk about things that we expect to happen based on the present situation.

- The sun is going down. It**'s going to be** dark soon.
- The bus is leaving! We**'re going to miss** it.

---

(4) We use **am/is/are going to** in negative sentences and questions in the following ways:

NEGATIVE

I	am			exercise
he/she/it	is	not	going to	take
we/you/they	are			win

QUESTIONS

Am	I		study ...?
Is	he/she/it	going to	clean ...?
Are	we/you/they		visit ...?

- I**'m not going to exercise** tonight. I'm too tired.
- "Jess will attend B.C. College." "That college is famous for journalism. **Is** she **going to study** that?"
- Ryan just bought a car. He**'s not going to take** the subway anymore.
- "**Are** you **going to clean** your room?" "Yes, but I'm going to take a shower first."
- We're losing now. We **aren't going to win** this game.
- "Jim and Sophie will come to our town." "**Are** they **going to visit** us?"

PRACTICE

A. Complete the sentences with **am/is/are going to** and the verbs in the box. Write negative sentences if necessary.

be	graduate	leave	~~read~~	relax	rent	take

1. I bought a new book. I *'m going to read* OR *am going to read* ____ it during my vacation.
2. OK, class. We _____ a break. Come back in 10 minutes.
3. "My plane _____ soon." "OK. Have a good trip!"
4. My friend wants to take another class at college. She _____ this year.
5. We _____ in the office next Monday. It's a holiday.
6. "You look tired." "Yes. I _____ for a few minutes."
7. I _____ that apartment. It's very old and dirty.

B. Look at the pictures and complete the sentences with **am/is/are going to** and the words in the box.

have a sale	~~play golf~~	take an exam	watch a movie

1. He *'s going to play golf* OR *is going to play golf* ____ .   3. They _____ .
2. She _____ .   4. She _____ .

C. Complete the sentences with **am/is/are going to** and the words in *italics*.

1. *(I, attend)* <u>I'm going to attend</u> OR <u>I am going to attend</u> ____ a seminar tomorrow. It's about African art.
2. *(Tina, meet)* "_____ us at the train station?" "Yes. At 10 o'clock."
3. *(I, see)* _____ the musical tonight. I'm so excited!
4. *(you, buy)* "_____ that car?" "I'm not sure."
5. *(Brian, join)* "_____ us for lunch." "Good! I haven't seen him for years."
6. *(they, get)* Andy proposed to Hannah. _____ married soon.
7. *(it, hurt)* "You have a cold. I'll give you a shot." "_____ ?"

D. Complete the conversation with **am/is/are going to** and the words in *italics*.

LINDA: I'm so hungry.
JAMES: Don't worry. [1.] <u>I'm going to make</u> ____ dinner soon. *(I, make)*
LINDA: Oh good. What are you going to cook?
JAMES: [2.] _____ chicken and rice. It's easy. *(I, cook)*
[3.] _____ ready in 30 minutes. *(it, be)*
LINDA: Great! [4.] _____ some help? *(you, need)*
JAMES: [5.] Thanks, but _____ your help. *(I, not need)*

LINDA

JAMES

ANSWERS p.271, REVIEW TEST 4 p.220

UNIT **024**

Grammar Gateway Basic

| ## She**'s leaving** tomorrow. *Future (3) Present progressive and Present simple*

🎧 025.mp3

(1)

She**'s leaving** tomorrow.

The plane **leaves** at 10 o'clock.

"is leaving" (*present progressive*) and **"leaves"** (*present simple*) are future events.

---

(2) We can use **am/is/are + -ing** to talk about future plans with a specific time or place (appointments, reservations, etc.).

- I**'m seeing** Bob on Friday. We**'re going** to the opera.
- Michelle and I **are having** dinner tonight. Will you join us?
- Sally **isn't moving** to Florida. She changed her mind.
- "**Is** Jack **returning** to the office today?" "Yes. At around 5 p.m."

In this case, **am/is/are + -ing** is about the future and not the present.

- I**'m starting** a new job tomorrow.
- George **is not coming** home tonight.

We can also use **am/is/are going to + open/run**/etc. instead of **am/is/are + -ing**.

- I**'m opening** my new business next month.
  OR I**'m going to open** my new business next month.
- **Are** you **running** in the marathon on Sunday?
  OR **Are** you **going to run** in the marathon on Sunday?

---

(3) We can use the *present simple* to talk about future events with fixed schedules (public transportation, class schedules, etc.).

- The train **arrives** in Paris at 7 p.m.
- "Why are you going to bed now? It's only 9 o'clock."
  "My class **starts** early in the morning."
- The TV show **doesn't end** at 5:30. It **ends** at 6.
- "**Does** your soccer team **play** here on May 13?" "Yes, and on June 13."

Note that we do not use the *present simple* to talk about personal plans. We use **am/is/are + -ing**.

- Terry and Rachel are getting married soon. They **are buying** a house next week.
  (*NOT* They buy)
- Carla **is not studying** in Sweden next year. She**'s going** to Finland instead.
  (*NOT* Carla studies, *NOT* She goes)

PRACTICE

A. Look at Stephanie's plans for next week and complete the sentences.

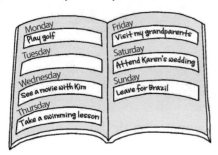

1. She *'s playing golf* OR *is playing golf* _____ on Monday.
2. She _____ with Kim on Wednesday.
3. She _____ on Thursday.
4. She _____ on Friday.
5. She _____ on Saturday.
6. She _____ on Sunday.

B. Look at each schedule and complete the sentences with the verbs in *italics*.

1 Movie Schedule		2 Flight Departures		3 Train Arrivals		4 Class Schedule	
5:30	*Funny People*	12:30	London	1:00	New York	9:00	Computer
6:30	*Space War*	2:15	Berlin	2:00	Boston	10:30	English

1. (start) Funny People *starts at 5:30* _____ .
2. (leave) I'm going to Berlin. My flight _____ .
3. (arrive) Jerome is coming from Boston. His train _____ .
4. (begin) My computer class _____ .

C. Complete the sentences with the words in *italics*. Use the *present progressive* or *present simple*.

1. (I, fly) "When are you going to China?" "*I'm flying* OR *I am flying* there tomorrow night."
2. (you, stay) "_____ at a hotel during your vacation?" "Yes. I've already made a reservation."
3. (the plane, depart) _____ in 30 minutes. Let's hurry.
4. (Brenda, move) _____ to a new house next month. She's very excited.
5. (it, begin) "When does the school holiday start?" "_____ next Wednesday."
6. (the meeting, finish) _____ at 10 p.m. I'll call you then.
7. (I, meet) Ms. Edmonds doesn't have much time this morning, so _____ her at noon.

D. The following is Amy's diary. Complete the sentences with the verbs in *italics* using the *present progressive* or *present simple*.

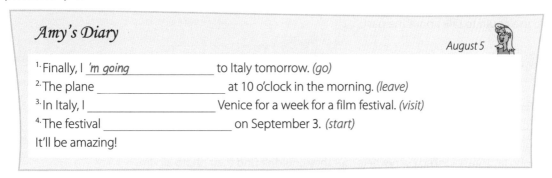

Amy's Diary   *August 5*

1. Finally, I *'m going* _____ to Italy tomorrow. (go)
2. The plane _____ at 10 o'clock in the morning. (leave)
3. In Italy, I _____ Venice for a week for a film festival. (visit)
4. The festival _____ on September 3. (start)

It'll be amazing!

ANSWERS p.271, REVIEW TEST 4 p.220

He **can** speak Italian. can, could

①

He **can speak** Italian.

He **can't speak** Japanese.

---

② can + **ride**/**eat**/etc.

We use **can** to say that someone has the ability to do something or that something is possible.

I/we/you/they he/she/it	can	ride eat dance sing

- I **can ride** a bike.
- We **can eat** at the hotel. It has a restaurant.
- Peter **can dance** well. He **can sing** well too.
- Wendy **can meet** me tomorrow. She doesn't have any classes.

---

③ We use **can** in negative sentences and questions in the following ways:

NEGATIVE

I/we/you/they he/she/it	cannot (= can't)	cook talk

QUESTIONS

Can	I/we/you/they he/she/it	play ...? take ...?

- I **cannot cook** very well, so my husband makes our meals.
- "**Can** you **play** the guitar?" "Yes. I've played for many years."
- "Peggy isn't answering her phone." "She **can't talk** to you now. She's in a meeting."
- "**Can** we **take** pictures inside the museum?" "No. Sorry."

---

④ We use **could** to talk about the past.

I/we/you/they he/she/it	could	swim see

NEGATIVE

I/we/you/they he/she/it	could not (= couldn't)	walk find

- Ten years ago, Liz **could swim** 50 meters in 30 seconds.
- Sorry I'm late. I **could not walk** fast because the streets were icy.
- The sky was clear yesterday evening, so we **could see** the stars.
- John and Stacy looked everywhere, but they **couldn't find** their photo album.

PRACTICE

A. Complete the sentences with **can/can't** and the verbs in the box.

fix	~~go~~	join	stay	talk	understand	wear

1. "Sara _can't go OR cannot go_ to the beach with us today." " Really? That's too bad."
2. You should take the computer to Tom. He _____ computers.
3. "Let's discuss this now. Where should we go?" "The meeting room is empty, so we _____ there."
4. "Tony! Let's go to the mall." "I _____ you. I have a lot of homework."
5. "You _____ shoes inside the house." "Sorry. I didn't know that."
6. "My friends are coming to our town for vacation. Can I bring them home?" "Sure. They _____ here."
7. Steve speaks very fast. I _____ him.

B. Complete the questions with **can** and the words in *italics*.

1. *(you, climb)* _Can you climb_ _____ that tree?
2. *(your parrot, talk)* _____ ?
3. *(Karen, help)* _____ you with your report?
4. *(you, attend)* _____ the company picnic?
5. *(your husband, drive)* _____ a truck?
6. *(you, tell)* _____ me the meaning of this word?

No. I can't.
Yes. It can say hello and goodbye.
No. She's busy.
Of course I can.
No, but he can drive a motorcycle.
Sure. What is the word?

Grammar Gateway Basic

C. Complete the sentences with **can/can't** or **could/couldn't** and the verbs in *italics*.

1. *(take)* "Where is City Hall?" "On Main Street. You _can take_ _____ the subway over there."
2. *(see)* Can we move to different seats? I _____ the movie well from here.
3. *(walk)* My brother is only 10 months old, but he _____!
4. *(buy)* When I was a child, I _____ a soda for 25 cents. Everything was so cheap.
5. *(remember)* "When is Lisa's birthday? I _____." "It's May 8."
6. *(ride)* Kelly _____ a bicycle last week, but now she can.
7. *(have)* "This room is too small for a party." "Then we _____ the party in another room."
8. *(answer)* "Ask Ron about this. He's smart." "I did, but he _____ it."

D. Complete the conversation with **can/could** and the words in *italics*.

JUSTIN

JUSTIN: I talked to an Italian man on the street today.
SANDY: Oh. 1. _Can you speak_ _____ Italian? *(you, speak)*
JUSTIN: A little. 2. But _____ English too. *(he, understand)*
SANDY: That's good. 3. _____ Italian when I was young. *(I, speak)*
        4. Now, _____ anything. *(I, not remember)*
JUSTIN: My friend is teaching me Italian every Friday night.
SANDY: Really? 5. _____ you? *(I, join)*
JUSTIN: Sure. 6. _____ if you want to. *(you, come)*

SANDY

ANSWERS p.271, REVIEW TEST 5 p.222

63

UNIT 027 | He **might** play soccer. might, may

🎧 027.mp3

①

He **might play** soccer.

He **might not play** soccer.

---

② might + **come**/**see**/etc.

We use **might** to say that something is possible now or in the future.

I/we/you/they he/she/it	might	come see be have

- I **might come** to work after lunch because I have a dentist appointment.
- Let's go to Hollywood! We **might see** a famous person.
- "Where's Eric?" "I'm not sure. He **might be** in his bedroom."
- "Do you have our room key?" "No. Ask Monica. She **might have** it."

---

③ We use **might** in negative sentences in the following way:

I/we/you/they he/she/it	might not	finish go enjoy remember

- I have a lot of work to do. I **might not finish** it all today.
- We **might not go** skiing this weekend. There's not much snow.
- Thomas **might not enjoy** this movie. He doesn't like comedies.
- Tina **might not remember** her uncle. She has met him only once.

---

④ We can also use **may** instead of **might**.

- Jeff **might work** late tonight. *OR* Jeff **may work** late tonight.
- Anne **might take** an art class next year. *OR* Anne **may take** an art class next year.

In everyday conversation, we use **might** more often.

- "I'll pick you up at 7 p.m." "6:30 **might be** better. We don't want to be late."

64

PRACTICE

A. Read the conversations and complete the sentences with **might**.

1. BILL — Are you meeting Jenny tomorrow? | I'm not sure. I'll ask her. — TOM

2. JANE — Are you traveling by train? | I'm thinking about it. — ROBERT

3. MACY — Are you going to Martin's wedding? | Maybe. — SUSAN

4. PETER — Are you moving next month? | I don't know yet, but it's possible. — RACHEL

1. Tom _might meet Jenny tomorrow_ .
2. Robert _____ .
3. Susan _____ .
4. Rachel _____ .

B. Complete the sentences with **might / might not** and the verbs in *italics*.

1. *(win)* Our soccer team is playing well. We _might win_____ the game.
2. *(help)* Fred isn't very busy today. He _____ us with our homework.
3. *(come)* "Emma is sick. She _____ with us." "That's too bad."
4. *(try)* "Have you been to that restaurant?" "No, but I _____ it next week."
5. *(fit)* This dress looks too small. It _____ me.
6. *(like)* Carla and Jake _____ seafood. Let's cook some steaks.
7. *(invite)* "Do you have plans for this Friday?" "Well, we _____ some friends to our house."
8. *(buy)* I _____ that suitcase. It's very expensive.
9. *(be)* "Where is Steve?" "He's not in the office. He _____ at the gym."
10. *(rain)* There are dark clouds in the sky. It _____ .

C. Complete the conversation with **might** and the verbs in the box. Write negative sentences if necessary.

be	go	have	~~play~~

PAUL: ¹·I _might play_____ soccer tomorrow. Can you come?
CHRIS: ²·I want to go, but I _____ time.
PAUL: Why not?
CHRIS: ³·I _____ to see my grandparents.
PAUL: How about Sunday?
CHRIS: ⁴·The weather _____ good. I heard it's going to rain.
PAUL: Well, OK. Maybe we can play together next week.

PAUL   CHRIS

ANSWERS p.271, REVIEW TEST 5 p.222

Can I use your phone?

Can/Could I . . .?, Can/Could you . . .?, May I . . .?

🎧 028.mp3

①

Can I use your phone?

Can you come to the party?

---

② We use **Can I . . .?** to ask for someone's permission.

- It's very late. **Can I** stay here tonight?
- "**Can I** bring my friend to the picnic?" "Of course."
- "I don't have a pen. **Can I** borrow yours?" "Here you go."
- "**Can I** pay by credit card?" "Sure."

We can also use **Could I . . .?** or **May I . . .?** instead of **Can I . . .?** to be more polite.

- "**Could I** ask you something?" "Sure. What is it?"
- "**May I** check my e-mail on your computer?" "All right."
- "I need that box from the top shelf, but I can't reach it." "**Could I** help you with that?"
- **May I** leave now? I have another meeting after this.

---

③ We use **Can you . . .?** to make requests.

- "**Can you** lend me 10 dollars?" "Sorry. I didn't bring my wallet."
- "It's hot in this room. **Can you** open the window for me?" "OK. Just a moment."
- "**Can you** recommend a good restaurant in this town?" "The Thai Grill is good."
- "**Can you** take my picture, please?" "Sure. Say cheese!"

We can also use **Could you . . .?** instead of **Can you . . .?** to be more polite.

- I'm sorry. **Could you** say that again?
- "**Could you** give this document to Jason?" "No problem."

> But we do not use **May you . . .?** instead of **Can/Could you . . .?**
>
> - **Can you** show me the way, please? *OR* **Could you** show me the way, please?
>   (*NOT* May you show me the way, please?)
> - **Can you** wash the dishes for me? *OR* **Could you** wash the dishes for me?
>   (*NOT* May you wash the dishes for me?)

PRACTICE

A. Look at the pictures and complete the questions with **Can I...?** and the words in the box.

| close the window | come in | get some water | take this seat |

1. _Can I come in_ ?
2. _____ _____ ?
3. _____ _____ ?
4. _____ _____ ?

B. Complete the questions with **May I...?** / **Can you...?** and the verbs in *italics*.

1. *(have)* " _May I have_____ a cup of coffee?" "OK. Do you want milk in it?"
2. *(help)* "These bags are heavy." "_____ you with them?"
3. *(call)* _____ me back in five minutes? I'm meeting with a client now.
4. *(look)* "I can't turn the heater on." "_____ at it for you?"
5. *(borrow)* _____ some money? I just need a few dollars.
6. *(check)* I sent you an e-mail this morning. _____ it?
7. *(buy)* Are you still at the supermarket? _____ me some eggs?

UNIT 028

C. Complete the questions with **Could you...?** and the words in *italics*.

1. *(take me home)* _Could you take me home_____ ?	Of course.
2. *(come to my office)* _____ ?	What time?
3. *(sign this form)* _____ , please?	OK.
4. *(read me another story)* _____ ?	No. It's time for bed.
5. *(move your car)* _____ ?	Sure.
6. *(tell me your name)* _____ ?	It's Jennifer.

D. Complete the conversation with **Can I...?** / **Can you...?** and the words in *italics*.

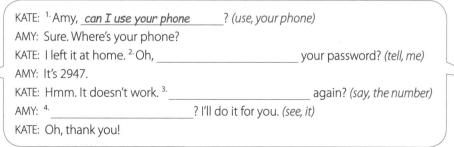

KATE: 1. Amy, _can I use your phone_____ ? *(use, your phone)*
AMY: Sure. Where's your phone?
KATE: I left it at home. 2. Oh, _____ your password? *(tell, me)*
AMY: It's 2947.
KATE: Hmm. It doesn't work. 3. _____ again? *(say, the number)*
AMY: 4. _____ ? I'll do it for you. *(see, it)*
KATE: Oh, thank you!

KATE

AMY

ANSWERS p.271, REVIEW TEST 5 p.222

He **must** wear a seat belt. must

(1)

You **must wear** your seat belt.

He **must wear** a seat belt.

---

 (2) must + **arrive/buy**/etc.

We use **must** to say that something is necessary.

I/we/you/they he/she/it	must	arrive buy show

- You **must arrive** on time for work.
- The concert isn't free. We **must buy** tickets.
- Travelers **must show** their passport before they get on the plane.

We do not use **must** to talk about the past. We use **had to.**

- Nancy **had to pay** for my lunch yesterday because I had no money.
- Mr. Smith had a lot of work last night, so he **had to stay** late.

---

(3) must not + **run/cross**/etc. *(negative)*

We use **must not** to say that it is wrong to do something.

I/we/you/they he/she/it	must not	run cross bring

- Children **must not run** near the pool.
- You **must not cross** the street when the light is red.
- Visitors **must not bring** any food into the museum.

---

 (4) We also use **must** to say that something is certainly true.

- "Elisa has lived in France for 10 years." "She **must speak** French very well."
- Jill and Peter **must like** each other a lot. They are always together.
- "We're leaving for Malaysia tomorrow." "You **must be** really excited!"

We use **must not** to say that something is certainly not true.

- Ken is still sleeping. He **must not have** class today.
- Shana's room is always dirty. She **must not clean** it often.
- This store **must not sell** hats. I don't see any here.

PRACTICE

A. Explain the signs with **must / must not** and the verbs in the box.

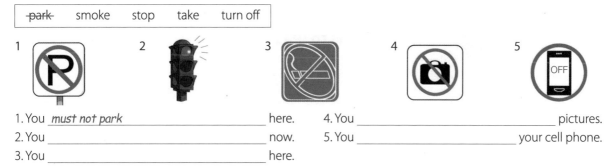

~~park~~	smoke	stop	take	turn off

1. You _must not park_ here.
2. You _____ now.
3. You _____ here.

4. You _____ pictures.
5. You _____ your cell phone.

B. Write **must / had to.**

1. "Can I borrow your car tonight, Dad?" "OK, but you _must_ be careful."
2. Mr. Smith wasn't in his office, so I _____ leave him a message.
3. Brenda _____ quit the softball team. She was too busy at school.
4. We _____ finish the report by 3 o'clock tomorrow.
5. The restaurant was full last night, so we _____ go to another place.
6. You _____ return this equipment before next Tuesday.

C. Complete the conversations with **must** and the verbs in the box. Write negative sentences if necessary.

~~be~~	feel	have	hurt	know	miss	read

1. The diamond on that ring is so big!
2. Sara caught a bad cold.
3. I haven't seen my mom for a year.
4. Nick just met Andrea for the first time.
5. I cut my finger.
6. The children are still playing outside.
7. Mark has so many books at home.

It _must be_ really expensive.
She _____ very well.
You _____ her.
He _____ her well.
It looks bad. It _____.
They _____ homework today.
He _____ a lot.

D. Complete the conversation with **must** and the verbs in *italics*. Write negative sentences if necessary.

JAMES: 1. Justin, you _must wear_ your seat belt. *(wear)*
JUSTIN: I know, Dad. Don't worry.
JAMES: Safety is very important, Justin.
2. You _____ that. *(forget)*
JUSTIN: I won't. 3. Also, I _____ all the mirrors before I drive. *(check)*
JAMES: Right. 4. And you _____ too fast. *(go)*

JAMES

JUSTIN

ANSWERS p.272, REVIEW TEST 5 p.222

🎧 030.mp3

(1)

I'm late. I **have to leave** now.

He **has to leave** now.

---

(2) **have/has to** + **hurry**/**wear**/etc.

We use **have/has to** to say that something is necessary.

I/we/you/they	have to	hurry
		wear
he/she/it	has to	return

- We **have to hurry**. The movie starts soon.
- Terry **has to wear** a suit tomorrow. He has a job interview.
- That's not my book. I **have to return** it to the library.

   We can also use **must** instead of **have/has to**. In everyday conversation, we use **have/has to** more often.

   - You **must be** quiet in the hall. *OR* You **have to be** quiet in the hall.

---

(3) **don't/doesn't have to** + **worry**/**see**/etc. *(negative)*

We use **don't/doesn't have to** to say that something is not necessary.

I/we/you/they	don't	have to	worry
			see
he/she/it	doesn't		go

- You **don't have to worry**. Everything will be OK.
- Scott canceled his appointment. He **doesn't have to see** the doctor today.
- We **don't have to go** to school this Friday. It's a national holiday.

Note that we use **don't/doesn't have to** and **must not** in different ways.

- Daisy lives near her office, so she **doesn't have to drive** to work. (Driving to work is not necessary.)
  Andy had a lot of wine, so he **must not drive** tonight. (It is wrong to drive tonight.)

---

(4) We use **had to** to talk about the past.

- It was cold last night, so I **had to put** on my jacket.

didn't have to . . . *(negative)*

- We **didn't have to cook** yesterday because we ordered pizza.

PRACTICE

A. Look at the pictures and complete the sentences with **have to** and the verbs in the box.

~~carry~~	see	use	wait

1. You *have to carry* an umbrella.

2. I _____ a dentist.

3. We _____ here.

4. We _____ the stairs.

B. Complete the sentences with **have/has to** or **don't/doesn't have to** and the verbs in the box.

ask	attend	call	pay	~~study~~	take	teach

1. Tim has a test tomorrow. He _*has to study*_____ tonight.
2. I've never played chess before. You _____ me.
3. Diane feels better today, so she _____ the medicine anymore.
4. Mr. Roy _____ me back. I'll visit his office.
5. "Can I leave work early today?" "You _____ Mr. Nelson first. He's right there."
6. The jeans are on sale, so I _____ a lot.
7. "Is Melanie joining us for lunch on Saturday?" "No. She _____ a wedding."

C. Complete the sentences with **have to / must** and the verbs in *italics*. Write negative sentences if necessary.

1. *(come)* The show starts at 7 p.m. You _*must not come*_____ late.
2. *(write)* Tim _____ the essay today. He can do it tomorrow.
3. *(run)* We _____. The bus isn't at the station yet.
4. *(be)* "Could I have a cup of tea?" "Sure, but it's very hot. You _____ careful."
5. *(park)* "You _____ in front of the entrance." "Sorry. I'll move my car."
6. *(pack)* We're going on camping this afternoon. We _____ now!
7. *(bring)* You _____ anything to the party. We already have enough food.
8. *(leave)* Bianca _____ now. She's going to miss the last train.

D. Complete the sentences with **had to / didn't have to** and the words in *italics*.

1. *(she, stay, in the hospital)* Gina hurt her leg, so _*she had to stay in the hospital*_____ last week.
2. *(we, stop, at the gas station)* _____ because we didn't have much gas.
3. *(I, tell, John)* _____ about my job. He already knew about it.
4. *(Allan, buy, a ticket)* The concert was free, so _____.
5. *(I, change, my clothes)* "Why are you late?" "Sorry. _____."

ANSWERS p.272, REVIEW TEST 5 p.222

(1)

You **should** go home.

He **should go** home.

---

(2) should + be/have/etc.

We use **should** to suggest that something is a good idea.

I/we/you/they he/she/it	should	be have see

- The soup is very hot. You **should be** careful.
- We **should have** a party. It'll be fun.
- "Samantha has a toothache." "Again? She **should see** a dentist."

---

(3) We use **should** in negative sentences in the following way:

I/we/you/they he/she/it	should not (= shouldn't)	drive drink smoke

- You look so tired. You **should not drive**.
- I'm going to bed soon. I **shouldn't drink** coffee.
- Frank **shouldn't smoke**. It's not good for his health.

---

(4) We use **Should I . . .?** to ask if something is a good idea.

- I think my hair is too long. **Should I get** a haircut?
- "**Should I bring** an umbrella?" "Yes. It might rain this afternoon."
- "**Should I wear** a tie to the wedding?" "No. You don't have to."
- "What **should I cook** for dinner tonight?" "How about chicken?"

---

(5) We often use **should** with **I think** or **I don't think**.

I think . . . should

- Sue is angry at me. **I think** I **should talk** to her.
- **I think** we **should go**. Our train arrives soon.

I don't think . . . should

- **I don't think** we **should buy** a new car.
- It's dark outside. **I don't think** you **should leave**.

PRACTICE

A. Look at the pictures and complete the sentences with **should** and the verbs in the box.

| buy | ~~call~~ | speak | wash |

1. He _should call_ _____ the police.
2. She _____ a new bicycle.

3. He _____ to the waiter.
4. He _____ his hands.

B. Complete the sentences with **should/shouldn't** and the words in *italics*.

1. *(we, give)* "Is it Jenny's birthday today?" "Yes. _We should give_ _____ her a gift."
2. *(children, watch)* _____ that movie. It's too scary.
3. *(you, return)* "Can I borrow this book?" "OK, but _____ it in three days."
4. *(we, take)* "Can we walk to the office?" "No. It's very far. _____ a taxi."
5. *(I, go)* "Do you have a cold?" "Yes. I have a fever. _____ to school today."
6. *(we, make)* The baby is sleeping. _____ any noise.

C. Complete the questions with **Should I . . . ?** and the words in the box.

| ~~cancel the trip~~ | change the channel | find a new job | go to the airport | invite |

1. The weather won't be good. _Should I cancel the trip_ _____?
2. My salary is not very high. _____?
3. My flight leaves at 8 p.m. What time _____?
4. "This TV show is boring." "_____?"
5. I'm planning Bill's birthday party. _____ Ben?

D. Read what each person says and write your opinion with **I think . . . should / I don't think . . . should** and the words in *italics*.

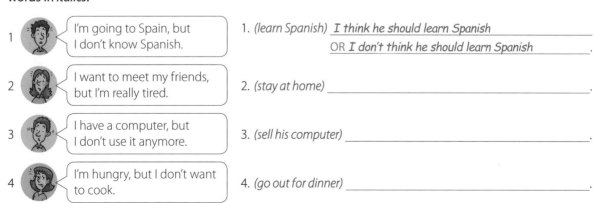

1. *(learn Spanish)* _I think he should learn Spanish_ _____
   OR _I don't think he should learn Spanish_ _____.

2. *(stay at home)* _____.

3. *(sell his computer)* _____.

4. *(go out for dinner)* _____.

ANSWERS p.272, REVIEW TEST 5 p.222

UNIT 032 | **Would** you help us, please? would

🎧 032.mp3

①

> Would you help us, please?

Would you help us, please?

---

② We use **Would you** + **close/get**/etc. . . .**?** to ask for a favor.

- I feel cold. **Would you close** the window, please?
- **Would you get** me a glass of water, please?
- "**Would you drive** me to work, please?" "Sure."

We can also use **Can/Could you . . .?** instead of **Would you . . .?**

- **Can you give** me some advice? *OR* **Could you give** me some advice?
- **Can you pass** me the pen? *OR* **Could you pass** me the pen?

---

③ **Would you like . . .?**

We use **Would you like . . .?** to offer something.

- "Did you enjoy your meal? **Would you like some dessert** now?" "That will be great."
- "**Would you like a newspaper**?" "No, thanks."

We use **Would you like to . . .?** to suggest doing something.

- "**Would you like to join** us for lunch?" "Sure."
- "**Would you like to go** fishing on Saturday?" "Sorry, I can't. I have to work."

---

④ I would like . . . (= **I'd like . . .**)

We use **I would like . . .** to ask for something.

- "Can I help you?" "Yes. **I would like two tickets**, please."
- "**I'd like a room**, please." "For one person?"

We use **I would like to . . .** to say that we want to do something.

- **I would like to introduce** you to Mr. Murphy.
- **I'd like to thank** you for your interest in our company.

74

PRACTICE

A. Complete the questions with **Would you . . .?** and the verbs in the box.

answer	bring	~~call~~	drive	show	turn off

1. _Would you call_____ me when you get this message?
2. David, I can't sleep. _____ the TV, please?
3. I feel sick. _____ me some medicine?
4. Karen, _____ the phone? I can't get it right now.
5. _____ me home? I didn't bring my car today.
6. _____ me the way to the hospital? It should be near here.

B. Look at the pictures and complete the questions with **Would you like . . .?** and the words in the box.

an orange	~~some cookies~~	some ice cream	some wine

1. _Would you like some_
    cookies ?
2. _____
    _____ ?
3. _____
    _____ ?
4. _____
    _____ ?

C. Complete the questions with **Would you like . . .?** / **Would you like to . . .?** and the words in *italics*.

1. *(a drink)* _Would you like a drink_____ ? Thanks, but I'm good.
2. *(go shopping)* _____ ? OK. Where?
3. *(some bread)* _____ ? No, thanks. I'm full.
4. *(a map)* _____ ? Yes, please.
5. *(see the menu)* _____ ? Thank you.
6. *(play golf)* _____ this Sunday? That sounds fun.

D. Complete the conversations with **I'd like . . .** / **I'd like to . . .** and the words in *italics*.

1. A: *(a coffee)* _I'd like a coffee_ OR _I would like a coffee_,
       please.
    B: Hot or cold?

2. A: *(study biology)* _____
       _____ in college.
    B: Me too!

3. A: Hello. Where are you traveling to?
    B: *(a ticket)* _____
       _____ to Boston.

4. A: *(invite you)* _____
       _____ to my Christmas party.
    B: That's very kind of you.

5. A: *(that blue sweater)* _____
       _____ , please.
    B: Here you are, ma'am.

6. A: Do you have any plans for vacation?
    B: *(visit Europe)* _____
       _____ .

ANSWERS p.272, REVIEW TEST 5 p.222

①

Active Someone **broke** the window.

Passive The window **was broken**.

"was broken" is the *passive*.

---

② We use the *passive* to say what happens to a person/thing.

am/is/are + **spoken/allowed/etc.** *(present simple)*

am/is/are	(not)	spoken allowed grown parked

Am	I	given ...? hurt ...?
Is	he/she/it	
Are	we/you/they	

- Spanish **is spoken** in Mexico.
- Children **are not allowed** in this pool.
- "**Is** wine **given** to every guest here?" "Yes. The hotel provides it for free."
- Bananas **are grown** in tropical countries.
- "Where's your car? It **isn't parked** outside." "I didn't bring it today."
- Did my dog bite you? **Are** you **hurt**?

---

③ **was/were** + **made/discovered/etc.** *(past simple)*

was/were	(not)	made discovered destroyed

- "This doll **was made** in Russia." "Wow! It's so pretty."
- Vitamin C is in food, but it **wasn't discovered** until 1928.
- Several buildings **were destroyed** during the storm.

---

④ **will/can/must/etc.** + **be** + **served/repaired/etc.**

will can must, etc.	(not)	be	served repaired answered

- Dinner **will be served** in a minute.
- Unfortunately, your phone **cannot be repaired**.
- All the questions on this form **must be answered**.

PRACTICE

A. Complete the sentences with the verbs in *italics*. Use the *present simple*.

1. *(lock)* The office door _is locked_ at 10 o'clock.
2. *(write)* I can't read this book. It _____ in Italian.
3. *(not require)* The museum is free, so tickets _____.
4. *(make)* Those shoes look great on you! _____ they _____ of leather?
5. *(deliver)* "Do you read the newspaper?" "Yes. It _____ to my home every morning."
6. *(not use)* Look at the old car. That kind of car _____ much these days.
7. *(bake)* "That bakery has fresh pies." "_____ those pies _____ every day?"

B. Complete the sentences with the words in *italics*. Use the *present simple* or *past simple*.

1. A: *(our team, move)* _Our team was moved_ _____ to the 3rd floor last week.
   B: Did any other teams change floors?

2. A: How old is that building?
   B: *(it, build)* _____ in 1910.

3. A: *(my dog, wash)* _____ _____ every weekend.
   B: Really? You take good care of your dog.

4. A: Did you go to the concert last night?
   B: *(it, cancel)* No. _____.

5. A: Is Tom a famous artist?
   B: *(his paintings, display)* Yes. _____ _____ at many galleries.

6. A: *(these photos, take)* _____ _____ last year.
   B: Your hair has grown a lot since then.

C. Complete the sentences with the given words.

announce	~~make~~	pay	show	wear

1. *(must not)* The same mistake _must not be made_ again.
2. *(can)* Casual clothes _____ to the office on Fridays.
3. *(cannot)* This movie _____ to children. There is too much violence in it.
4. *(will not)* The winners of the contest _____ until tomorrow.
5. *(must)* The credit card bill _____ every month.

D. Choose the correct one.

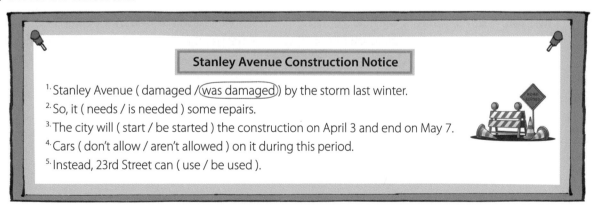

Stanley Avenue Construction Notice

1. Stanley Avenue (damaged / (was damaged)) by the storm last winter.
2. So, it (needs / is needed) some repairs.
3. The city will (start / be started) the construction on April 3 and end on May 7.
4. Cars (don't allow / aren't allowed) on it during this period.
5. Instead, 23rd Street can (use / be used).

ANSWERS p.273, REVIEW TEST 6 p.224

She **caught** a fish. A fish **was caught**. *Active vs. Passive*

🎧 034.mp3

①

She **caught** a fish.

A fish **was caught**.

② We use the *active* to say what a person/thing does.

- Nate **washes** the floors every evening.
- Helen **didn't pay** the phone bill.
- **Did** someone **invite** Jane?
- I **will fix** the bicycle.
- You **can find** the stapler on my desk.

We use the *passive* to say what happens to a person/thing.

- The floors **are washed** every evening.
- The phone bill **wasn't paid**.
- **Was** Jane **invited**?
- The bicycle **will be fixed**.
- The stapler **can be found** on my desk.

③ We use **by** in passive sentences to show who or what does the action.

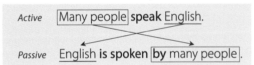

	Active	*Passive*
(*am/is/are*)	• Ms. Wright **teaches** my son.	→ My son **is taught by** Ms. Wright.
	• The farmers **grow** these pears.	→ These pears **are grown by** the farmers.
(*was/were*)	• Shakespeare **wrote** *Hamlet*.	→ *Hamlet* **was written by** Shakespeare.
	• The airline **canceled** all flights.	→ All flights **were canceled by** the airline.
(*will, can, must*, etc.)	• The company **will hold** a seminar.	→ A seminar **will be held by** the company.
	• Visitors **must not touch** the painting.	→ The painting **must not be touched by** visitors.

PRACTICE

A. Look at the pictures and complete the sentences with the verbs in the box using the active or passive. Use the *past simple.*

find	grow	hit	~~make~~	send

1. The vase *was made* _____ in 1563.
2. The flowers _____ by John.
3. A ball _____ the girl.
4. The rice _____ in China.
5. They _____ a box under the bed.

B. Complete the sentences with the verbs in the box using the passive. Use the *present simple* or *past simple.*

keep	repair	~~sell~~	tell	use	wear

1. Our house *was sold* _____ yesterday. We're moving to a new house next week.
2. "The meeting starts at 4:30." "Are you sure? I _____ 5:00."
3. "Excuse me, where is the ham?" "It _____ in the big fridge, next to the beef."
4. My car _____ this morning. I can drive to work now.
5. Computers _____ in almost every house today.
6. Those shoes are expensive because they _____ by Elvis Presley when he was alive.

C. Find and change any mistakes in each sentence. Put ✓ if the sentence is correct.

1. The house cleans on Saturdays. _____*cleans → is cleaned*_____
2. The pizza will deliver to your home. _____
3. I hope you were enjoyed your meal. _____
4. Beef must cook at a high temperature. _____
5. My sunglasses stole yesterday at the mall. _____
6. These magazines are published every month. _____
7. Does food allow in the library? _____
8. Jimmy was broken his leg twice last year. _____

D. Rewrite the sentences with **by** using the passive.

1. My husband wrote the letter. _____*The letter was written by my husband*_____ .
2. The Millers invited me. _____ .
3. Mr. Lee designed those buildings. _____ .
4. The author will sign the book. _____ .
5. Many tourists visit this place. _____ .
6. John Baird invented the television. _____ .
7. An accident can cause a traffic jam. _____ .

ANSWERS p.273, REVIEW TEST 6 p.224

035.mp3

①

The water **is** hot.

QUESTION **Is** the water hot?

---

② We can ask questions with **be**, **have/has** *(present perfect)*, and **will/can**/etc. in the following ways:

be

Am/Is/Are Was/Were	subject	...?

- **Are you** from Canada?
- "**Was the weather** good in Miami?" "Yes. It was sunny."

present perfect

Have Has	subject	tried ...? arrived ...?

- **Have you tried** Indian food before?
- Carl hasn't come yet. **Has Dave arrived**?

will/can/etc.

Will Can, etc.	subject	become ...? open ...?

- **Will Bob become** a famous actor?
- I can't open this jar. **Can you open** it?

---

③ We use **do/does/did** when we ask questions without **be**, **have/has**, and **will/can**/etc. In this case, we use **do/does/did** before the *subject*.

Do Does Did	subject	know ...? live ...? meet ...?

- **Do you know** this song?
- "Jenna lives in England." "**Does she live** in London?"
- "We met Mr. Jacobs last night." "**Did you meet** his wife too?"

Note that we do not use **be** instead of **do/does/did**.

- "**Do** you **have** a pen?" "No, but I have a pencil." *(NOT Are you have …?)*
- "**Does** this computer **work**?" "I think so." *(NOT Is this computer work?)*
- "**Did** Jerry **come** to your wedding?" "Yes, he did."

---

④ We can also ask questions with **who/what**/etc. In this case, we use **who/what**/etc. before the *verb*.

- "**Who is** your best friend?" "Michelle."
- "**What did** you **eat** for breakfast?" "Pancakes."
- I was worried about you. **Where have** you **been** all day?
- "**When will** you **be** home tonight?" "Around midnight."
- "**How can** you **forget** my birthday?" "I'm so sorry."

PRACTICE

A. Put the words in *italics* in the correct order.

1. *(go / you / will)* You don't look very well. _Will you go_____ to the doctor today?
2. *(are / the cookies)* "_____ in the oven." "Oh, I forgot about that."
3. *(Ted / done / has)* "Can I take Ted to the park with me?" "_____ his homework?"
4. *(live / Mitchell / does)* "_____ with his parents?" "No. With his brother."
5. *(Julie / was / sleeping)* "_____ when you called?" "Yes. I woke her up."
6. *(should / take / we)* We've studied for three hours. _____ a break.
7. *(you / found / have)* "_____ your keys yet?" "No. I'm still looking for them."
8. *(ask / I / you / can)* "I'm sorry, but _____ a question?" "Sure. What is it?"

B. Complete the questions with **be/do/have** in the correct form.

1. _Is_____ Kristin a nurse? — No. She's a doctor.
2. _____ you talked to Jane lately? — Yes. I spoke to her yesterday.
3. _____ Tina work in China? — Yes. She's in Beijing.
4. _____ Debbie spend a lot of money last weekend? — Not too much.
5. _____ you going to the seminar next month? — I haven't decided yet.
6. _____ Mr. Riley sold his car yet? — I'm not sure. I'll ask him.
7. _____ you wearing a new tie yesterday? — Yes. Did you like it?
8. _____ you have any plans for Saturday? — I'm visiting my parents.

C. Find and change any mistakes in each sentence. Put ✓ if the sentence is correct.

1. Are you remember that woman's name? _____ _Are → Do_
2. Should I sign on this paper? _____
3. Where was Joel grow up? _____
4. Does Kelly travel a lot for work? _____
5. Who the girl is in the picture? _____
6. Has Jenny called you yet? _____
7. What you bought at the grocery store yesterday? _____

D. Put the words in *italics* in the correct order.

1. A: I found my wallet!
   B: *(was / your car / in / it)*
   _Was it in your car_____ ?

2. A: *(are / moving to / Australia / you / when)*
   _____ ?
   B: Next year.

3. A: I'm seeing Thomas tonight.
   B: *(him / will / meet / where / you)*
   _____ ?

4. A: *(you / my office / come to / can)*
   _____ by 10 a.m.?
   B: Sure. I'll be there.

ANSWERS p.273, REVIEW TEST 7 p.226

🎧 036.mp3

(1) We use **who** to ask about people.

- A: **Who** is he?
  B: He's my favorite singer.
- "**Who** are you meeting tonight?" "Billy."
- "**Who** will you ask for help with this project?" "Gwen and Brian."
- "**Who** did you see at the mall?" "My roommate Sam."

Who is he?

He is my favorite singer.

(2) We use **what** to ask about things or to ask for information.

- A: **What** is it?
  B: It's a gift for my friend.
- "**What** can I do for you?" "Can I have a drink?"
- "**What** do you usually wear to work?" "A suit."
- This box is heavy. **What**'s in it?

We can also use **what** + *noun*.

- "**What magazine** are you reading?" "*Home Design*."
- "**What time** does the class start?" "It starts at 5 o'clock."

What is it?

It's a gift for my friend.

(3) We use **which** to ask about things.

- A: **Which** do you want?
  B: Tea, please.
- **Which** is closer, Chicago or Dallas?
- "**Which** does Joe want, cake, pie, or a muffin?" "He wants cake."
- We're going to the mall. **Which** should we take, the train or the bus?

We can use **which** + *noun* to ask about people/things.

- "**Which boy** is Jack?" "He's wearing jeans."
- "**Which dress** do you like best?" "The black one."

Which do you want?

Tea, please.

(4) **which** and **what**

We usually use **which** to ask for a choice from two or more things.

- "We have chicken and fish. **Which** would you like?" "I'll have the fish."
  (**Which** is used to ask for a choice between chicken and fish.)
- "**Which** sport do you like, baseball, basketball, or soccer?" "Baseball is my favorite."
  (**Which** is used to ask for a choice among baseball, basketball, and soccer.)

We usually use **what** to ask for information and not a choice.

- "**What** do you want for dinner tonight?" "Anything is OK."
  (**What** is used to ask for the dinner menu.)
- "**What** year were you born?" "1994."
  (**What** is used to ask for the birth year.)

PRACTICE

A. Look at the pictures and complete the questions with **who/what** and the words in *italics*. Use the *past simple*.

 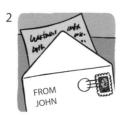  

1. *(she, pay)* " Who did she pay ?" "Jill."
2. *(John, send)* "_____?" "A letter."
3. *(they, visit)* "_____?" "Larry."
4. *(he, eat)* "_____?" "Some pizza."

B. Put the words in *italics* in the correct order.

1. *(what / your major / was)* " What was your major _____ in college?" "I studied art and history."
2. *(sports / what / you / play / do)* "_____?" "Basketball."
3. *(you / inviting / are / who)* "I'm having a party next week." "_____?"
4. *(that store / sell / what / does / fruit)* "_____?" "Apples and pears."
5. *(should / who / I / contact)* "_____ for reservations?" "John Murphy."
6. *(the problem / what / is)* "_____?" "Nothing. Everything is fine."

C. Look at the pictures and complete the questions with **which** and the nouns in the box.

book	car	~~restaurant~~	shirt

1. Which restaurant should we go to?
2. _____ should I buy?
3. _____ do you recommend?
4. _____ do you like?

D. Write **who/what/which**. Choose the most appropriate one.

1. Who _____ did you meet at Ken's wedding?
2. I'm not sure how to get outside. _____ door is the exit?
3. "_____ does Mr. Taylor teach?" "History."
4. "_____ is that woman?" "My neighbor."
5. _____ island did you visit in Indonesia, Java or Bali?
6. "_____ did you do last night?" "I stayed at home."
7. "Korea and Greece are having a soccer match tomorrow." "_____ team do you think will win?"
8. "_____ time does the next bus come?" "It comes at 9 o'clock."

ANSWERS p.273, REVIEW TEST 7 p.226

🎧 037.mp3

(1)

Where is the bathroom?

Over there.

Where is the bathroom?

We use **where** to ask about places.

- "**Where** is Ralph working these days?" "At a hospital."
- That necklace is so pretty. **Where** did you get it?
- "**Where** can I find an ATM?" "Across the street."
- "**Where** are we meeting Mr. Kim?" "In the lobby."

We often use **Where . . . from?**

- "**Where** are you **from**?" "I'm from Brazil."
- "**Where** did this package come **from**?" "It's from my company."

(2)

When is your flight?

When is your flight?

We use **when** to ask about time or dates.

- "**When** is Cindy's birthday?" "March 21."
- "**When** does the new museum open?" "Next month."
- "I'm sorry, but I'm busy now. I'll call you later." "**When** can you call me back?"
- "**When** do you watch TV?" "I watch TV after dinner."

(3)

Why are you crying?

I'm reading a sad story.

Why are you crying?

We use **why** to ask about reasons.

- "**Why** are you studying Italian?" "I use it at work."
- "**Why** did you take a taxi?" "Because I was in a hurry."
- "**Why** has Terry been in her room all day?" "She isn't feeling well."
- "Jeff is in Africa right now." "Really? **Why** did he go there?"

PRACTICE

A. Write **where/when/why**.

1. _When_ does the next train for Chicago leave?
2. _____ is Tom upset?
3. _____ did Simon get married?
4. _____ can I return these shoes?
5. _____ are your hands dirty?
6. _____ should I go on vacation?

At 12 o'clock.
He lost his cell phone.
Last month.
The customer service counter.
I was fixing the car.
How about Mexico?

B. Put the words in *italics* in the correct order.

1. (quit / did / why / you) _Why did you quit_ your job? I thought you liked it.
2. (be / will / your parents / when) "_____ home?" "I'm not sure."
3. (do / live / where / you) I live in Seattle. _____?
4. (why / wear / should / I) "_____ sunglasses?" "The sun is very strong today."
5. (bringing / you / why / are) _____ a coat? Are you going somewhere?
6. (where / from / is / she) "That's the new student in my class." "Really? _____?"
7. (Sharon / leaving / when / is) _____ for London? Is it next week?

C. Write questions with **where/when/why**.

1. _Where do you park your car_ ?
2. _____ ?
3. _____ ?
4. _____ ?
5. _____ ?

I park my car on Ivory Street.
Ivan left the office an hour ago.
The bus comes in 10 minutes.
The mall is closed because it's a holiday.
You can find the elevator in the lobby.

D. Chris is on the phone with Uncle Simon. Choose the correct one.

CHRIS: Hello. Uncle Simon! Thank you for inviting me to Greece.
SIMON: Chris, I miss you so much.
     1. ((When) / Where) are you coming?
CHRIS: Next Monday. 2. (Where / Why) should we meet?
SIMON: Let's meet at the airport.
     3. (When / Where) does your flight arrive?
CHRIS: At 3:30. 4. (When / Where) are we going after we meet?
     Can we go to Santorini first?
SIMON: 5. Sure, but (where / why) do you want to go there?
CHRIS: I saw some pictures online. It looks very beautiful there.

CHRIS

SIMON

ANSWERS p.273, REVIEW TEST 7 p.226

How can I help you?   *Questions (4)* **how**

🎧 038.mp3

①

How can I help you?

How can I help you?

We use **how** to ask about ways to do something.

- "**How** can I get to the library?" "Take Bus 202."
- **How** do you say "tree" in German?
- "**How** did Jim break his leg?" "He fell while he was skiing."
- "**How** do I open this door?" "Here, use this key card."

② **how + be**

- **How is** the weather today?
- "**How was** your trip to Hong Kong?" "It was so much fun!"
- "**How are** you these days?" "I'm very busy."

③ **how +** *adjective/adverb*

How	adjective/adverb		
" How	long	have you known Lucy?"	"For six years."
" How	far	is the train station?"	"Just a few kilometers."
" How	fast	can a cheetah run?"	"I'm not sure."
" How	often	do you exercise?"	"Twice a week."

④ We use **how many/much** to ask about the number or quantity.

- "Could I have some cookies, please?" "**How many** do you want?"
- "Put some salt in the soup." "**How much** should I put?"

   We also use **how much** to ask about the price.

   - "This is a nice watch. **How much** is it?" "That one is $800."

We can also use **how many/much +** *noun*.

- "**How many guests** are coming for dinner?" "Maybe 10."
- "**How much time** do you need?" "It will take about 30 minutes."

PRACTICE

A. Put **how** and the words in *italics* in the correct order.

1. *(I / can / contact)* <u>How can I contact</u> _____ you?
2. *(you / come / did)* _____ to Germany?
3. *(can / turn off / I)* _____ the heater?
4. *(do / get to / your kids)* _____ school?
5. *(prepare / we / should)* _____ for the party?

Here's my phone number.
I took a train from Italy.
Just push that button.
They usually walk.
Let's cook some food first.

B. Complete the questions with **how + be**.

1. <u>How are you</u> _____ today? Are you still sick?
2. _____ ? Was it good?
3. _____ ?
4. _____ ?
5. _____ in Hawaii?

I'm OK. I feel better.
Yes. The concert was excellent.
The food tastes bad. I don't like it.
My parents are fine.
My holiday was great.

UNIT
038

Grammar Gateway Basic

C. Complete the questions with **how** and the words in the box.

| far | ~~fast~~ | long | many | much | much | often | old | tall |

1. " <u>How fast</u> _____ was Dan driving?" "I don't know, but it was over the speed limit."
2. "Your little brother is very cute. _____ is he?" "He's six years old."
3. "These apples were on sale." " _____ were they?"
4. " _____ do you check your e-mail?" "Once a day."
5. " _____ is the park from your house?" "Three miles."
6. "Sorry, but you have to wait. The restaurant is full." " _____ do we have to wait?"
7. " _____ cash do you have? Can I borrow some?" "I only have credit cards."
8. " _____ is Carl?" "I think he's 180 cm."
9. " _____ children do you have?" "I have two daughters."

D. Put the words in *italics* in the correct order.

Clerk: Hello. ¹·<u>How can I help you</u> _____ ? *(how / help / you / can / I)*
AMY: I'd like to buy some perfume for my friend.
Clerk: Try this new perfume.
²· _____ ? *(scent / how / is / the)*
AMY: It's nice. I want to buy it.
³· _____ ? *(is / how / much / it)*
Clerk: It's $50. If you want, I can deliver it to your friend's house.
AMY: ⁴· _____ ? *(long / will / how / take / it)*
Clerk: It'll take two or three days.

Clerk

AMY

ANSWERS p.274, REVIEW TEST 7 p.226

🎧 039.mp3

(1)

The stars are very pretty, **aren't they?**

The stars are very pretty, **aren't they?**

"aren't they?" is a *tag question*. A *tag question* comes at the end of a statement.

We use *tag questions* to ask for agreement or to make sure something is correct.

- It's going to rain tomorrow, **isn't it**?
- You aren't reading this book, **are you**?

(2) *Tag questions* can be negative or positive. We always use **she/you**/etc. *(pronouns)* as the *subject* in a *tag question*.

We use negative *tag questions* after positive statements.

positive statement			*negative tag question*	
Julie	is	pretty,	**isn't**	**she**?

- It was a long trip, **wasn't it**?
- Ellen enjoys surfing, **doesn't she**?
- You can drive, **can't you**?
- "Mark and Tina will come to see us tonight, **won't they**?" "I'm not sure."

We use positive *tag questions* after negative statements.

negative statement			*positive tag question*	
You	are not	angry,	**are**	**you**?

- The roller coaster wasn't scary at all, **was it**?
- Sam doesn't like me, **does he**?
- You haven't seen Bob lately, **have you**?
- "Sophie can't speak French, **can she**?" "I don't know."

(3) When we answer *tag questions*, we say **Yes** for positive answers and **No** for negative answers.

- "You know this song, **don't you**?" "**Yes**, I do." (= Yes, I know this song.)
- "The food was very good, **wasn't it**?" "**No**, it was awful." (= No, the food wasn't very good.)
- "You haven't heard this story, **have you**?" "**Yes**, I've heard it many times!"
- "Jack doesn't smoke, **does he**?" "**No**, he doesn't."

PRACTICE

A. Read the following positive statements and write tag questions in the correct form.

1. These sunglasses are yours, _aren't they_ ?   4. Mary has been to Morocco, _____ ?
2. You locked the door, _____ ?   5. You can fix the computer, _____ ?
3. Your parents live in New York, _____ ?   6. Tomorrow is Tuesday, _____ ?

B. Read the following negative statements and write tag questions in the correct form.

1. Bill doesn't like sports, _does he_ ?   4. Joseph can't play the guitar, _____ ?
2. You haven't met Ronald, _____ ?   5. You aren't coming to the meeting, _____ ?
3. I'm not wrong, _____ ?   6. We don't work this weekend, _____ ?

C. Read the following statements and write tag questions in the correct form.

1. You went shopping today, _didn't you_ ?	Yes, I did.
2. The soccer game was great, _____ ?	Yes, it was exciting.
3. You can't speak Japanese, _____ ?	No, I can't.
4. It's not cold outside, _____ ?	No. It's very warm today.
5. You have ridden a horse before, _____ ?	Yes, I have.
6. Your sister doesn't like spaghetti, _____ ?	No, she doesn't.
7. Tom and Megan are having a baby next year, _____ ?	Yes, they are.

D. Write **Yes** or **No**.

1. You are from Russia, aren't you?	_Yes_ , I'm Russian.
2. Sally can't swim, can she?	_____ . She is afraid of water.
3. This umbrella is mine, isn't it?	_____ , it's yours.
4. You haven't had lunch yet, have you?	_____ . I'm very hungry.
5. You don't drink soda, do you?	_____ , I never drink it.
6. Jane's children are cute, aren't they?	_____ . They're nice too.

E. Justin is looking at stars. Write tag questions in the correct form.

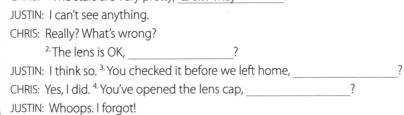

CHRIS: [1.] The stars are very pretty, _aren't they_ ?
JUSTIN: I can't see anything.
CHRIS: Really? What's wrong?
      [2.] The lens is OK, _____ ?
JUSTIN: I think so. [3.] You checked it before we left home, _____ ?
CHRIS: Yes, I did. [4.] You've opened the lens cap, _____ ?
JUSTIN: Whoops. I forgot!

CHRIS   JUSTIN

ANSWERS p.274, REVIEW TEST 7 p.226

UNIT
039

Grammar Gateway Basic

Do you know **where the station is**? *Indirect questions*

🎧 040.mp3

①

*Do you know **where the station is**?*

Where is the station?
↓
Do you know **where the station is**?

"**where the station is**" is an *indirect question*. An *indirect question* is a question inside a sentence.

---

② We can ask *indirect questions* with **who/what**/etc. *(question words)*. In this case, we use *subject + verb* after the *question words*.

Indirect questions

question word + subject + **be/have/can**/etc.

- Who is Holly?
- How has Peter been? → I don't know
- Where can we find a gas station?

who Holly is.
how Peter has been.
where we can find a gas station.

Indirect questions

question word + subject + **like/close**/etc.

- What do you like?
- When does the store close? → Could you tell me
- Why did Carol leave early?

what you like?
when the store closes?
why Carol left early?

We do not use **do/does/did** in *indirect questions*.

- Can you tell me **what you study in college**? *(NOT* Can you tell me what do you study in college?)
- I'm not sure **where Jason lives**. *(NOT* I'm not sure where does Jason live.)

---

③ We use **if/whether** when we ask *indirect questions* without *question words*. In this case, we use *subject + verb* after **if/whether**.

Indirect questions

if/whether + *subject* + **speak/come**/etc.

- Does Sam speak Greek?

if Sam speaks Greek.
whether Sam speaks Greek.

→ I wonder

- Is Jane coming to the meeting?

if Jane is coming to the meeting.
whether Jane is coming to the meeting.

PRACTICE

A. Put the words in *italics* in the correct order.

1. *(where / is / the bus stop)* Could you tell me <u>where the bus stop is</u> ?
2. *(Emily / why / was / late)* Do you know _____ ?
3. *(I / parked / my car / where)* I don't remember _____ .
4. *(in the report / I / should / what / write)* I don't know _____ .
5. *(John / will / be back / when)* I'm not sure _____ .
6. *(called / why / the manager / me)* Do you know _____ ?
7. *(you / answer / how / can / this question)* Please tell me _____ .

B. Tony and Sue are Tina's new neighbors, and she wants to know about them. Write Tina's questions with **Do you know.**

1. When did they move here?
2. Where did they live before?
3. What does Tony do?
4. How many children do they have?
5. What are their hobbies?

TINA

<u>Do you know when they moved here</u> ?
_____ ?
_____ ?
_____ ?
_____ ?

UNIT 040

Grammar Gateway Basic

C. Read the following questions and complete the new sentences with **if/whether**.

1. Did Greg finish his report? — I don't know <u>if (OR whether) Greg finished his report</u> .
2. Did many people come to the party? — I'm not sure _____ .
3. Is Annie going to visit us tomorrow? — Could you tell me _____ ?
4. Have you seen my brother? — I wonder _____ .
5. Can Joey play the violin? — I'm not sure _____ .
6. Has Hannah gone home? — Do you know _____ ?

D. Amy has just met a tourist. Put the words in *italics* in the correct order.

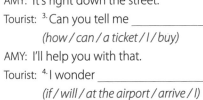

Tourist: ¹·Excuse me. Could you tell me <u>how I can get to the airport</u> ?
   (get / can / how / I / to the airport)
AMY: Sure. It's easy. You can take the subway.
Tourist: ²·Do you know _____ ? *(the station / where / is)*
AMY: It's right down the street.
Tourist: ³·Can you tell me _____ ?
   (how / can / a ticket / I / buy)
AMY: I'll help you with that.
Tourist: ⁴·I wonder _____ by 5 p.m.
   (if / will / at the airport / arrive / I)
AMY: Don't worry. It only takes 30 minutes.

Tourist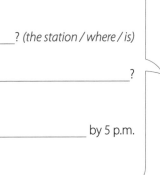

AMY

ANSWERS p.274, REVIEW TEST 7 p.226

| **Exercising** is good for health. <small>-ing and to . . .</small>

🎧 041.mp3

①

Exercising is good for health.

---

② We can use **-ing** as the *subject* in a sentence.

- **Painting** is fun. I really enjoy it.
- **Traveling** can cost a lot of money.
- "I'm still sleepy. I have to wake up."   "**Drinking coffee** might help."

We can also use **-ing** as the *object* in a sentence.

- I enjoy **playing cards**.
- We just finished **cleaning the house**.
- "Do you mind **opening the window**? It's hot in here."   "No. Go ahead."

---

③ We can use various words after **-ing** as in the following sentences:

- Learning a foreign language | takes a long time.
- Washing your hands before meals | is important.

- Jack avoids | taking the subway in the morning.
- I suggest | wearing that blue dress to the party.

---

④ We can use **to . . .** as the *object* in a sentence.

- I didn't expect **to see you**. What brings you here?
- Benny wants **to buy a car**.
- Lisa isn't good at math, so her brother offered **to help her**.

We can also use **to . . .** as the *subject* in a sentence, but we use **-ing** more often.

- **Smoking** is not allowed in this restaurant. (= To smoke)
- It's raining. **Bringing an umbrella** was a good idea. (= To bring an umbrella)

---

⑤ We can also use various words after **to . . .** as in the following sentences:

- Is Megan planning | to study in Europe next year?
- We hope | to work with you again.

PRACTICE

A. Complete the sentences with the verbs in the box using **-ing**.

~~collect~~	lose	make	plant	swim	watch	wear

1. I have a lot of comic books at home. _Collecting_ them is my favorite hobby.
2. _____ weight is hard. I exercise every day, but it doesn't help.
3. I want to avoid _____ a reservation for a room on Saturday. It's too expensive.
4. You should put on your sunglasses. _____ them protects your eyes.
5. "What do you usually do on weekends?" "I enjoy _____ old movies."
6. _____ in this lake is not safe. It's very deep.
7. _____ trees helps the environment.

B. Put the words in *italics* in the correct order using **-ing**.

1. *(to work / drive)* Traffic is bad in the morning. _Driving to work_ takes a long time.
2. *(read / that book)* I finished _____ last night. It was very good.
3. *(about her / talk)* I think Bill likes Diane. He keeps _____.
4. *(eat / too much food)* _____ can cause a stomachache.
5. *(with these old shoes / run)* _____ hurts my feet. I should get new ones.

C. Choose the one you agree with and write sentences using **-ing**.

make friends	☐ easy	☐ difficult
ride a roller coaster	☐ exciting	☐ scary
take a taxi	☐ cheap	☐ expensive
travel alone	☐ safe	☐ dangerous
play chess	☐ fun	☐ boring

1. _Making friends is easy_ OR _Making friends is difficult_ .
2. _____.
3. _____.
4. _____.
5. _____.

D. Read what each person says and complete the sentences with the verbs in *italics* using **to . . .** Use the *present simple.*

JOE — (Can we go camping this weekend?)
1. *(want)* Joe _wants to go camping this weekend_ .

MILA — (I should visit my grandparents tomorrow.)
4. *(plan)* Mila _____.

HENRY — (I will be home by 6.)
2. *(promise)* Henry _____.

DANIEL — (My dream is to win a Nobel Prize.)
5. *(hope)* Daniel _____.

BELLA — (I have to finish the report by Monday.)
3. *(need)* Bella _____.

LUCY — (The interview went well. Maybe I'll get the job.)
6. *(expect)* Lucy _____.

ANSWERS p.274, REVIEW TEST 8 p.228

UNIT
041

Grammar Gateway Basic

UNIT 042 | He **enjoys cooking**. -ing/to ... as *objects*

042.mp3

①

He is making pizza.

He **enjoys cooking**.

He **wants to open** a restaurant.

"**cooking**" is the *object* of the *verb* "**enjoys**."
"**to open**" is the *object* of the *verb* "**wants**."

---

② We use **-ing** as the *object* of the following *verbs*:

enjoy	finish	keep	mind	**-ing**
avoid	give up	practice	suggest	(writing, raining, waiting, etc.)

- "I **finished writing** my essay." "Great. Can I read it?"
- It **kept raining** for three days.
- "Do you **mind waiting** a moment?" "No problem."
- Sophie is **avoiding going** to the dentist because she is scared.
- "Ken will **give up teaching** and go to law school." "Really? Does he want to be a lawyer?"
- Jane and I take a Chinese class together. We **practice speaking** Chinese every day.
- We don't **suggest staying** at that hotel. The service isn't good.

  We do not use **to ...** with these *verbs*.

  - Jake **finished painting** the fence. (*NOT* finished to paint)

---

③ We use **to ...** as the *object* of the following *verbs*:

want	need	hope	expect	**to ...**
decide	plan	promise	offer	(to worry, to get, to see, etc.)
choose	ask	learn	refuse	

- "Alan, are you OK?" "You don't **need to worry** about me. I'm fine."
- I **hope to get** a reply from you soon.
- We can **expect to see** a lot of snowfall this winter.
- "Have you **decided to take** the job?" "Yes. I will start next week."
- "What are you doing this weekend?" "I'm **planning to attend** a wedding on Saturday."
- Ben **promised to be** here at 4, but he hasn't arrived yet.
- "Jackie and Allison **offered to bring** some cake to the party." "That's great!"

  We do not use **-ing** with these *verbs*.

  - I **promised to go** out for dinner with you tonight, but I can't. (*NOT* promised going)

PRACTICE

A. Choose the correct one.

1. "The meeting is at 3:30, right?" "It was, but Ms. Bill asked (changing /(to change) the time."
2. I've been busy with too much work, so I suggested (hiring / to hire) more people.
3. "You promised (doing / to do) all your homework tonight." "OK, I'll do it."
4. I was going to offer (helping / to help) with your report, but you already finished it.
5. My roommate is practicing (singing / to sing) in her room.
6. I told John some ghost stories, but he refused (believing / to believe) in them.

B. Look at the pictures and complete the sentences with the words in the box using -ing or to . . .

| buy this house | clean the bathroom | ~~get some gas~~ | look at me | open the door | play the flute |

1. We need _to get some gas_ _____ .

2. Do you mind _____ _____ for me?

3. I finished _____ _____ .

4. We decided _____ _____ .

5. I plan _____ _____ at a concert.

6. He keeps _____ _____ .

C. Complete the sentences with the given words using -ing or to . . .

| become | drive | ~~ride~~ | smoke | spend |

1. *(learn)* "When did you _learn to ride_ _____ a motorcycle?" "Last year."
2. *(choose)* "Why did you _____ a writer?" "I love writing short stories."
3. *(avoid)* Julie _____ a car at night.
4. *(expect)* I didn't _____ so much money at the mall today.
5. *(give up)* "My father _____ a year ago." "You must be proud of him."

D. Complete the conversation with the verbs in *italics* using -ing or to . . .

LINDA

JAMES

LINDA: What are you thinking about, James?
JAMES: [1.] I _want to open_ _____ a restaurant. *(want, open)*
LINDA: [2.] But you _____ to your office. *(enjoy, go)*
JAMES: [3.] I do, but I _____ my own business. *(hope, have)*
LINDA: It will be hard, you know.
JAMES: I know. [4.] But I don't _____ hard. *(mind, work)*

ANSWERS p.275, REVIEW TEST 8 p.228

UNIT 043 | They **like visiting/to visit** museums. *Verb + -ing/to . . .*

🎧 043.mp3

①

They **like visiting** museums.

OR They **like to visit** museums.

---

② We can use **-ing** or **to . . .** after the following *verbs*:

like	love	prefer	hate	**-ing** (skating, living, etc.)
start	begin	continue		**to . . .** (to skate, to live, etc.)

- Polly **loves skating**. *OR* Polly **loves to skate**.
- Do you **prefer living** in the city or in the country?
  OR Do you **prefer to live** in the city or in the country?
- I **hate doing** the dishes. *OR* I **hate to do** the dishes.
- When did you **start studying** French? *OR* When did you **start to study** French?
- Leaves **begin falling** in October. *OR* Leaves **begin to fall** in October.
- Harry will **continue working** at the bank. *OR* Harry will **continue to work** at the bank.

---

③ We can also use **-ing** or **to . . .** after the following *verbs*, but there are differences in meaning:

stop	**-ing** not do something anymore
	to . . . not do something to do something else

- Please **stop making** noise. I can't sleep.
  (= Please don't make noise anymore.)
- There are some nice dresses at that store. Let's **stop to look**.
  (= Let's not do what we're doing now to look at the dresses.)
- Paula **stopped listening** to the radio and turned on the TV.
- "Can we **stop to eat** something?" "Sure. What do you want?"

try	**-ing** do something to see what happens
	to . . . do something with effort

- "Planning a wedding is so tiring." "You should **try hiring** a wedding planner."
  (= You should hire a wedding planner to see what happens.)
- After graduating, Tina will **try to get** a job at a marketing company.
  (= Tina will look for a job with effort.)
- "My computer isn't working." "You should **try turning** off its power and on again."
- I **tried to talk** to Jessica, but she was still upset.

PRACTICE

A. Complete the sentences with the verbs in *italics* using **-ing** or **to . . .**

1. *(find)* We expected _to find_ Mr. Miller in his office, but he wasn't there.
2. *(go)* We avoid _____ to the mall on Sundays. It's very crowded.
3. *(feel)* "When did you begin _____ sick?" "This morning."
4. *(join)* Greg and I refused _____ the golf club because it cost too much.
5. *(write)* Thomas continued _____ the novel until it was finished.
6. *(drive)* I don't like _____ in the snow. It's very dangerous sometimes.
7. *(learn)* My grandmother keeps _____ new things. She's learning about smartphones these days.

B. Complete the sentences with **stop** and the verbs in the box.

ask	buy	laugh	take	~~walk~~	worry

1. Can we _stop walking_ now? My feet hurt.
2. The movie was so funny. I couldn't _____.
3. "I think we're lost." "We should _____ for directions."
4. "I'm so nervous about my speech." "_____ about it so much."
5. Can we _____ some milk at the store? We don't have any at home.
6. Let's _____ a picture here. The view from this mountain is beautiful.

C. Complete the conversations with the verbs in the box.

call	finish	go	~~invite~~	take

1. Why wasn't Joel at the party?
2. Are you done writing the report?
3. Have you been to the new theater?
4. I've never done yoga.
5. Did you speak to Bob?

I tried _to invite_ him, but he was busy.
Almost. I'll try _____ it by 2.
No. Let's try _____ there tomorrow.
You should try _____ a lesson.
No. I'm trying _____ him now.

D. Find and change any mistakes in each sentence. Put ✓ if the sentence is correct.

Picasso – A great artist

1. Picasso started studying art when he was four.   ✓
2. He practiced to draw at school until he was 16.   _____
3. Picasso always loved experiencing new things.   _____
4. So, he decided moving to Paris.   _____
5. He was very poor, but he didn't give up to paint.   _____
6. He continued making artwork until he died in 1973.   _____

ANSWERS p.275, REVIEW TEST 8 p.228

(1)

> I want you to clean the room.

She **wants him to clean** the room.

---

(2) want + *person* + to ...

- I'm really tired, so I **want you to drive**.
- Jenny didn't **want Albert to buy** the TV. It was too expensive.
- I'm going to the store. Do you **want me to get** anything for you?

  We can also use **want + to ...**, but there is a difference in meaning.

  - I **want to help** him. (= I think I should help him.)

    I **want you to help** him. (= I think you should help him.)

---

(3) We can also use *person* + to ... after the following *verbs*:

advise	allow	ask	expect	teach	tell

	verb	person	to ...
The doctor	advised	Judy	to drink more water.
We didn't	expect	Fred	to win the race.
Can you	teach	me	to dance?

---

(4) make/have/let + *person* + base form

	make/have/let	person	base form	
Bob and Helen	made	me	wait	for an hour.
Erin	had	Tom	move	some furniture.
	Let	me	introduce	myself.

In this case, we do not use **to ...**

- Exercising **makes me feel** healthy. (*NOT* makes me to feel)

---

(5) help + *person* + base form

	help	person	base form	
Can you	help	me	find	the post office?
I	helped	Sean	do	his homework.

We can also use **help + *person* + to ...**

- I'll **help you hang** that picture. *OR* I'll **help you to hang** that picture.

PRACTICE

A. Complete the conversations with **want** and the words in *italics*.

1. A: *(you, come)* I _want you to come_ to my wedding.
   B: Of course! I'll be there.

2. A: Let's stay at home tonight.
   B: *(us, have)* Actually, Leo and Marcy _____ _____ dinner with them.

3. A: *(me, move)* Do you _____ those boxes upstairs?
   B: Thanks, but I can do it.

4. A: John isn't here yet.
   B: *(you, call)* I don't have my phone now, so I _____ _____ him.

B. Read what each person says and complete the sentences with the verbs in *italics*. Use the *past simple*.

JOE — < Bill, can you close the window? >
1. *(ask)* Joe _asked Bill to close the window_ .

JAY — < Ben, you can use the camera. >
2. *(allow)* Jay _____ .

LYNN — < Brian, could you answer the phone? >
3. *(tell)* Lynn _____ .

DIANA — < David will call back soon. >
4. *(expect)* Diana _____ .

TIM — < Nick, please speak louder. >
5. *(want)* Tim _____ .

ANNA — < Nancy, you should go to bed. >
6. *(advise)* Anna _____ .

C. Complete the sentences with the right person (her, etc.) and the verbs in the box.

| ~~bake~~ | buy | drive | pay | run | stay |

1. Lana makes delicious cookies, so I had _her bake_ some for me.
2. My wife wants me to lose weight. She makes _____ every morning now.
3. "Where is Larry?" "I had _____ some eggs and butter."
4. I want to use Dad's car, but he won't let _____ it.
5. "Did you and Lucy find a hotel?" "No, but my friend let _____ at her house."
6. Jim and Cody broke a vase in the store, so the clerk made _____ for it.

D. Complete the conversations with **help** and the verbs in the box.

| answer | carry | find | ~~prepare~~ | wash |

1. I have to make dinner.
2. I lost my passport.
3. These bags are heavy.
4. I don't understand this question.
5. My dog is so dirty.

I can _help you prepare_ OR _help you to prepare_ it.
I will _____ it.
I can _____ them.
I can _____ it.
I will _____ your dog.

ANSWERS p.275, REVIEW TEST 8 p.228

They're running **to catch** the bus. to ... of purpose

🎧 045.mp3

They're running **to catch** the bus.

We can use **to . . .** to talk about the purpose of an action.

- I must study hard **to pass** the exam.
- "How can I help you?" "I'm here **to meet** Mr. Johnson."
- We usually go to a bar **to drink** some wine on Friday nights.
- "Where's Fred?" "He went out **to play** baseball."

We can also use **in order to . . .** instead of **to . . .** In everyday conversation, we use **to . . .** more often.

- A lot of effort is necessary **(in order) to succeed**.
- Tickets are required **(in order) to enter** the theater.

It's **time to go**.

We can use *noun* + **to . . .** to talk about the purpose of something.

time	to go
key	to open
line	to buy
place	to stay
money	to spend

- "Do you have a **key to open** this cabinet?" "It's not locked."
- The **line to buy** tickets for last night's game was very long. We had to wait for an hour.
- Are there any hotels nearby? I need a **place to stay**.
- I can't go shopping. I have no **money to spend**.

PRACTICE

A. Look at the pictures and complete the sentences with the right place (hair salon, etc.) and the words in the box using **to ...**

| get a haircut | return a book | see the pandas | send a package | visit his friend |

1. She went to the _hair salon to get a haircut_ .
2. He went to the _____.
3. He went to the _____.
4. She went to the _____.
5. They went to the _____.

B. Complete the sentences with the words in the box using **to ...**

| buy some ice cream | get some fresh air | help him |
| make an appointment | stay healthy | take a nap |

1. Derek got up at 5 o'clock this morning. He wanted to go home early _to take a nap_ .
2. I opened the window _____.
3. A boy fell down the stairs, so Ben stopped _____.
4. I'm going to the supermarket _____.
5. You should exercise regularly _____.
6. I'm not feeling well, so I'm calling the doctor's office _____.

C. Put the words in *italics* in the correct order using **to ...**

1. *(sit / place)* There's no _place to sit_ here. We should go to another café.
2. *(time / visit)* I don't have _____ my grandparents these days.
3. *(ask / questions)* Can we meet this afternoon? I have some _____ you.
4. *(games / play)* I'm bored. Do you have any _____?
5. *(book / read)* It'll be a long trip. You should take a _____.
6. *(share / snacks)* "Let's have a picnic tomorrow." "Should I bring some _____?"

D. Put the words in *italics* in the correct order using **to ...**

JAMES: [1.] Linda, it's _time to go_ ! *(go / time)*
LINDA: I need five more minutes.
　　　[2.] I just have a few _____. *(things / do)*
JAMES: Please hurry! [3.] I have _____. *(finish / work)*
　　　[4.] I've also got _____. *(meetings / attend)*
LINDA: OK. [5.] Then, there's no _____. *(talk / time)*
JAMES: All right. I'll wait in the car.

JAMES

LINDA

ANSWERS p.275, REVIEW TEST 8 p.228

🎧 046.mp3

1

a **bag**   three **bags**

a **bag** → three **bags**
singular   *plural*

We use *singular nouns* for one person/thing and *plural nouns* for two or more people/things.

Singular	a **bag**	one **girl**	this **car**	my **son**
Plural	three **bags**	some **girls**	these **cars**	your **sons**

2 We usually add -s at the end of *nouns* to make *plural nouns*.

this desk → these desk**s**	a cat → some cat**s**	one apple → two apple**s**	my friend → my friend**s**

- These **desks** are made of wood.
- "My **friends** bought a birthday gift for me." "What did you get?"

But we add -es/-ies/etc. at the end of some *nouns* to make *plural nouns*.

-sh/-ch/-s/-x/-z/-o + -es	dish → dish**es**	church → chur**ches**	potato → potat**oes**	*BUT:* kilo → kilo**s**
-y → -ies	baby → bab**ies**	lady → lad**ies**	party → part**ies**	*BUT:* day → day**s**
-f/-fe → -ves	calf → cal**ves**	knife → kni**ves**	self → sel**ves**	wife → wi**ves**

- Steve usually washes the **dishes** after dinner.
- Look at those **babies**. They're so cute!
- "Can you put these **knives** in the drawer?" "Sure."
- Americans usually attend many **parties** during the holiday season.
- "The weather is very nice these **days**." "Yes. It's perfect for a picnic."

More about spelling rules: Appendix p.249

3 Some *plural nouns* are irregular.

a **person** → some **people**	my **foot** → my **feet**
a **woman** → many **women**	a **child** → a lot of **children**

- Some **people** can write with both hands.
- I can't walk anymore. My **feet** hurt.
- There are many **women** in our office.
- A lot of **children** don't eat vegetables.

PRACTICE

A. Write the plural form of each noun.

1. doctor → *doctors*
2. foot → _____
3. day → _____
4. lady → _____

5. child → _____
6. bench → _____
7. party → _____
8. wife → _____

9. knife → _____
10. kilo → _____
11. loaf → _____
12. friend → _____

B. Look at the pictures and write the appropriate singular or plural nouns.

1

2

3

4

1. There are some _cats_____ in the basket.
2. He is carrying _____.

3. The _____ are crying.
4. She is buying some _____.

C. Find and change any mistakes in each sentence. Put ✓ if the sentence is correct.

1. "How many day do you work each week?" "Only three." ⟶ _____ *day → days*
2. I need to buy two loaf of bread. _____
3. How many child do you have? _____
4. I wear a uniform at work. _____
5. My daughter likes peach, so she eats them every day. _____
6. Two boy are playing in the pool. Who are they? _____
7. Many womans go shopping on the day after Christmas. _____
8. "I want to sit down." "Oh, there is a bench." _____
9. Jody took a photography class. She enjoys taking photoes. _____
10. I've lived in many big cities since I was young. _____

D. Paul and Chris are going on a camping trip. Complete the conversation with the nouns in *italics*.

PAUL

PAUL: What can I bring for the camping trip?
CHRIS: [1.] Can you bring five _potatoes_____? *(potato)*
PAUL: Sure. [2.] Do you have a camping _____? *(knife)*
CHRIS: [3.] I have three camping _____. *(knife)*
        I'll bring them.
PAUL: Good. [4.] How many _____ are coming? *(person)*
CHRIS: Six. [5.] And don't forget to wear a warm _____. *(jacket)*
        It's cold in the mountains.
PAUL: OK.

CHRIS

ANSWERS p.275, REVIEW TEST 9 p.230

🎧 047.mp3

① *Nouns* can be countable or uncountable.

Countable nouns

a girl   three hats

| girl | hat | dog | apple |
| brother | pen | bird | flower |

Uncountable nouns

water   music

| water | music | snow | sugar |
| air | time | money | news |

More about uncountable nouns: Appendix p.252

② *Countable nouns* can be singular or plural.

- Do you have a **pencil**?
- I have a **brother** and two **sisters**.
- Have you seen my **gloves**? I can't find them.

We usually use **a/an** before *singular countable nouns*.

- Does Leo have **a dog**?
- I ate **an egg** for breakfast.

   We use **a** before *countable nouns* that start with a consonant sound (b, c, g, etc.).

   - **A boy** is standing by the window.
   - Joseph teaches physics at **a university**. (**university** is pronounced "youniversity")

   We use **an** before *countable nouns* that start with a vowel sound (a, e, i, o, u).

   - I think I lost **an earring**.
   - Mr. Roberts is out, but he'll return in **an hour**. (**hour** is pronounced "our")

③ We do not use **one/two**/etc. before *uncountable nouns* or add **-s** at the end.

- I bought **water** and **milk** at the store. (*NOT* one water and one milk)
- "Do you enjoy listening to **music**?" "Yes. I really like pop songs." (*NOT* musics)
- I asked Tony for **information** about the seminar.

We also do not use **a/an** before *uncountable nouns*.

- There is **snow** on the road. Drive carefully. (*NOT* a snow)
- Can you give me some **advice**? (*NOT* an advice)

PRACTICE

A. Complete the sentences with the nouns in *italics*. Add **a/an** if necessary.

1. *(rice)* I'd like _rice_ with my steak, please.
2. *(air)* This city has clean _____.
3. *(rain)* There will be _____ this evening.
4. *(umbrella)* I'd like to get _____.
5. *(taxi)* Let's take _____ to the airport.
6. *(salt)* Could you bring me some _____?
7. *(man)* I saw _____ with purple hair.
8. *(orange)* Can I have _____?

B. Look at the pictures and complete the sentences with the nouns in the box. Add **a/an** or use the plural form if necessary.

| apple | bicycle | ~~milk~~ | snow | sugar |

1. The man is drinking _milk_ .
2. There are _____ on the tree.
3. There is a lot of _____ on the street.
4. She is riding _____ .
5. There is _____ in the jar.

| baby | dog | flower | music | water |

6. She is holding _____ .
7. He is walking with _____ .
8. He is listening to _____ .
9. There is _____ in the glass.
10. She has _____ in her garden.

C. Find and change any mistakes in each sentence. Put ✓ if the sentence is correct.

1. I wanted to take a shower, but there was no hot waters.   _waters → water_
2. Robert exercises for half an hour in the morning.   _____
3. I need some egg and butter for the cake.   _____
4. I'd like to get an information about the train schedule.   _____
5. Ann is teacher. She teaches history.   _____
6. I forgot my wallet. Could you lend me some money?   _____
7. I don't have much times now. I'll call you later.   _____

ANSWERS p.276, REVIEW TEST 9 p.230

| some **fish**, **a glass of** water · *Countable* and *uncountable nouns* (2)

🎧 048.mp3

① The following *nouns* have the same singular/plural forms:

Singular	a **fish**	a **sheep**	a **deer**
Plural	some **fish**	eight **sheep**	many **deer**

- Look! Some **fish** are swimming in the water.
- Mr. Anderson has eight **sheep** and a horse on his farm.
- We saw many **deer** during our camping trip.

② The following *nouns* that refer to things with two parts are always plural.

pajamas	scissors	jeans	shorts
glasses	pants	headphones	

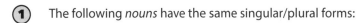

- I like my **pajamas**. They're very comfortable.
- Can I borrow your **scissors** for a minute?
- "Do you wear **jeans** often?" "No, I don't."

glasses

pajamas

We can use **a pair of**, **two pairs of**, etc. before these *nouns* to talk about the number of them.

- I got **a pair of shorts** for my birthday.
- I have **two pairs of glasses**. I use one pair at home and the other pair at work.

③ We can use **a glass of**, **two cans of**, etc. before some *uncountable nouns* to talk about quantity.

a glass of water	two cans of soda	three bottles of juice

a glass of water	**a can of** soda	**a bottle of** juice
a cup of coffee	**a loaf of** bread	**a piece of** cake/paper
a carton of milk	**a box of** cereal	**a slice of** pizza

- Can I have **a glass of water**?
- I need **two loaves of bread** and **a box of cereal**.
- "What did you have for lunch?" "I ate **two slices of pizza**."

In this case, we do not add -s at the end of *nouns* after **two bottles of**, **cartons of**, etc.

- "Are there any drinks?" "There are **two bottles of juice** in the fridge." (*NOT* two bottles of juices)
- How many **cartons of milk** are sold in a week? (*NOT* cartons of milks)

We can also use **a/an** or **one/two**/etc. with **soda**, **coffee**, etc. when we order them.

- Would you like **a soda**? *OR* Would you like **a can of soda**?
- **Two coffees**, please. *OR* **Two cups of coffee**, please.

PRACTICE

A. Complete the sentences with the nouns in *italics*. Add **a/an** or use the plural form.

1. *(glove)* I bought new _gloves_____ , but they are too small for me.
2. *(pant)* "I'd like to buy these _____." "Sure. What size do you need?"
3. *(fish)* "I went fishing last weekend." "Did you catch many _____?"
4. *(key)* "I found _____ on the floor." "Oh, it's mine."
5. *(glass)* Cindy has worn _____ for many years.
6. *(sheep)* Some _____ are sleeping on the grass. They look peaceful.
7. *(apple)* _____ is good for breakfast if you're busy in the morning.

B. Look at the picture and complete the sentences with **a glass of / two bottles of /** etc.

> **I am buying ...**
> 1. *(wine)* _two bottles of wine_____ .
> 2. *(milk)* _____ .
> 3. *(cake)* _____ .
> 4. *(soda)* _____ .
> 5. *(bread)* _____ .

C. Find and change any mistakes in each sentence. Put ✓ if the sentence is correct.

1. I'll have an orange juice, please.   ✓
2. Julia bought two box of cereals for her kids.   _____
3. The market on Hill Street sells many fish and vegetables. _____
4. "My feet are cold." "Well, you're not wearing sock."   _____
5. When I went hiking last weekend, I saw three deers.   _____
6. "Would you like a coffee?" "Yes. With some sugar, please." _____
7. We will bring a bottle of wine to dinner tomorrow.   _____
8. There is a lot of snows on the street.   _____
9. "I need two pieces of papers." "OK. Here you go."   _____

D. Complete the conversation with **of** and the nouns in *italics*. Use the plural form if necessary.

LINDA

LINDA: ¹·Could I have three _pieces of cake_____ ? *(piece, cake)*
      ²·And four _____ , please. *(slice, pizza)*
Waiter: Certainly. Would you like anything to drink?
LINDA: ³·Yes, a _____ and
      two _____ . *(cup, coffee) (can, soda)*
      ⁴·Oh, and a _____ . *(bottle, water)*
Waiter: Really? You're ordering a lot!
LINDA: Yes. My husband and two sons are coming.

Waiter

ANSWERS p.276, REVIEW TEST 9 p.230

UNIT
048

Grammar Gateway Basic

🎧 049.mp3

(1)

We need **a lamp**.

They need **a lamp**.

"**a lamp**" means one lamp that is not specific.

We use **a/an** to talk about one person/thing that is not specific.

● **A woman** is walking down the street. (= one woman that is not specific)
● Brenda is looking for **an office** to rent. (= one office that is not specific)
● "Do you have **a car**?" "Yes. I bought one a month ago."

(2)

It's too bright!

The lamp is too bright.

"**The lamp**" means one specific lamp.

We use **the** to talk about specific people/things.

● I saw you on the street. Who was **the woman** with you? (= one specific woman with you)
● It's almost 6 o'clock. I'm leaving **the office**. (= one specific office)
● "Is **the car** in front of the store yours?" "Yes, it is."

We do not use **the** to talk about people/things in general.

● I like **cats**. (= cats in general)
  The cats in this shop are so cute. (= specific cats in the shop)
● Winter is my favorite season. I don't like hot **weather**.
  "What was **the weather** like in California?" "It was very warm."

(3) We use **a/an** to talk about someone or something for the first time. We use **the** to talk about them again.

● I got **an e-mail** from Jenny this morning. **The e-mail** was about today's meeting.
  (an e-mail = The e-mail)
● I ate **a sandwich** and **a salad** for lunch. **The sandwich** was very good, but I didn't like **the salad**.
  (a sandwich, a salad = The sandwich, the salad)

PRACTICE

A. Look at the pictures and complete the sentences with **a/an** or **the** and the nouns in the box.

apple	bill	~~bus~~	car	office	ticket

1. Let's take *the bus* _____ .

2. Can I have _____ ?

3. I'd like _____ , please.

4. Is Ms. Lee in _____ ?

5. Did you pay _____ ?

6. Hi. We want to buy _____ .

B. Complete the conversations with **a/an** or **the** and the words in the box.

accident	cake	exam	~~food~~	funny joke	heater	phone	window

1. A: How was _the food_ at that Thai restaurant?
   B: It was very good.

2. A: Why is the traffic so slow?
   B: I think there was _____ .

3. A: Which dessert do you want?
   B: I want _____ on the blue plate.

4. A: Why are you smiling?
   B: I just heard _____ .

5. A: Look out _____ . It's snowing!
   B: Let's go outside and make a snowman!

6. A: Can you answer _____ ? I'm busy.
   B: Of course.

7. A: Is there _____ in here? It's cold.
   B: Yes. I'll turn it on for you.

8. A: Do we have _____ tomorrow?
   B: Yes, we do. Did you study for it?

C. Complete the sentences with **a/an** or **the** and the nouns in *italics*.

1. *(gloves)* Nancy sent me some nice gloves. _The gloves_ are very warm.
2. *(question)* "I have _____ for you." "OK. Go ahead."
3. *(water)* _____ in this river is very clear.
4. *(umbrella)* It's raining outside. Do you have _____ ?
5. *(key)* I need to open the cabinet. Where is _____ ?
6. *(book)* "I'm reading an interesting book." "What's _____ about?"
7. *(problem)* I have _____ with my computer. I should take it to the repair shop.
8. *(mountain)* There is _____ near my hometown. I often go hiking there.
9. *(suit)* I got a suit and a book for my birthday. My wife gave me _____ .
10. *(orange)* I'd like to buy _____ . Do you have any?

ANSWERS p.276, REVIEW TEST 9 p.230

1 We usually use **the** before the following *nouns*:

the				
	Only one in the world	**the world**	**the sun**	**the moon**
	Nature	**the sky**	**the sea**	**the ocean**
	Only one in a country or city	**the army**	**the police**	**the government**
	Media	**the radio**	**the Internet**	

- I want to travel **the world**.
- Look at the color of **the sky**. It's beautiful.
- John was in **the army** 20 years ago.
- I always listen to **the radio** in the morning.

We also use **the** before musical instruments.

- "Can you play **the guitar**?" "Not very well."
- Helen practices **the piano** every day, so she's good at it.

the sun

the radio

the police

the piano

2 We do not use **the** before the following *nouns*:

~~the~~			
	Sport	**basketball**	**football**	**tennis**
	Subject	**biology**	**history**	**marketing**
	Meal	**breakfast**	**lunch**	**dinner**

- Ted and Mike play **basketball** every Sunday.
- My daughter is studying **biology** at college.
- "Have you eaten **breakfast** yet?" "Yes, I have."

3 We use **the** when we say that we are going to the following places:

go to the movies	**go to the station**	**go to the bank**
go to the theater	**go to the airport**	**go to the post office**

- "Do you want to **go to the movies** tomorrow?" "Sure."
- Dad **went to the bank** yesterday.
- "Which subway line **goes to the airport**?" "The blue line."
- "Are you **going to the post office**?" "Not now. I'm going there this afternoon."

But we usually do not use **the** before **home** or **work**.

go home	**go to work**
at home	**at work**

- Joanne **went home** early because she had a cold.
- "How do you know Jonathan?" "We met **at work**."

More about **the**: Appendix p.252

PRACTICE

A. Look at the pictures and complete the sentences with the nouns in the box. Add **the** if necessary.

golf	math	moon	~~piano~~	radio

1. She is playing _the piano_____ .
2. She is listening to _____ .
3. He is playing _____ .
4. They are looking at _____ .
5. He's studying _____ at school.

B. Complete the sentences with the nouns in *italics*. Add **the** if necessary.

1. *(lunch)* I had _lunch_____ with Eric today. We went to a Mexican restaurant.
2. *(ocean)* Michael likes to go surfing in _____ .
3. *(history)* "Are you taking _____ classes this year?" "No, I'm not."
4. *(Internet)* "What time does the flight arrive?" "Let me check on _____ ."
5. *(government)* _____ is going to build a new road in my hometown.
6. *(baseball)* I like watching _____ . It's very exciting.
7. *(breakfast)* I usually eat pancakes for _____ .
8. *(world)* "How many countries are there in _____ ?" "Maybe around 200?"

C. Complete the sentences with **go (to)** and the nouns in the box. Add **the** if necessary.

airport	bank	home	movies	~~post office~~	work

1. Would you send these packages when you _go to the post office_____ ?
2. I must _____ now. My parents are coming, and I need to clean the house.
3. Let's _____ early. I don't want to miss our flight.
4. "Would you like to _____ tonight?" "Sure. I haven't seen any films recently."
5. "What time do you _____ in the morning?" "I have to be in the office by 8:30."
6. "I have to _____ to get some money." "It closes at 4, so you should hurry."

D. Find and change any mistakes in each sentence. Put ✓ if the sentence is correct.

1. I need to go to station. Can you give me a ride?   _go to station → go to the station_
2. I called police because someone stole my car.   _____
3. "Where were you last night?" "I was at work."   _____
4. You shouldn't look at sun directly. You can damage your eyes.   _____
5. We usually don't stay at the home during the summer. We like to travel.   _____
6. "Did you go to the theater yesterday?" "Yes. I saw a funny play."   _____
7. Do you study the politics in college?   _____

ANSWERS p.276, REVIEW TEST 9 p.230

UNIT 051 | **She** is my friend. *Pronouns*

(1)

> This is Kate. **She** is my friend.
> I met **her** in high school.

This is <u>Kate</u>.

She is my friend.
I met **her** in high school.

"She" and **"her"** are *pronouns* that refer to "Kate."

---

(2) We use **I/we/you**/etc. *(pronouns)* as the *subject* of a sentence.

person	
I	
We	
You	saw Danny.
He	
She	
They	

thing	
It	was beautiful.
They	were beautiful.

- I'm thirsty. Can **I** have some water?
- "Is Stephanie home?" "**She** is in her room."
- "Have **you** met your new neighbors?" "Yes. **They**'re very nice."
- **We** washed our car on the weekend. **It** looks nice and clean now.

---

(3) We use **me/us/you**/etc. *(pronouns)* as the *object* of a sentence.

	person
	me.
	us.
Danny saw	you.
	him.
	her.
	them.

	thing
I bought	it.
	them.

- My dad drives **me** to school every day.
- "Have you seen Ryan lately?" "I met **him** last week."
- I sent **you** some flowers. Did you get **them**?
- This hat is for Rob. I bought **it** in Sweden.

We can use **me/us/you**/etc. after **with/to**/etc. *(prepositions)*, but we do not use **I/we/you**/etc.

- I'm going to the park. You should come **with me**. (*NOT* with I)
- Is Bianca in her office? I'd like to talk **to her** for a minute. (*NOT* to she)

PRACTICE

A. Choose the correct one.

1. "Is Laura back yet?" "I'm not sure. I haven't seen (**her** / she)."
2. "Did your package arrive today?" "Yes. I received (them / **it**) this morning."
3. "Is Steve feeling okay?" "No. (**He** / Him) has a headache."
4. "I want to move this sofa to my room. Can you help (I / **me**)?" "Of course."
5. "Do you remember Matthew and Julie?" "(**They** / Them) were in our class, right?"
6. My brother and I are going to the beach. You should join (we / **us**).

B. Look at the pictures and write **I/me**, **we/us**, etc. Use each of them only once.

1. _I_ am Sam.
   People call _me_ Sammy.

2. I know _____ very well.
   _____ lives next door.

3. _____ is my uncle. I don't
   see _____ very often.

4. I like _____.
   Do _____ like me?

5. _____ are friends.
   People like _____.

6. _____ are my grandparents.
   I love _____ very much.

C. Complete the conversations with the appropriate pronouns.

1. Do you enjoy movies?
2. What are they building over there?
3. You should call Mr. Green now.
4. Are we going to the party?
5. Would you like some tomatoes?
6. Did you and Tim go to the museum yesterday?

Yes, but I don't watch _them_ often.
_____ is a new hotel.
I'm busy. I'll contact _____ later.
Yes. Bruce invited _____.
No, thanks. _____ don't look fresh.
Yes. _____ saw many beautiful paintings.

D. Find and change any mistakes in each sentence. Put ✓ if the sentence is correct.

1. "Nicole hasn't arrived yet." "Then we should wait for she."   _she → her_
2. "Look at this photo from high school." "Us look so young!"   _____
3. "Do you need help with the report?" "No. I'm almost done."   _____
4. "Where did you get that sweater?" "My grandmother gave it to I."   _____
5. "What's this?" "It is a gift for you."   _____
6. "Are those earrings diamonds?" "No. Them are made of glass."   _____

ANSWERS p.276, REVIEW TEST 9 p.230

UNIT **052** | **It** is Monday. *it* for time, date, etc.

🎧 052.mp3

①

It is Monday.

It is snowing.

---

② We can use **it** as the *subject* of a sentence to talk about the following things:

Time
- "What time is **it** now?" "**It**'s 5 o'clock."
- **It**'s noon. Let's go to lunch.
- **It**'s time to go. We should leave now.

Date
- "What's the date today?" "**It**'s October 10th."
- **It**'s the first day of September. Time has gone so fast.
- We're going to a concert. **It**'s on March 2nd.

Day
- "What day is **it** today?" "**It**'s Friday."
- **It**'s Saturday. What should we do?
- **It** can't be Monday already! I'm so sad.

Weather
- Let's go on a picnic. **It**'s very sunny today.
- **It**'s raining outside. Did you bring an umbrella?
- **It**'s going to be hot all week.

Distance
- Don't worry. **It**'s only one kilometer to the gas station.
- "Is your house close?" "Yes. **It**'s a short walk from here."
- "How far is **it** from London to Paris?" "**It**'s about 300 miles."

Season
- **It**'s snowing! Is **it** winter already?
- **It**'s almost spring. It is my favorite season of the year.

---

③ **It** does not refer to a specific thing when **it** is used to talk about time, date, etc.
- **It**'s 1:50 right now. The meeting will start soon.
  "What's in the box?" "A belt. **It**'s a gift for my dad." (It = A belt)
- **It** was very windy at the beach last weekend.
  I enjoyed this book. **It** was very interesting. (It = this book)

114

PRACTICE

A. Complete the conversations with **it** and the words in the box.

12:30	close	summer	~~Thursday~~	warm

1. Is today Wednesday?
2. What time is it?
3. How is the weather today?
4. Is it far from here to the hospital?
5. What season is it now in Australia?

No, _it's Thursday_ OR _it is Thursday_ .
_____ .
_____ .
No, _____ .
_____ there.

15 miles	8 o'clock	~~cloudy~~	December 25th	Tuesday

6. _It's cloudy_ OR _It is cloudy_ outside.
7. _____ today.
8. _____ to the museum.
9. _____ tomorrow!
10. _____ already.

Yes. It's going to rain this afternoon.
Is it? I thought it was Monday.
That's far. We should take a taxi.
I know! I love Christmas.
Really? I should get ready for work.

B. Write the appropriate pronouns.

1. "How's your brother?" " _He_ 's doing well, thanks."
2. I can't open the door. _____ 's locked.
3. These boots were on sale, so _____ weren't very expensive.
4. "I called you this morning, but _____ didn't answer." "I didn't have my phone with me."
5. _____ 's almost midnight. You should go to bed.
6. "Sam and I have great news. _____ are getting married!" "Congratulations!"
7. "What is today's date?" " _____ 's February 1st."
8. " _____ 's already winter." "I hope it doesn't snow a lot."

C. Amy sent a postcard to Kate from Italy. Complete the sentences with **it** and the words in *italics*.

Dear Kate,

1. _It's July 11th_ OR _It is July 11th_ today, and I'm in Capri, Italy. *(July 11th)*
2. _____ there? *(midnight)*
3. _____ here, and I just finished my lunch. *(2 p.m.)*

What's the weather like there?

4. _____ here, so _____ . *(summer) (very warm)*

Capri is so beautiful. You should come with me next time!

Love, Amy

ANSWERS p.277, REVIEW TEST 9 p.230

That's **my** camera. *Possessives (1)*

🎧 053.mp3

(1) We use **my/our/your**/etc. *(adjectives)* before *nouns* to talk about possession.

I	we	you	he	she	they	it
my	our	your	his	her	their	its

That's **my camera!**

- A: What's this?
  B: That's **my camera!**
- Brian and I are getting married. **Our wedding** is on April 21.
- "What's **your name**?" "I'm Bella Smith."
- I can't find Mr. Tyler. He's not in **his office**.

What's this?

Note that we use **its** and **it's** (= **it is**) in different ways.

- I don't wear this jacket these days. **Its** zipper is broken, and **it's** too small.
- There's a flower in my yard. I don't know **its** name, but **it's** beautiful.

(2) We use **mine/ours/yours**/etc. *(pronouns)* to talk about something that belongs to someone.

I	we	you	he	she	they
my	our	your	his	her	their
mine	ours	yours	his	hers	theirs

This car is **mine.**

- This car is **mine**. I got it yesterday.
- Excuse me? I think these seats are **ours**.
- That's my cup. **Yours** is on the table.
- "Is this Tom's backpack?" "Yes, it's **his**."

We do not use a *noun* after **mine/ours/yours**/etc.

- I lent Diane my laptop because **hers** was not working. (*NOT* hers laptop)
- My neighbors have a son. My son often plays with **theirs**. (*NOT* theirs son)

(3) We do not use **a/an** or **the** before **my/our/mine/ours**/etc.

- I have a meeting with **my boss** tomorrow. (*NOT* a my boss)
- "Which phone is **yours**?" "The small one." (*NOT* the yours)

(4) We use **Whose + noun ...?** to ask who owns something.

- "**Whose scissors** are these?" "Sophie was just here. Maybe they're hers."
- "**Whose magazine** is this?" "It's mine. Do you want to read it?"
- "There are some gloves on the sofa." "**Whose gloves** are they?"
- "**Whose party** are you attending tonight?" "Paul's. It's his birthday."

PRACTICE

A. Look at the pictures and complete the sentences with **my/our/your**/etc. and the nouns in *italics*.

1. *(house)* This is
   our house .

2. *(bag)* This is
   _____ .

3. *(key)* It's
   _____ .

4. *(dog)* This is
   _____ .

5. *(ball)* It's
   _____ .

B. Complete the conversations with **mine/ours/yours**/etc.

1. Is this your ticket?   Yes, it's _mine_____ .
2. Can I borrow this book?   Ask Bill. It's _____ .
3. Is this Rachel's purse?   No, it's not _____ .
4. Cody, are these my socks?   Yes, they are _____ .
5. Is this Mr. and Mrs. Brown's car?   No, it's not _____ .

C. Write **my/our**/etc. or **mine/ours**/etc.

1. "I lost my pen." "You can use _mine_____."
2. The book has an interesting title, but _____ story wasn't very good.
3. "Where's _____ office?" "I work in a building downtown."
4. We didn't sleep well last night. _____ neighbors were too noisy.
5. "Did Ms. Spears bring a suitcase?" "Yes. The black one is _____."
6. "Does this house belong to your aunt and uncle?" "Yes, and that car is _____ too."

D. Complete the conversations with the words in *italics*. Add **Whose** in the questions.

1. A: *(tent)* _Whose tent_____ can I borrow?
   B: *(we)* You can use _ours___ .

2. A: *(glasses)* _____ are these?
   B: *(he)* Ask Jim. Maybe they're _____ .

3. A: *(wallet)* _____ is this?
   B: *(you)* Oh, I thought it was _____ .

4. A: *(scarf)* _____ is on the chair?
   B: *(she)* Kim was wearing it. It must be _____ .

E. Complete the conversation with **my/our**/etc. or **mine/ours**/etc.

JUSTIN

JUSTIN: Chris! ¹·Is this _your_____ camera? I found it in Ginger's house.
CHRIS: ²·Yes, that's _____! Ginger, you bad dog!
JUSTIN: And look, there is a watch. ³·Is it _____ too?
CHRIS: No. ⁴·Dad lost _____ watch a few days ago.
   ⁵·It's probably _____.
JUSTIN: And Ginger also took a ball from someone!
CHRIS: Um, Justin. That's Ginger's ball.

CHRIS

ANSWERS p.277, REVIEW TEST 9 p.230

UNIT
053

Grammar Gateway Basic

It's **Amy's** book. *Possessives (2) -'s*

①

"It's my book."

It's **Amy's** book.

---

② We use -'s to talk about possession. We add -'s at the end of a *person*.

Mr. Wright's	job	⊙ "What's **Mr. Wright's job**?" "He's a lawyer."
Karen's	room	⊙ **Karen's room** is upstairs. She's probably in her room.
children's	toys	⊙ "Where are the **children's toys**?" "I put them in the closet."
brother's	name	⊙ My **brother's name** is Jeff. He's at university.

But we only add -' at the end of *people* that end with **s**.

parents'	anniversary	⊙ Today is my **parents' anniversary**.
the Grays'	house	⊙ "Is this **the Grays' house**?" "No. Theirs is next door."
artists'	paintings	⊙ There are many **artists' paintings** in this museum.
neighbors'	garden	⊙ Our **neighbors' garden** is beautiful. It has many flowers.

---

③ We can use -'s without a *noun* when the meaning is clear.

- ⊙ "I like your hat." "Thanks. It's **my sister's**." (= my sister's hat)
- ⊙ "Whose bicycle is that?" "It's **our kids'**." (= our kids' bicycle)
- ⊙ "Is that your suit?" "No. It's **Jim's**. I borrowed it for my job interview."
- ⊙ This isn't my laptop. It's **Tammy's**.

---

④ We usually use **of** for things.

- ⊙ "Can you play chess?" "No. I don't know **the rules of the game**."
- ⊙ **The time of the flight** has changed. It will leave at 7:40.
- ⊙ The company is on **the 10th floor of the building**.
- ⊙ "I found a good restaurant downtown." "What's **the name of the restaurant**?"

But we usually use -'s for people.

- ⊙ Do you know **Jessie's phone number**? (*NOT* phone number of Jessie)
- ⊙ Excuse me. Are you **Mr. Green's wife**? (*NOT* wife of Mr. Green)
- ⊙ "Have you seen my blue skirt?" "Yes. It's in **Sally's closet**."
- ⊙ "Is he **Jason's brother**?" "Yes. His name is Toby."

PRACTICE

A. Complete the sentences with the given words. Add -' or -'s.

boat	husband	~~name~~	presents	problems	voice

1. *(your dentist)* "What's <u>your dentist's name</u>?" "John Williams."
2. *(Laura)* "What does _____ do?" "He is an engineer."
3. *(our kids)* My wife and I wrapped _____ on Christmas Eve.
4. *(your brother)* "Is that _____?" "Yes. He sometimes uses it to go fishing."
5. *(Richard)* _____ is amazing. He's a great singer.
6. *(her friends)* Wendy always listens to _____. She's a good friend.

B. Look at the pictures and complete the sentences for each one.

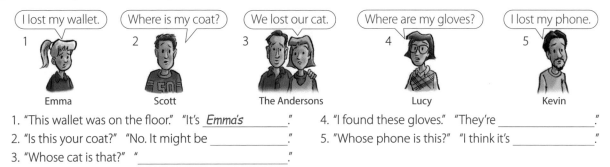

1. "This wallet was on the floor." "It's <u>*Emma's*</u>."
2. "Is this your coat?" "No. It might be _____."
3. "Whose cat is that?" "_____."
4. "I found these gloves." "They're _____."
5. "Whose phone is this?" "I think it's _____."

C. Put **of** and the words in *italics* in the correct order.

1. *(this street / the name)* "Do you know <u>the name of this street</u>?" "Yes. It's 3rd Avenue."
2. *(this chair / the price)* "What's _____?" "It's $200."
3. *(the title / the book)* "I'm looking for a book." "What's _____?"
4. *(the number / your hotel room)* Could you tell me _____?
5. *(the mountain / the top)* We walked to _____. It was beautiful.
6. *(the year / the start)* Patricia moved to England at _____.

D. Find and change any mistakes in each sentence. Put ✓ if the sentence is correct.

1. I found the watch of Sam under the desk.   <u>the watch of Sam → Sam's watch</u>
2. The ending of the program was very surprising.   _____
3. "Whose car is that?" "It's my parents's."   _____
4. Please write your name at the page's top.   _____
5. My husband and I couldn't go to Rose' wedding.   _____
6. Andrew's favorite sport is soccer.   _____
7. "Where is Jack?" "He is in Mr. Cowan office."   _____
8. Do you know the meaning of this word?   _____
9. The best friend of Mia is Natalie.   _____
10. We're going to stay at the Smiths' house this summer.   _____

ANSWERS p.277, REVIEW TEST 9 p.230

🎧 055.mp3

①

She is looking at **herself**.
    subject   *object*

"herself" refers to the same person as **"She."**

② **myself/yourself/himself**/etc.

I	you (singular)	he	she	we	you (plural)	they
me	you	him	her	us	you	them
myself	**yourself**	**himself**	**herself**	**ourselves**	**yourselves**	**themselves**

- I'm going to start learning piano this year. I promised **myself**.
- You can do it. You have to trust **yourself**.
- Gary isn't careful. He often cuts **himself** while shaving.
- Tom and Jenny are taking a photo of **themselves**.

③ We use **-self** as the *object* when the *subject* and *object* refer to the same person.

I'm so handsome!

- **Justin** is talking to **himself**. (Justin = himself)
- "Where did you learn English?" "I taught **myself**." (I = myself)
- **Alison** made **herself** a salad.

We use **me/him**/etc. as the *object* when the *subject* and *object* do not refer to the same person.

You look great!

- **Justin** is talking to **him**. (Justin ≠ him)
- **My brother** taught **me** English. (My brother ≠ me)
- Tina was hungry, so **Alison** made **her** a salad.

④ We use **by -self** to mean "alone" or "without any help."

- I've lived **by myself** since 2008. (= I've lived alone since 2008.)
- "Can you carry the table **by yourself**?" "Sure. It's not heavy." (= Can you carry the table without any help?)

⑤ We use **make yourself at home** to mean "relax like you are in your own home."

- Welcome to my place. Please **make yourself at home**.

We use **help yourself** to mean "take something freely."

- "Can I have some more bread?" "Of course. **Help yourself**."

PRACTICE

A. Write **myself/yourself**/etc.

1. Susan became the captain of her football team. She must be proud of _herself_ .
2. "I'll see you next week." "OK. Take care of _____."
3. The meeting didn't go well, but it's not our fault. We shouldn't blame _____.
4. "These paintings are nice. Did you take an art class?" "No. I taught _____."
5. "Why is Carlos in the hospital?" "He injured _____ during the baseball game."

B. Look at the pictures and write **himself/herself** or **him/her**.

1
They're so cute!

2

3
Please stop, sir.

4
MAGGIE

5

6
I'm Dave.

1. She is talking to _herself_ .
2. She cut _____ with a knife.
3. The police officer stopped _____.

4. Maggie is giving _____ a present.
5. He hurt _____.
6. He is introducing _____.

C. Complete the conversations with **by -self**.

1. Did you go to the beach alone?
2. Did your mom make dinner for you?
3. Did Jake go to the park with his friends?
4. Kevin, were you shopping alone?
5. Was Claire playing games with her friend?
6. Are you and your wife traveling with your kids?

Yes. _I went to the beach by myself_ .
No. _____.
No. _____.
Yes. _____.
No. _____.
No. _____.

D. Complete the conversation with **myself/yourself**/etc. or **me/you**/etc.

AMY: Kate, come in. ¹·Make _yourself_ at home.
KATE: ²·Thanks for inviting _____ to your Halloween party.
AMY: There are some cookies on the table. ³·Help _____.
KATE: ⁴·Did you make these cookies by _____?
AMY: No. ⁵·My mom made _____.
KATE: What about the room decorations? They're very nice.
AMY: Thanks. ⁶·I did them by _____.

AMY

KATE

ANSWERS p.277, REVIEW TEST 9 p.230

UNIT 055

Grammar Gateway Basic

🎧 056.mp3

①

How much is **this**?
How much are **these**?

How much is **that**?
How much are **those**?

② We use **this** to talk about someone or something that is near us.

- "**This** is my cousin, Alex."
  "It's nice to meet you."
- **This** tastes really good. Did you make it?
- "Can I try **this** on?"
  "Sure. The fitting room is over here."

We use **these** for two or more people/things.

- **These** are my friends. Their names are Dave and Janine.
- "Which shoes should I buy?" "**These** are nice."
- "Whose pens are **these**?"
  "They're mine."

We use **that** to talk about someone or something that is not near us.

- "Is **that** your cousin?"
  "I'm not sure. I can't see him very well."
- **That** smells very delicious. What did you cook?
- "Can I try **that** on?"
  "Sure. I'll get it for you if you wait here."

We use **those** for two or more people/things.

- "Are **those** your friends over there?"
  "Yes, they are."
- I'd like **those** on the shelf, please.
- "Whose pens are **those** on the table?"
  "They're Fred's."

③ We can use **this/these** or **that/those** with *nouns*.

this + *singular/uncountable noun*

- **This box** is very light. What's in it?
- Thank you again for visiting our museum.
  The exit is **this way**.

these + *plural noun*

- Here you are. Try **these sandwiches**.
- I'm sorry, but you can't sit here. **These seats** are reserved.

that + *singular/uncountable noun*

- Is **that box** heavy? Do you need some help?
- You took the wrong road.
  The museum is **that way**.

those + *plural noun*

- Jerry made **those sandwiches** for our picnic.
- "Where should we sit?"
  "**Those seats** are ours."

PRACTICE

A. Look at the pictures and complete the sentences with **this/that** and the nouns in *italics*.

1. *(word)* What does _this word_ mean?
2. *(book)* Is _____ yours?
3. *(painting)* Look at _____!
4. *(ring)* I'll take _____!

B. Choose the correct one.

1. "These scissors aren't sharp." "Here, try (these / those)."
2. "What is (this / that) on the wall over there?" "It looks like a spider!"
3. (These / Those) are my brother's friends. Let's go and say hello.
4. "Are you wearing a new suit?" "Yes, (this / that) is new."
5. "What is (this / that) on the water?" "I'm not sure. It's too far away."
6. "(This / That) restaurant is amazing." "I know. I come here often."
7. Can you see (these / those) buildings across the street?
8. "What are you holding in your hand?" "(These / Those) are the invitations for my birthday party."

C. Look at the pictures and ask the price of each item with **this/these** or **that/those** and the nouns in *italics*.

1	2	3
4	5	6

1. *(lamp)* _How much is this lamp_ ?
2. *(socks)* _____ ?
3. *(cake)* _____ ?
4. *(spoons)* _____ ?
5. *(perfume)* _____ ?
6. *(sunglasses)* _____ ?

D. Complete the conversation with **this/these** or **that/those**.

KATE: 1. Amy, do you like _this_ shirt?
AMY: Not really. 2. I like _____ shirt over there.
KATE: 3. But it looks very nice with _____ shoes here.
AMY: Really? 4. I think _____ shoes on that shelf are better.
KATE: 5. _____ are for men!

KATE

AMY

ANSWERS p.277, REVIEW TEST 9 p.230

UNIT 057 | How about this **one**? one, ones

🎧 057.mp3

①

How about this **one**?

How about these fresh **ones**?

We use **one**/**ones** when we do not want to repeat a *noun*.

- "May I borrow **a pencil**?" "Sure. You can take **one**." (one = a pencil)
- "I like these **socks**." "Well, I prefer the **ones** with stripes." (ones = socks)

② We use **one** for *singular nouns*.

- "Which **boy** is your son?" "The **one** in the white shirt." (one = a boy)
- I'm looking for **a hotel**. Could you suggest **one**? (one = a hotel)
- "You should take **a taxi**." "Where can I catch **one**?"

We use **ones** for *plural nouns*.

- We want to be **cheerleaders**. The **ones** at our school are very popular. (ones = cheerleaders)
- Can you bring me my **glasses**? They are the **ones** on the desk. (ones = glasses)
- "Which **jeans** are on sale?" "The **ones** outside the store."

③ We can use **one**/**ones** with *adjectives*.

a/**an**/**the**/etc. + *adjective* + **one**

- "That is a famous building."
  "It looks like **an old one**."
- All of these ties are nice, but I think I'll buy **the blue one**.
- "This store has a lot of dolls."
  "Yes. I really like **this little one**."

some/**the**/etc. + *adjective* + **ones**

- Let's buy some snacks. There are **some good ones** at this store.
- The small envelopes are $2, and **the large ones** are $3.
- Let's get some roses. **These yellow ones** are pretty.

④ We use **Which one**/**ones** . . .? to ask about a choice from a group of people/things.

- "**Which one** is your bicycle?" "It's the red one on the left."
- "Ally can speak four languages." "Really? **Which ones**?"
- There are so many dogs. **Which one** is yours?
- **Which ones** do you like better, the red gloves or the purple ones?

The speech bubbles in image ①: "I'd like to buy **a melon**." / "How about this **one**?" / "I'd also like some **oranges**." / "How about these fresh **ones**?"

PRACTICE

A. Complete the conversations with **one/ones**.

1. Do you have a pet?
2. Which painting is your favorite?
3. What do you think of these pants?
4. I need to find a good dentist.
5. Does anyone have an eraser?
6. These sodas are warm.

No, I don't have _one_ _____.
I like the _____ with bright colors.
I think the black _____ are better.
I know a good _____. He's very kind.
I have _____. Here you go.
The _____ in the fridge are cold.

B. Complete the sentences with **one/ones** and the adjectives in the box. Add **a/an** or **some**.

| bigger | ~~black~~ | cheap | chocolate | exciting | important | new |

1. "Do you have any brown boots?" "No, we don't. But we have _some black ones_ _____."
2. "Our toaster is very old." "You're right. We need _____."
3. These earphones are expensive. Do you have _____?
4. There is a meeting tomorrow. It's _____, so I have to go.
5. "Did you bake blueberry cookies?" "Yes. Try _____ too. I just made them."
6. "I can't put all these clothes in the suitcase." "I have _____. You can borrow it."
7. Did you watch the baseball game last night? It was _____.

C. Look at the pictures and complete the questions with **Which one/ones . . . ?**

1. _Which one_ is Andy?
2. _____ are Mary's?
3. _____ is Ted's house?
4. _____ goes to London?
5. _____ do you like?

D. Complete the conversation with **one/ones** and the words in *italics*.

LINDA: Hello. I'd like to buy a melon.
Clerk: 1. How about _this one_ _____? It's from Turkey. *(this)*
LINDA: No, thank you. 2. I want the _____ over there. *(big)*
         I'd also like some apples.
         3. Do you have any _____? *(green)*
Clerk: 4. No. We only have _____. *(red)*
LINDA: OK. I'll take them.

LINDA

Clerk

ANSWERS p.278, REVIEW TEST 9 p.230

There are **some** children on the bus. some and any

🎧 058.mp3

①

There are **some children** on the bus.

There aren't **any children** on the bus.

We usually use **some** in positive sentences.

- We spent **some time** in the mountains last weekend.
- "What did you buy for Sandra?"
  "I got **some flowers**."

We usually use **any** in negative sentences and questions.

- I'm tired today because I didn't get **any sleep** last night.
- "Do you have **any plans** for Saturday?"
  "Yes. I'm visiting my parents."

But when we offer or request something, we usually use **some** in questions.

- "Can I offer you **some advice**?" "Of course."

② We can use **some** or **any** without a *noun*.

- "We have some ice cream." "Oh, I want **some**."
- "Did you see any dolphins at the zoo?" "No. There weren't **any**."

③ We use **someone/anything**/etc. for people/things/places.

Person	someone/somebody	anyone/anybody
Thing	something	anything
Place	somewhere	anywhere

- "**Someone** left this briefcase in the lobby." "Oh. That's mine."
- I'm going to the supermarket. Do you need **anything**?
- "Where is Jen's office?" "It's **somewhere** on Washington Avenue."

We usually use **someone/something**/etc. in positive sentences and **anyone/anything**/etc. in negative sentences and questions.

- "**Something** smells great!" "It's my perfume. Do you like it?"
- "Is **anyone** sitting here?" "No. Have a seat."
- We haven't traveled **anywhere** lately.

But when we offer or request something, we usually use **someone/something**/etc. in questions.

- "Can you bring **something** to drink here?" "Sure."

PRACTICE

A. Complete the sentences with **some/any** and the nouns in the box.

| friends | money | ~~pancakes~~ | paper | rest | snow | sports | trains |

1. "What are you cooking?" "I'm making _some pancakes_____ for breakfast."
2. It was warm last winter, so there wasn't _____.
3. We need to buy _____ for the printer.
4. "Does Sandra play _____?" "I think she plays hockey."
5. "There aren't _____ to London tonight, right?" "Actually, we have one at 8."
6. Jacob used to live in Australia, so he has _____ there.
7. You should get _____. You look very tired.
8. I lost my wallet, so I don't have _____ now.

B. Write **some/any**.

1. It's so quiet in this room.	Should we turn on _some_____ music?
2. Let's buy some shampoo.	I have no money right now. Do you have _____?
3. There are no chairs in this room.	Oh, I'll bring _____.
4. The weather is very clear today.	Yes. There aren't _____ clouds in the sky!
5. Have you seen any movies lately?	No, I haven't watched _____.
6. Can I have a steak?	Sure. Would you like _____ wine with it?

C. Look at the pictures and complete the sentences with **someone/somebody/something/somewhere**.

1
> Where is my umbrella?

2
> I'm hungry.

3
> Who is it?

4
> Where are they going?

1. _Someone_ OR _Somebody_____ took his umbrella.
2. He wants _____ to eat.
3. _____ is knocking on the door.
4. They're going _____.

D. Write **someone/something**/etc. or **anyone/anything**/etc.

1. "Did _anyone_ OR _anybody_____ call me?" "Yes. Your sister left a message for you."
2. "Where does Sienna live?" "She lives _____ in Brooklyn."
3. William is angry because _____ parked a car in front of his house again.
4. "Are you busy?" "No. I'm not doing _____ right now."
5. "Would you like _____ to read?" "A newspaper, please."
6. "I haven't seen Ben _____ today." "He went to his brother's wedding."
7. _____ is wrong with the washing machine. It's not working.
8. "Has _____ heard from John?" "He called me this morning."

ANSWERS p.278, REVIEW TEST 10 p.232

There are **no** rooms. <small>no, none</small>

🎧 059.mp3

(1)

Sorry, all the rooms are full.

PRIME HOTEL

There are **no rooms**.

---

(2) **no** + *noun*

- Ms. White has three sons but **no daughters**.
- That sofa is too big for our apartment. There's **no space** for it.
- "I want to meet you this afternoon." "Sorry, I have **no time**."

---

(3) We can use **not . . . any** + *noun* instead of **no** + *noun*.

- I have **no questions**. *OR* I don't have **any questions**.
- There are **no girls** in my class. *OR* There aren't **any girls** in my class.

---

(4) We can also use **none** instead of **no** + *noun*.

- "How much pizza is left?" "**None**. Jeff ate it all." (= No pizza)
- "Do you have any pets?" "No. I have **none**." (= no pets)

   Note that we use a *noun* after **no**, but we do not use a *noun* after **none**.

   - I checked for messages, but there were **none**. (*NOT* none messages)
   - "Did you buy an umbrella?" "No. The store had **none**." (*NOT* none umbrella)

---

(5) We use **no one / nobody / nothing / nowhere** for people/things/places.

Person	**no one / nobody**
Thing	**nothing**
Place	**nowhere**

- "Who is that boy?" "He must be new to this town. **No one** knows him."
- We have **nothing** to eat. We should go to the grocery store.
- "Where did you go last weekend?" "**Nowhere**. I stayed at home."

---

(6) We do not use **no** + *noun* / **no one** / **nothing** / etc. with **not**.

- There are **no classes** on Sunday. (*NOT* There aren't no classes)
- Claire told a joke, but **nobody** laughed. (*NOT* nobody didn't laugh)

PRACTICE

A. Complete the sentences with **no** and the nouns in the box.

bread	children	choice	money	rain	~~seats~~	tickets	windows

1. There were _no seats_____ on the bus, so I had to stand.
2. "I want to make some sandwiches." "We have _____ at home. Should we go to the bakery?"
3. There's _____ in my wallet. I spent it all.
4. There are _____ for the 11 a.m. show. They're sold out.
5. "Why are you moving to Dubai?" "My company is moving there. I have _____."
6. _____ are allowed in the playground after 8 p.m.
7. It was cloudy last night, but there was _____.
8. Our garage has _____, so it's always dark.

B. Write **no/any/none**.

1. "How many people are coming today?" " _None_____. The meeting was canceled."
2. I couldn't take _____ pictures in the museum. _____ cameras were allowed.
3. Mike bought two suits at the mall, but I bought _____.
4. There weren't _____ buildings here 10 years ago. Those are all new.
5. The library was very quiet. There was _____ noise.
6. There aren't _____ cups on the table. Could you get some?
7. "How many cousins do you have?" " _____."

C. Write **no one / nobody / nothing / nowhere**.

1. " _No one_ OR _Nobody_____ was hurt in the accident." "That's good news."
2. "There's _____ to park the car here." "Let's try the next street."
3. "What's that sound?" "It's _____. Just the wind."
4. "This gallery is boring." "Yes. There's _____ to see here. Let's go."
5. I have to get a bookshelf. There's _____ to put these new books.
6. If _____ wants the last piece of pizza, I'll eat it.

D. Complete the conversation with **no/any/none**.

PAUL

PAUL: Hello. Is there a room here?
Clerk: Yes, there is one. How many people are staying?
PAUL: [1.] There are _no_____ other people. It's just me.
How much is the room?
Clerk: [2.] It's $30 for a night, but it has _____ wi-fi.
PAUL: [3.] Well, the other hotels didn't have _____ rooms. I'll take that one.
Clerk: OK. Do you have any bags? I'll help you with them.
PAUL: [4.] I have _____ . Thanks for the offer.

Clerk

ANSWERS p.278, REVIEW TEST 10 p.232

①

There are **many cars** on the road.

There isn't **much sugar** in the spoon.

many + *plural noun*

- I invited **many friends** to my house.
- There are **many birds** in the garden.

We use **many** in positive/negative sentences and questions.

- Ted can speak **many different languages**.
- **Many stores** don't open on Sundays.
- How **many brothers** do you have?

much + *uncountable noun*

- We haven't had **much rain** lately.
- Do you use **much oil** in your cooking?

We usually use **much** in negative sentences and questions.

- I don't have **much work** to do today.
- Did you get **much sleep** last night?
- How **much time** does it take to get to the airport?

② **a lot of / lots of**

We can also use **a lot of / lots of** instead of **many/much**. We can use *plural* or *uncountable nouns* after **a lot of / lots of**.

- **A lot of people** go shopping at the mall before the holidays.
- My mom gives me **lots of advice** about life.

We use **a lot of / lots of** in positive/negative sentences and questions.

- I'm so full! I ate **a lot of food** for dinner.
- Luke likes music, but he doesn't attend **a lot of concerts**.
- "Did you visit **lots of places** in New Zealand?" "Yes, I did."

③ We can use **many/much** without a *noun*.

- Maria likes flowers. She grows **many** in her yard. (= many flowers)
- "Do we have any cheese for the burgers?" "Yes, but there isn't **much**." (= much cheese)

But we do not use **a lot of / lots of** without a *noun*. We use **a lot**.

- "How much money did you spend today?" "**A lot**." (= A lot of money)
- "I want to buy these shoes. They're very pretty!" "But you already have **a lot**." (= a lot of shoes)

PRACTICE

A. Look at the pictures and complete the sentences with **There are many / There isn't much** and the nouns in *italics*.

1. *(book)* <u>There are many books</u> on the bookshelf.
2. *(space)* _____ in the fridge.
3. *(money)* _____ in the wallet.
4. *(kids)* _____ on the playground.
5. *(bread)* _____ in the basket.

B. Complete the sentences with **many/much** and the nouns in *italics*. Use the plural form if necessary.

1. *(orange)* <u>Many oranges</u> are grown in Florida.
2. *(interest)* "Do you like playing basketball?" "No. I don't have _____ in sports."
3. *(furniture)* We don't have _____ in our house. Let's buy some this weekend.
4. *(cup)* "How _____ do we need?" "Well, there are 12 guests."
5. *(dog)* There are _____ in my neighborhood. They bark too much.
6. *(information)* "Did you find _____ for your trip?" "No, not yet."
7. *(time)* Hurry up! We don't have _____.

C. Complete the sentences with **a lot of** and the nouns in the box.

~~books~~ coffee fun noise vegetables

1. "Do you have to read <u>a lot of books</u> for your history class?" "Yes. The class is very hard."
2. You should stop drinking _____. It might be bad for your health.
3. "Do you eat _____?" "Yes. I especially like carrots."
4. "Did you have _____ yesterday?" "Yes, I did."
5. My roommates were making _____ last night. I couldn't sleep.

D. Write **much / a lot / a lot of**.

1. "Let's go out!" "I can't. I have <u>a lot of</u> things to do."
2. It's raining a lot, but there isn't _____ wind.
3. "Can you bring me a pen from the desk?" "Which one do you want? There are _____."
4. "Are there many mistakes in my report?" "Yes. You made _____."
5. This lamp doesn't use _____ electricity.
6. The meeting is very important. We should prepare _____.
7. "Are there _____ parks in your city?" "No. There's only one."
8. "How many people bought that book?" "_____. I think it'll be a best-seller."
9. I spend _____ time with my family on weekends.
10. Please don't put _____ salt in the soup. It'll taste bad.

ANSWERS p.278, REVIEW TEST 10 p.232

| **(a) few** cookies, **(a) little** milk (a) few and (a) little

🎧 061.mp3

①

There are **a few cookies**.

There is **a little milk**.

We use **a few** or **a little** to mean "not many/much but some."

a few + *plural noun*

- Sue bought **a few magazines** at the store.
- Can I talk to you for **a few minutes**?
- It's late, but **a few restaurants** might be open.

a little + *uncountable noun*

- Nick had **a little wine** at dinner.
- Can I have **a little salt** in my soup?
- There's **a little ice** on the streets. Walk carefully.

②

There are **few cookies**.

There is **little milk**.

We use **few** or **little** to mean "almost none."

few + *plural noun*

- We see **few stars** in the sky these days.
- The store just opened, so it has **few customers**.
- There were **few cars** on the road this morning.

little + *uncountable noun*

- Eric spends **little money** on clothes.
- I have **little knowledge** about physics.
- We had **little snow** this year.

③ Note that we use **a few** / **a little** and **few/little** in different ways.

- The party was fun. **A few** people came.
  (= Not many but some people)

  The party was boring. **Few** people came.
  (= Almost no people)

- I don't have to leave now. I have **a little** time.
  (= not much but some time)

  I have to leave now. I have **little** time.
  (= almost no time)

④ We can use **(a) few** / **(a) little** without a *noun*.

- My brother reads many books, but I read **few**. (= few books)
- "Is there any paper in the printer?" "There's **a little**." (= a little paper)

PRACTICE

A. Look at the pictures and complete the sentences with **a few / a little** and the nouns in the box. Use the plural form if necessary.

~~hair~~	rose	ticket	water

1   2   3   4

1. He has *a little hair* _____ .
2. There is _____ in the cup.
3. There are _____ in the vase.
4. She has _____ .

B. Complete the sentences with **few/little** and the nouns in the box. Use the plural form if necessary.

car	information	letter	space	~~student~~	sugar

1. The test was very difficult. *Few students* _____ passed it.
2. The police are still looking for the thieves. They have _____ about them.
3. _____ were on the road after midnight. It was almost empty.
4. There is _____ in this pie, so it's not very sweet.
5. I can't put this sofa in the garage. There is _____ .
6. People write _____ these days. They usually use e-mail.

C. Write **a few / a little** or **few/little**.

1. Tim is out of the office. He'll be back in *a few* _____ hours.
2. My sister has _____ interest in cooking. She always eats out.
3. "Could you give me _____ help? I don't understand this question." "Sure."
4. "Would you like some grapes?" "Yes, I'll have _____ ."
5. I found _____ errors in your report. You did a good job.
6. I had _____ time to prepare for my speech, so it wasn't good.
7. "Would you like some pepper on your pasta?" "_____ , please."
8. Our baseball team didn't play well this year. They won _____ games.

D. Complete the conversation with **a few / a little** or **few/little**.

JUSTIN

JUSTIN: We should eat something before we leave for the movie.
AMY: [1.] But we just ate *a little* _____ chocolate. You also had some cake.
JUSTIN: [2.] Yes, but I had _____ pieces. I'm still hungry.
AMY: [3.] We have _____ tomatoes in the fridge.
We can make some soup.
JUSTIN: That will take too long. [4.] There's _____ time.
AMY: OK. [5.] Let's just get _____ snacks at the theater then.

AMY

ANSWERS p.278, REVIEW TEST 10 p.232

UNIT 062 | **All** dogs have tails. <small>**all** and **every**</small>

①

All dogs have tails.

OR **Every dog** has a tail.

---

② **all/every**

all + *plural/uncountable noun*

- Nancy often goes to the zoo. She loves **all animals**.
- **All bread** at this bakery is baked every morning.
- There are restrooms on **all floors** of the building.

every + *singular noun*

- **Every book** in this library is in English.
- I open **every window** when I get up.
- **Every painting** in this gallery is for sale.

---

③ We use *plural verbs* after **all** + *plural noun* and *singular verbs* after **all** + *uncountable noun*.

- **All banks close** on Sundays. (*NOT* All banks closes)
- "**Is all wine** made from grapes?" "No. There are many different kinds." (*NOT* Are all wine)

We use *singular verbs* after **every** + *singular noun*.

- In my school, **every class has** 30 students. (*NOT* every class have)
- I couldn't get into the office because **every door was** locked. (*NOT* every door were)

---

④ We use **all** + **day/week/month**/etc. to mean "one entire day/week/month/etc."

- I'm hungry. I haven't eaten anything **all day**. (= one entire day)
- Tanya went to London in June and stayed there **all month**. (= one entire month)

We use **every** + **day/week/month**/etc. to mean "each individual day/week/month/etc."

- I take a shower **every day**. (= each day)
- "Do you visit your parents often?" "Yes. I visit them **every week**." (= each week)

---

⑤ We use **everyone/everybody/everything/everywhere** for people/things/places.

Person	**everyone/everybody**	
Thing	**everything**	
Place	**everywhere**	

- The concert was amazing. **Everyone** enjoyed it.
- "How was your vacation?" "**Everything** was perfect."
- You need to clean your room. Your clothes are **everywhere**.

PRACTICE

A. Write all/every.

1. _Every_ desk in our classroom is new.
2. I like _____ kinds of ice cream.
3. _____ shop on the street was crowded.
4. _____ flights were canceled yesterday.
5. There are books on _____ shelf in the library.
6. _____ plants need water and sunlight.

B. Look at the pictures and complete the sentences with the given words. Use the plural form if necessary.

| ~~cat~~ flower man seat student |

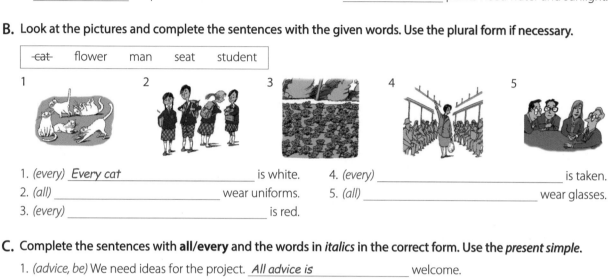

1. (every) _Every cat_ is white.
2. (all) _____ wear uniforms.
3. (every) _____ is red.
4. (every) _____ is taken.
5. (all) _____ wear glasses.

C. Complete the sentences with all/every and the words in *italics* in the correct form. Use the *present simple*.

1. (advice, be) We need ideas for the project. _All advice is_ welcome.
2. (languages, have) _____ rules of grammar.
3. (story, have) _____ a beginning and an ending.
4. (children, need) _____ parents' care.
5. (rain, come) _____ from clouds.
6. (table, be) " _____ taken. We have to wait." "OK."

D. Complete the conversations with all/every and the nouns in *italics*.

1. Did you sleep much last night?
2. What do you do on the weekend?
3. Do you read a lot of books?
4. You promised to call me, but you didn't.
5. Did you have fun at the beach yesterday?
6. How often do you jog?

(night) No. I watched TV _all night_ .
(weekend) I go to the mountains _____.
(month) Yes. I read 10 books _____.
(week) Sorry. I've been busy _____.
(day) Yes. We swam _____.
(morning) I jog _____.

E. Write everyone/everybody/everything/everywhere.

1. Thank you for the meal. _Everything_ was so good!
2. Mr. and Mrs. Adams traveled _____ in Asia after they retired.
3. I've tried _____, but the computer is still not working.
4. "Has _____ arrived?" "No. Ken isn't here yet."
5. There are clothes _____. You need to pick them up.

ANSWERS p.279, REVIEW TEST 10 p.232

🎧 063.mp3

①

I want **both.**

He wants **both.**

(= He wants the bagel and the muffin.)

We use **both** (+ *plural noun*) to refer to two people/things together.

- Alan likes baseball and basketball. He enjoys playing **both.** (= He enjoys playing baseball and basketball.)
- I've been to Rome twice. **Both times** were wonderful.
- "Does Karen speak English or Spanish?" "She can speak **both.**"
- Look **both ways** before you cross the street.

②

Either is fine.

Either is fine.

(= The bagel or the muffin is fine.)

We use **either** (+ *singular noun*) to refer to any one of the two people/things.

- "Do you want chicken or fish?" "**Either** is OK." (= Chicken or fish is OK.)
- We can stay at **either hotel.** Both seem nice.
- "Do you want to go to the beach or the lake?" "I'm fine with **either.**"
- "Should we meet at your house or mine?" "**Either place** is good."

③

I like **neither.**

He likes **neither.**

(= He doesn't like the bagel and the muffin.)

We use **neither** (+ *singular noun*) to refer to none of the two people/things.

- I'm not buying these dresses. **Neither** looks good on me. (= None of these dresses look good on me.)
- "Which house has a garage?" "**Neither house** has one."
- I have two printers at home, but **neither** is working.
- "Which should we take, the bus or the subway?" "Let's take **neither.** We should take a taxi."

PRACTICE

A. Look at the pictures and complete the sentences with **both/neither** and the nouns in *italics*. Use the plural form if necessary.

1

2

3

4

5

6

1. *(man)* _Neither man_____ is wearing glasses.
2. *(woman)* _____ have long hair.
3. *(seat)* _____ is taken.
4. *(car)* _____ are in the garage.
5. *(store)* _____ is open.
6. *(baby)* _____ are one year old.

B. Write **both/either/neither**.

1. "Do you like horror movies or action movies?" " _Neither_____ . I like comedies."
2. "Which bag is yours?" " _____ are mine. I brought two."
3. "Should I leave the box here or on your desk?" "It doesn't matter. Just leave it _____ place."
4. "How were your math and science exams?" "Terrible. _____ was easy."
5. Our company always uses _____ sides of a paper to save money.
6. "Could we meet on Friday or Saturday?" "You can pick a date. I can see you _____ day."

C. Complete the conversations with **both/either/neither** and the nouns in *italics*. Use the plural form if necessary.

1. Where should we park our car?
2. Who wrote these books?
3. Which has two bedrooms?
4. Which month is better for you to visit, May or June?
5. Do you want some juice? I have apple and lemon.

(side) _Either side_____ of the street is fine.
(novel) _____ were written by Sam.
(house) _____ have two bedrooms.
(month) _____ is OK.
(kind) No. _____ sounds good.

D. Complete the conversation with **both/either/neither**.

LINDA: Do you want a muffin or a bagel, Justin?
JUSTIN: ¹· _Neither_____ . I already ate some toast.
LINDA: OK. What about you, Amy?
AMY: ²· _____ is fine. I don't mind.
JAMES: ³· Linda, I want _____ . And some butter, please!
LINDA: No, James. ⁴· You can have _____ a bagel or a muffin.
     ⁵· You can't have _____ . Please choose one.

JUSTIN

AMY   JAMES

LINDA

ANSWERS p.279, REVIEW TEST 10 p.232

Grammar Gateway Basic

all of the pie, **most of** the pie all/most/some/none of

🎧 064.mp3

①

all of the pie   **most of** the pie   **some of** the pie   **none of** the pie

② We can use **of** after **all/most/some/none** to talk about a part of a group or the whole group.

| all most some none | of | the/my/these/etc. + noun |
| | | it/us/you/them |

- **All of my friends** like playing football.
- "Have you talked to your new classmates?" "Yes. **Most of them** are friendly."
- **Some of the clothes** in the store are on sale.
- We took a taxi to the airport because **none of us** could drive.

③ We use **all/most/some/none of** + *noun* to talk about specific people/things in a group.

- I've met **all of the people** in our company.
  (specific people in our company)
- **Most of these cars** are expensive.
  (these specific cars)
- **Some of the songs** on this album are good.
- I've read **none of the books** on the shelf yet.

We use **all/most/etc.** + *noun* to talk about people/things in general.

- **All people** have secrets.
  (people in general)
- **Most cars** use gas.
  (cars in general)
- I like to listen to **some songs** when I'm jogging.
- **No books** are published without titles.

④ We can also use **of** after **both/either/neither**.

| both either neither | of | the/my/these/etc. + plural noun |
| | | us/you/them |

- **Both of my parents** are teachers. (= My father and mother)
- "Should I wear a red tie or a blue one?"
  "**Either of those colors** matches your suit." (= The red or the blue color)
- "Have Brad and Andy arrived?"
  "No. **Neither of them** is here yet."

PRACTICE

A. Look at the pictures and complete the sentences with **all/most/some/none of them**.

1-4

5-8

1. _All of them_ are in the kitchen.
2. _____ are standing.
3. _____ are sitting at the table.
4. _____ are wearing yellow shirts.

5. _____ have red ribbons.
6. _____ have green ribbons.
7. _____ are open.
8. _____ are under the Christmas tree.

B. Put the words in *italics* in the correct order.

1. *(our neighbors / of / have children / some)* _Some of our neighbors have children_ .
2. *(those fish / all / of / did you / catch)* _____ ?
3. *(none / of / liked it / us)* The movie was boring. _____.
4. *(some / I / my cousins / often visit / of)* _____ in New York.
5. *(the shops / of / most / are expensive)* I don't really like this street. _____.
6. *(of / were here / these buildings / none)* _____ 10 years ago.
7. *(put / most / I / mine / of)* My sister never saves her money, but _____ in a bank.

C. Complete the sentences with the words in *italics*. Add **of** if necessary.

1. *(none, you)* Why did everyone come late? Did _none of you_ know the schedule?
2. *(some, animals)* _____ sleep during the day.
3. *(most, the work)* "Do you need help with the dishes?" "No. _____ is done."
4. *(all, animals)* We should protect _____. They're important for the environment.
5. *(most, trees)* _____ lose their leaves in the winter.
6. *(some, these muffins)* "Would you like _____?" "Sure. I'll take one."
7. *(all, them)* I've tried on these sweaters, and I want to buy _____.
8. *(none, my friends)* The hotel had a nice pool, but _____ could swim.

D. Complete the sentences with **both/either/neither of** and the words in *italics*.

1. *(them)* "Which table do you want to sit at?" " _Either of them_ is OK."
2. *(our cars)* _____ are in the repair shop. Can you give us a ride?
3. *(his parents)* "Jason is really tall." " _____ is tall, so it's very unusual."
4. *(the restaurants)* I'm fine with _____. You can choose.
5. *(us)* My friend and I like singing, but _____ likes dancing.
6. *(you)* Jenna will need _____. Those chairs are heavy, so three people should carry them.

ANSWERS p.279, REVIEW TEST 10 p.232

UNIT **064**

Grammar Gateway Basic

🎧 065.mp3

①

He's wearing a **black** jacket.

He's **tall**.

"**black**" and "**tall**" are *adjectives*.

② We use *adjectives* to describe someone or something.

nice/pretty/etc. *(adjectives) + noun*

- "Have you met Dr. Morris?" "Yes. He's a **nice man**."
- We bought a house with a **pretty garden**.
- Frank is writing a **short story** about his family.
- My sister has **blond hair**, and I have **brown hair**.
- "What is your **favorite sport**?" "Hockey."
- "Let's eat out tonight." "OK. How about **Mexican food**?"

be + thirsty/hot/etc. *(adjectives)*

- "**I'm thirsty**. Can I have a glass of water?" "Of course."
- Don't touch that pan. It**'s hot**.
- Charlie's old apartment **wasn't big**, but it **was expensive**.
- "**Is** that new restaurant **good**?" "No. I'll never go there again."
- Let's go home. It'll **be dark** soon.
- "Can I help you carry your bags?" "No, thanks. They **aren't heavy**."

③ We often use *adjectives* after the following *verbs*:

look	- You **look sad**. What happened? - "Tony **looks different** today." "Really? Well, I didn't notice."
smell	- What is this? It **smells strange**. - This perfume **smells nice**. I'd like to buy it.
sound	- Claire told a joke, but it didn't **sound funny** at all. - Do you know this song? It **sounds great**.
taste	- This cake **tastes sweet**. Try some. - The soup **tastes great**. Can I have some more?
feel	- My daughter graduated from college. I **feel proud**. - William lives alone, so he **feels lonely** sometimes.

PRACTICE

A. Look at the pictures and complete the sentences with the words from each box.

| blue | ~~cloudy~~ | long | old | + | car | ~~day~~ | eyes | hair |

1. It is a *cloudy day* _____.
2. She has _____.

3. They are driving an _____.
4. He has _____.

B. Complete the sentences with the given words.

| cold | empty | medical | ~~new~~ | pink |

1. *(suit)* "Are you wearing a *new suit* _____?" "Yes. I bought it yesterday."
2. *(weather)* I don't like _____, so I hate winter.
3. *(roses)* I ordered some _____ for my wife, but I got red ones!
4. *(seats)* On the subway, we had to stand because there were no _____.
5. *(school)* "Is your brother a student?" "Yes. He goes to _____."

UNIT
065

C. Look at the pictures and complete the sentences with **look/smell/sound/taste/feel** and the adjectives in *italics*.

1. *(nice)* You *look nice* _____.
2. *(delicious)* It _____.
3. *(scared)* I _____.
4. *(good)* It _____.
5. *(great)* It _____.
6. *(happy)* They _____.

D. Complete the conversation with the adjectives in the box.

| black | kind | tall | ~~old~~ |

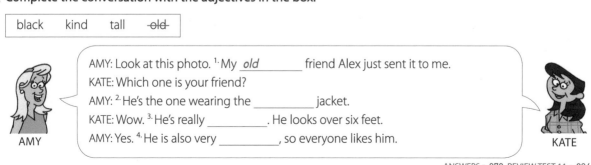

AMY: Look at this photo. [1.] My *old* _____ friend Alex just sent it to me.
KATE: Which one is your friend?
AMY: [2.] He's the one wearing the _____ jacket.
KATE: Wow. [3.] He's really _____. He looks over six feet.
AMY: Yes. [4.] He is also very _____, so everyone likes him.

AMY

KATE

ANSWERS p.279, REVIEW TEST 11 p.234

141

①

They are walking **carefully**.

"**carefully**" is an *adverb*.

---

② We use *adverbs* to describe how something happens. We usually add **-ly** at the end of *adjectives* to make *adverbs*.

Adjective	clear	quick	quiet	regular	slow
Adverb	clear**ly**	quick**ly**	quiet**ly**	regular**ly**	slow**ly**

- I bought new glasses, so now I can see **clearly**.
- Jack, come **quickly**! It's snowing outside!
- Please shut the door **quietly**. Everybody is sleeping.
- "Do you visit the dentist **regularly**?"   "Yes. I go once a year."
- Traffic was moving **slowly** because of an accident.

---

③ We add **-ily/-ically**/etc. at the end of some *adjectives*.

-y → -ily	easy → eas**ily**	busy → bus**ily**
-le → -ly	gent**le** → gent**ly**	comfortab**le** → comfortab**ly**
-ic → -ically	dramat**ic** → dramat**ically**	automat**ic** → automat**ically**
BUT:	**good → well**	

More about spelling rules: Appendix 3, p.249

- Most children can learn foreign languages **easily**.
- Jenna **gently** held her baby in her arms.
- This city has changed **dramatically** since last year. There are many new buildings.
- Our computer is very old, but it still runs **well**.
- Firefighters are **busily** spraying water on the fire.
- "What are you going to do this weekend?"   "I'll stay and watch TV **comfortably** at home."
- I wake up **automatically** at 6 o'clock. It's an old habit.

---

④ The following words end with **ly**, but they are *adjectives* and not *adverbs*:

friendly	**lovely**	**silly**	**ugly**	**lonely**

- My new neighbors are **friendly**. I really like them.
- "Where did you get that **lovely** dress?"   "At the mall."
- "Sorry. I made a **silly** mistake."   "That's OK."
- "Should we get that lamp?"   "No. I think it's **ugly**."
- "My grandfather lives alone."   "You should visit him often. He might feel **lonely**."

PRACTICE

A. Look at the pictures and complete the sentences with the adjectives in the box. Change the adjectives into adverbs.

| bright | comfortable | nervous | quick | ~~sudden~~ |

1. _Suddenly_____, the door closed.
2. He is running _____ across the road.
3. They are waiting _____.
4. He is sitting _____.
5. The sun is shining _____.

B. Complete the sentences with the appropriate adverbs.

1. Your paintings are wonderful. You paint pictures _wonderfully_____.
2. There will be heavy rain tomorrow. It will rain _____.
3. Peter is a simple person. He likes to live _____.
4. Our wedding was perfect. Everything was planned _____.
5. My neighbor's dog is so noisy. The dog barks _____.
6. The Tigers and the Eagles are both good teams. They always play _____.
7. The computer program is automatic. It will be updated _____.

C. Complete the sentences with the words from each box.

| drive | solve | speak | ~~visit~~ | walk | + | angrily | ~~happily~~ | loudly | quickly | safely |

1. I like my grandmother, so I always _visit_____ her house _happily_____.
2. Would you _____? I can't hear you.
3. "Why did Collin _____ out of the room _____?" "We just had a fight."
4. "It's too dark. You might not see other cars very well." "Yes. I'll _____."
5. You studied a lot. I think you can _____ these questions _____.

D. Find and change any mistakes in each sentence. Put ✓ if the sentence is correct.

1. Olivia is a friend girl. Everyone likes her.   _friend → friendly_
2. This is a lovely scarf. It looks well on you.   _____
3. "I saw a ghost!" "Don't be silly. It was a shadow."   _____
4. People should talk quiet in public places.   _____
5. "Can you hear the beautifully violin sound?" "Yes. Who's playing it?" _____
6. I don't like living abroad. It feels lonely.   _____
7. Oh, I forgot to call you. I'm terrible sorry about that.   _____
8. The temperature has dropped dramatically this morning.   _____

ANSWERS p.280, REVIEW TEST 11 p.234

He's **nervous**. He's waiting **nervously**.

Adjectives vs. Adverbs

🎧 067.mp3

①

He's **nervous**.

He's waiting **nervously**.

We use *adjectives* to describe someone or something.

- Jake is a **nice** guy. Everyone likes him.
- Our new bed is **comfortable**.
- This book has a **happy** ending.
- The music is **loud**.
- Mike got a **bad** grade on his test.
- Why does Sam look **angry**?
- Jane is a **quick** runner.

We use *adverbs* to describe how something happens.

- Jake always dresses **nicely**.
- We slept **comfortably** last night.
- The story ends **happily**.
- Tom is playing the guitar **loudly**.
- Mike did **badly** on his test.
- Sam just walked out **angrily**. What's wrong?
- Look! Why is Jane running so **quickly**?

② We can use the following words as both *adjectives* and *adverbs*:

	Adjective	*Adverb*
late	It's **late**. It's almost midnight.	I got home **late** last night. Everyone was asleep.
long	Sarah has **long** hair.	Let's walk to the park. It doesn't take **long**.
hard	My father is a **hard** worker.	The soccer team is practicing **hard**.
fast	Nicole's car is **fast**.	Nicole talks **fast**.
early	I had an **early** breakfast.	Mr. Jenkins arrived **early** for his interview.

PRACTICE

A. Choose the correct one.

1. "Which shoes do you like?" "These ones. They feel ((comfortable)/ comfortably)."
2. I don't like history. It is not (interesting / interestingly) to me.
3. Ben and Anna were talking (serious / seriously) when I saw them just a minute ago.
4. Lisa is a very (smart / smartly) student. She knows everything.
5. "Today is Valerie's birthday." "Oh no! I (complete / completely) forgot."
6. It was raining (heavy / heavily) when I woke up this morning.
7. I heard a (strange / strangely) sound last night. Did you hear anything?
8. You should exercise (regular / regularly) to stay healthy.

B. Complete the sentences with the adjectives in the box. Change the adjectives into adverbs if necessary.

| beautiful | ~~exciting~~ | fast | hard | late | safe |

1. "How was the soccer game?" "It was so _exciting_ ! Our team won."
2. We need to get to the theater _____. The show starts in 10 minutes.
3. "The concert was great. The singer sang _____." "I agree. I loved her voice."
4. We finally finished the project! Thank you for your _____ work.
5. I'm sorry I'm _____. There was so much traffic.
6. Did the train arrive _____? I was worried because of the bad weather.

C. Find and change any mistakes in each sentence. Put ✓ if the sentence is correct.

1. Please walk slowly. We don't need to hurry.   _____✓_____
2. Golf isn't an easily sport. You must practice often.   _____
3. I visit that café frequent. It's my favorite place.   _____
4. I have to get up early tomorrow. I'm going to the airport.   _____
5. "What happened?" "I don't know. The car stopped sudden."   _____
6. This painting is lovely! We should buy it.   _____
7. Your car looks nice. Is it newly?   _____
8. The children are playing noisy on the playground.   _____

D. Complete the conversation with the adjectives in the box. Change the adjectives into adverbs if necessary.

| late | long | nervous | quick | ~~terrible~~ |

LINDA: What's wrong, Justin? You look sick.
JUSTIN: ¹·I have a _terrible_ toothache. It hurts a lot.
LINDA: ²·You should see the dentist _____.
JUSTIN: ³·But I feel _____ when I go to the dentist.
LINDA: ⁴·Please don't wait too _____.
      ⁵·Go before it's too _____!

JUSTIN

LINDA

ANSWERS p.280, REVIEW TEST 11 p.234

| He **always** eats cereal for breakfast. always, often, never, etc.

🎧 068.mp3

①

| MON | TUE | WED | THU | FRI | SAT | SUN |

He **always** eats cereal for breakfast.

② We use the following *adverbs* to talk about how often something happens:

| always | usually | often | sometimes | rarely | never |

- I **always** take a shower in the morning.
- John **usually** wakes up around 7 a.m.
- You **often** give me advice. It helps a lot.
- We **sometimes** invite some neighbors to our house on weekends.
- It **rarely** snows here in October.
- Diana **never** drinks coffee at night.

③ We use **always**, **often**, **never**, etc. in the following positions:

before **check/cook**/etc.

- Ben **always** <u>checks</u> his e-mail when he arrives at the office.
- We **rarely** <u>cook</u> dinner these days. We **usually** <u>eat</u> out.
- I **often** <u>travel</u> abroad with a friend, but I **sometimes** <u>go</u> alone.

after **be**

- This hotel <u>is</u> **usually** full during the summer.
- I <u>am</u> **rarely** late for work, but my coworkers <u>are</u> **often** late.

after **will/can**/etc.

- I <u>will</u> **never** take a taxi to the airport again. It cost over $50!
- You <u>can</u> **always** call me when you need help.
- We <u>should</u> **often** visit our parents when we have time.

between **have/has** and **been/lived**/etc. *(past participle)*

- We <u>have</u> **never** <u>been</u> to Africa.
- Lynn <u>has</u> **always** <u>lived</u> in this town.

PRACTICE

A. Choose the correct one.

1. The bus (rarely / (usually)) comes late, so I don't take it to school.
2. "You used to go fishing (often / rarely). Do you still go regularly?" "No. I'm very busy these days."
3. "Do you drive a lot?" "Only (always / sometimes). I prefer to walk most places."
4. Tommy (never / usually) eats breakfast at home. He eats at a café every morning.
5. We (rarely / sometimes) go to bed late. We are always asleep before 10 p.m.
6. The shopping mall (always / never) has clothing sales, but there weren't any lately.
7. I see you and your dog on 2nd Street a lot. Do you (never / usually) walk there?

B. Read the questions and write about yourself with **always/often/never**/etc.

How often do you …?

1. wear jeans
2. exercise
3. watch movies
4. read books
5. clean your room
6. listen to music

I always wear jeans OR *I never wear jeans* _____ .
_____ .
_____ .
_____ .
_____ .
_____ .

YOU

C. Put the words in *italics* in the correct order.

1. (a lot of traffic / is / usually / there) _There is usually a lot of traffic_____ in the morning.
2. (always / smiling / is / she) Julia seems happy all the time. _____ .
3. (often / plays / Nick) _____ chess with his sister.
4. (never / we / will / move) _____ to the city. We enjoy living in the country.
5. (should / never / you / leave) _____ a baby alone.
6. (Danny / meets / sometimes) _____ his cousins from Belgium.
7. (always / can / you / talk) _____ to me when you have any problems.
8. (finish / rarely / we) _____ work before 8 o'clock.
9. (I / free / am / usually) _____ on Sundays.

D. Complete the conversations with the adverbs in *italics*. Use the *present perfect*.

1. Have you visited that restaurant?	(often) I _'ve often visited_ OR _have often visited__ there.
2. Has your son ever been late for class?	(rarely) No. He _____ late for class.
3. Have you wanted to go to Spain?	(always) Yes. We _____ to go.
4. Has Lily ridden in a boat before?	(never) No. She _____ in a boat before.
5. Have you ever felt lonely?	(sometimes) Yes. I _____ lonely.

ANSWERS p.280, REVIEW TEST 11 p.234

🎧 069.mp3

It's **too** small!

The bag is **too small**.

---

2 **too** + *adjective/adverb*

We use **too** to mean "more than necessary."

- Our washing machine is **too old**. We need a new one.
- "I lost my wallet again!" "You lose things **too easily**."
- Can I turn on the heater? The room is **too cold**.

---

3 We can use **for** + *person* or **to . . .** after **too** + *adjective*.

too + *adjective* + **for** + *person*

- Can you help me? This box is **too heavy for me**.
- This movie is **too scary for kids**.
- "Is the tea **too hot for you**?" "No, it's OK."

too + *adjective* + **to . . .**

- You're only 15 years old. You're **too young to drive**.
- The supermarket is already closed. It's **too late to buy** groceries.
- I was **too excited to sleep** before the trip, so I stayed awake all night.

---

4 We can use **too** before **many** or **much**.

too many + *plural noun*

- **Too many people** are waiting in line. Let's come back later.
- I made **too many mistakes** on my exam.

too much + *uncountable noun*

- Don't spend **too much time** on the Internet.
- The children are making **too much noise**. I can't read my book here.

We can use **too many / too much** without a *noun*.

- "I'm taking eight classes a day." "Eight? You're taking **too many**." (= too many classes)
- I don't have money for my bills. I spent **too much** last month. (= too much money)

PRACTICE

A. Look at the pictures and complete the sentences with **too** and the adjectives in the box.

dark	fast	high	long	~~small~~

1. This bag is
   _too small_____.

2. It's _____
   _____.

3. It's _____.
   I can't see you.

4. They're _____
   _____.

5. It's _____
   _____.

B. Complete the sentences with **too ... for ...** and the adjectives in the box.

~~big~~	early	expensive	hard	spicy

1. Do you want half of my burger? It's _too big for me_____.
2. We cannot afford to buy that sofa. It's _____.
3. This soup is _____. Can I have a glass of water?
4. Andrew didn't do well on the test. The questions were _____.
5. "Let's meet at 7 p.m." "Henry and Cathy finish work at 8 o'clock. 7 p.m. will be _____."

C. Complete the sentences with the words from each box.

too busy	~~too full~~	too heavy		~~to eat~~	to go	to lift
too large	too sick		**+**	to take	to see	

1. "Would you like some ice cream?" "No, thanks. I'm _too full to eat_____ dessert."
2. I've got a bad cold. I'm _____ to class today.
3. "Should I move the piano in my room?" "It weighs more than 50 kg. It's _____ by yourself."
4. "This museum is huge." "Yes. It's _____ everything in one day."
5. I'm so tired, but I'm _____ a break.

D. Complete the sentences with **too many / too much** and the nouns in *italics*. Use the plural form if necessary.

1. *(salt)* Jenny is not a good cook. She always puts _too much salt_____ in her food.
2. *(rain)* "How was your trip?" "I didn't enjoy it because there was _____."
3. *(word)* This article is very long. It has _____.
4. *(car)* There are _____ on the road. Let's just walk to the station.
5. *(food)* I have a stomachache. I had _____.
6. *(tourist)* _____ visit the Louvre Museum. It's always crowded.

ANSWERS p.280, REVIEW TEST 11 p.234

1 *adjective/adverb* + **enough**

We use **enough** to mean "equal to what is necessary."

These pants aren't **big enough.**

- His pants don't fit. They aren't **big enough**.
- Did I write this report **quickly enough**? It only took me two days.
- Mike can get into law school. He's **smart enough**.
- Tina was late for work. She didn't wake up **early enough**.

adjective + **enough** + **for** + *person*

- This book is **easy enough for children**.
- "Is the TV **loud enough for you**?" "Yes, it's fine."

adjective + **enough** + **to . . .**

- The weather is **cold enough to go** ice skating today.
- I like Mary, but I'm not **brave enough to tell** her.

2 **enough** + *noun*

We can use **enough** before *plural/uncountable nouns*.

- There aren't **enough seats** on the bus.
- I got **enough sleep** last night.
- "Can we stay at your house tonight?"
  "Of course. There are **enough bedrooms**."
- "Do we have **enough bread** for lunch?"
  "I'm not sure. Maybe we need some more."

enough + *noun* + **for** + *person*

- I'll drive. There's **enough space for everyone** in my car.
- Jane didn't buy **enough tickets for all of us**. She only bought four.

enough + *noun* + **to . . .**

- Did you save **enough money to pay** the rent?
- I don't have **enough time to finish** my homework.

3 We can use **enough** without a *noun*.

- "Do we need to stop for gas?" "No. We have **enough**." (= enough gas)
- "I'd like some cream for my coffee." "Here you go. Is that **enough**?" (= enough cream)

PRACTICE

A. Look at the pictures and complete the sentences with **enough** and the adjectives in the box.

large	long	loud	~~strong~~	tall

1. She is *strong enough* .
2. Her voice isn't _____ .
3. The space is _____ .

4. The boy is _____ .
5. His arm isn't _____ .

B. Complete the sentences with **enough** and the words in the box.

close	hungry	information	~~jobs~~

1. The new company will provide *enough jobs* for 500 people.
2. I'm just going to have a salad. I'm not _____ for a steak.
3. Let's walk to the mall. It's _____ from here.
4. I couldn't find _____ on the Internet for my essay.

doctors	hard	paper	wide

5. Is there _____? I have to print out over 100 pages.
6. Ray tried to score a goal, but he didn't kick the ball _____ .
7. We always have to wait at that hospital. There aren't _____ .
8. "Do you think this table will fit in the elevator?" "Yes. The door is _____ ."

C. Complete the sentences with **enough** and the words in *italics*. Add **for/to**.

1. *(good, sell)* Tim's paintings are *good enough to sell* . He's an excellent artist.
2. *(big, two people)* The hotel room had a very small bed. It wasn't _____ .
3. *(old, drink)* My daughter isn't _____ beer. She's only 15.
4. *(comfortable, me)* I'm not going to buy these shoes. They're not _____ .
5. *(lucky, meet)* During my trip to LA, I was _____ my favorite actor.

D. Put **enough** and the words in *italics* in the correct order.

1. *(cook / potatoes / to)* I'm going to the grocery store. I don't have *enough potatoes to cook* .
2. *(for / books / the students)* Our school library doesn't have _____ .
3. *(get to the station / to / time)* "We're late!" "Don't worry. There's _____ ."
4. *(stay healthy / to / exercise)* Eric should jog more often. He doesn't do _____ .
5. *(for / toys / all of our cousins)* It's Christmas, so I brought _____ .

ANSWERS p.280, REVIEW TEST 11 p.234

UNIT
070
Grammar Gateway Basic

| The mountain is **so** high. so

The mountain is **so high**.

so + *adjective/adverb*

We use **so** to mean "very." We use it before *adjectives* or *adverbs* to emphasize their meanings.

- This cake is **so good**. Can I have some more?
- Can you slow down? You're walking **so fast**.
- Are you getting married? I'm **so happy** for you!
- I am tired because I got up **so early** this morning.

We can use **so** before **many** or **much**.

so many + *plural noun*

- Katie received **so many gifts** on her birthday.
- I made **so many friends** during the trip.
- "Why do you need **so many boxes**?" "I'm moving to a new apartment."
- "I'm sorry. I made **so many mistakes**." "Don't worry. It's OK."

so much + *uncountable noun*

- My kids bring me **so much joy**.
- You should stop drinking **so much coffee**. Then, you'll sleep better.
- "How was the concert?" "It was great. We had **so much fun**."
- I spend **so much time** on the Internet. Maybe I should do something else.

We can use **so many** / **so much** without a *noun*.

- I don't know how many guests were at the party. There were **so many**. (= so many guests)
- Did you eat all the ice cream? You've eaten **so much**! (= so much ice cream)
- "Which book do you want to borrow?" "You have **so many**. It's hard to choose."
- Mr. Pitt taught history, art and math. I've learned **so much** from him.

PRACTICE

A. Look at the pictures and complete the sentences with **so** and the adjectives in the box.

~~full~~	heavy	long	small	tall

1. I'm _so full_ _____.
2. It's _____ _____.
3. These bags are _____.
4. The line is _____.
5. His hands are _____.

B. Complete the sentences with **so many / so much** and the nouns in *italics*.

1. *(snow)* "I've never seen _so much snow_ _____ in my life!" "Me neither. It's very beautiful."
2. *(passengers)* "There were _____ on the bus." "Was it during rush hour?"
3. *(food)* "Jason cooked _____." "Right. We couldn't eat it all."
4. *(questions)* "I have _____ for you." "OK. You can ask me now."

C. Complete the sentences with **so many / so much** and the nouns in the box.

clothes	countries	gas	languages	sisters	~~space~~	sugar	water

1. "How's your new room?" "I love it. It has _so much space_ _____."
2. I have _____. I need another closet.
3. "I can speak English, French and Japanese." "Wow! You speak _____"
4. I'm not going to buy that car. It uses _____.
5. You're wasting _____. Please turn off the shower.
6. You shouldn't eat _____. It's not good for your health.
7. Rick has been to _____. He visited every part of Europe.
8. Carla has _____. She comes from a large family.

D. Complete the conversation with **so** and the words in *italics*. Add **many/much** if necessary.

LINDA: Look, James! ^{1.} The trees and mountains are _so beautiful_ _____! *(beautiful)*
JAMES: ^{2.} Yes, and it's _____ here. *(quiet)*
     ^{3.} There are _____ in the city. *(people)*
LINDA: I know. Well, let's start climbing the mountain.
JAMES: ^{4.} But the mountain is _____! *(high)*
     ^{5.} It'll take _____. *(time)*
LINDA: Oh, come on, James. Let's just go!

LINDA

JAMES

ANSWERS p.281, REVIEW TEST 11 p.234

UNIT 071

Grammar Gateway Basic

| An airplane is **faster**. *Comparatives* (1)

①

A car is fast.

An airplane is **faster**.

"faster" is a *comparative*.

fast   faster

---

② We use **harder**, **higher**, etc. *(comparatives)* to compare two people/things. We usually add **-er** at the end of *adjectives/adverbs* to make *comparatives*.

Adjective/Adverb	hard	high	cold	quiet
Comparative	hard**er**	high**er**	cold**er**	quiet**er**

- "Japanese is hard to learn." "I think Chinese is **harder**."
- This roller coaster goes high, but that one goes **higher**.
- Take your jacket. It might get **colder** tonight.
- This café is noisy. Do you know a **quieter** place?

---

③ **comparative + than**

We often use **than** after *comparatives*.

- Silver is **cheaper than** gold.
- Ms. Jenner is **kinder than** Mr. Carter.
- Sound travels **slower than** light.
- I want a **lighter** racket **than** this one. Can you show me another one?

---

④ We can use the following two forms after **than**:

than	me/him/you/etc.
	I am / he is / you do / etc.

- Larry is one year **older than me**. *OR* Larry is one year **older than I am**.
- Frank is tall, but his brother is **taller than him**. *OR* Frank is tall, but his brother is **taller than he is**.
- I always come to work **earlier than you**. *OR* I always come to work **earlier than you do**.

But we use **me/him**/etc. more often than **I am** / **he is** / etc.

- Sharon is **stronger than me**.
- "How old is Mr. Brown's wife?" "She is five years **younger than him**."

PRACTICE

A. Complete the sentences with the comparatives of the adjectives/adverbs in the box.

cold	old	small	~~soft~~	soon	sweet

1. This lotion is great. My skin feels _*softer*_ now.
2. These sandals are too big. Do you have a _____ size?
3. "I think this sauce needs to be _____." "OK. I'll add some more sugar."
4. This winter is _____ than the last one.
5. "I'll finish the report by Friday." "I need it _____. How about Thursday?"
6. "Do you have any sisters?" "Yes. I have two _____ sisters. They're 25 and 28."

B. Complete the sentences with **than** and the comparatives of the adjectives in the box.

long	short	warm	~~young~~

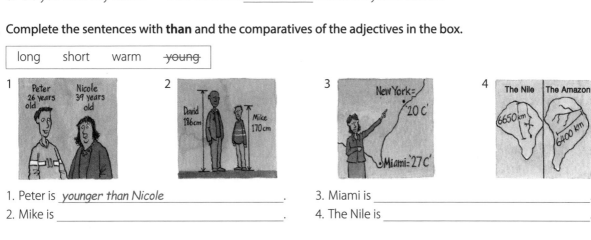

1. Peter is _*younger than Nicole*_ .
2. Mike is _____ .
3. Miami is _____ .
4. The Nile is _____ .

C. Read the sentences and complete the new ones with the comparatives in *italics*.

1. One pound is lighter than one kilogram.
   → *(heavier)* One kilogram _*is heavier than one pound*_ .
2. Theo has higher grades than Nathan.
   → *(lower)* Nathan _____ .
3. Beth has lighter hair than Jessie.
   → *(darker)* Jessie _____ .
4. Steel is stronger than aluminum.
   → *(weaker)* Aluminum _____ .
5. The countryside is quieter than the city.
   → *(noisier)* The city _____ .

D. Complete the sentences with **comparative + than** using **me/him**/etc. or **I am / he is** / etc.

1. Sean is rich, but Matt is _*richer than him* OR *richer than he is*_ .
2. I'm smart, but my brother is _____ .
3. My wife and I are tall, but our children are _____ .
4. Mary is fast, but John is _____ .
5. I can dive deep, but my dad can dive _____ .
6. High school students study hard, but college students usually study _____ .

ANSWERS p.281, REVIEW TEST 11 p.234

①

The sofa is **bigger** than the chair.

The chair is **more expensive** than the sofa.

② We add **-r/-ier**/etc. at the end of some *adjectives/adverbs* to make *comparatives*.

Adjective/Adverb	nice	wide	big	thin	early	pretty
Comparative	nic**er**	wid**er**	bi**gger**	thi**nner**	earl**ier**	prett**ier**

- I can't decide which car to buy. This one is **nicer**, but that one is **bigger**.
- "Does the movie start at 8:30?" "No. It's **earlier** than that. It starts at 7:45."
- I like this TV, but I still want a **wider** one.
- "Have you seen Jeff lately? He has gotten **thinner**." "Yes. He has been sick for two weeks."
- "Lucy changed her hairstyle." "I just saw her. She looks **prettier**."

More about spelling rules: Appendix 3, p.250

③ We use **more** before long *adjectives/adverbs*.

Adjective/Adverb	beautiful	carefully	comfortable	expensive
Comparative	**more** beautiful	**more** carefully	**more** comfortable	**more** expensive

- I think roses are **more beautiful** than lilies.
- "I fell off my bike again." "You should ride **more carefully**."
- Let's sit there. Those chairs look **more comfortable**.
- Diamonds are usually **more expensive** than pearls.

Note that we do not use **more** before *comparatives* that end with **er**.

- Can you walk **faster**? I'm in a hurry. (*NOT* more faster)
- Water is **healthier** than soda. (*NOT* more healthier)

④ Some *comparatives* are irregular.

Adjective/Adverb	good	bad	far
Comparative	**better**	**worse**	**farther**

- We should listen to others to make **better** decisions.
- I put some salt in this soup, and now it tastes **worse**!
- Which is **farther** from here, LA or San Francisco?

PRACTICE

A. Write the comparative of each adjective/adverb.

1. long   → _longer_
2. thin   → _____
3. easy   → _____
4. interesting → _____
5. bad   → _____

6. low   → _____
7. early   → _____
8. big   → _____
9. serious → _____
10. far   → _____

11. wide   → _____
12. close   → _____
13. good   → _____
14. strong   → _____
15. important → _____

B. Look at the pictures and complete the sentences with the given words. Use the comparatives of the adjectives.

| expensive   far   fast   heavy   ~~high~~ |

1. _(Mt. Fuji)_ Mt. Everest is _higher than Mt. Fuji_____.
2. _(the brown cap)_ The blue cap is _____.
3. _(Seattle)_ Vancouver is _____.
4. _(the man)_ The horse is _____.
5. _(the white box)_ The black box is _____.

C. Complete the sentences with the comparatives of the adjectives/adverbs in the box.

| carefully   cheap   ~~close~~   happy   hot   large   useful |

1. I moved into a new apartment. It's _closer_____ to my office.
2. "I don't see my red boots here." "Try looking _____."
3. This summer is _____ than last year. We use the air conditioner all day long.
4. "I'm writing an essay, but the textbook isn't helping." "Use the Internet. You'll find _____ information."
5. These pants are too small for me. Do you have a _____ size?
6. "Are you taking a plane?" "No, it's too expensive. The train is _____."
7. "Do you like your new job?" "Yes. I'm _____ than before."

D. Find and change any mistakes in each sentence. Put ✓ if the sentence is correct.

1. The meeting room is too small. We need a more big place.   _more big → bigger_
2. Health is more important than wealth.   _____
3. This puzzle is too difficult. Let's do the more easy one.   _____
4. Can you speak louder? I can't hear you.   _____
5. Riding a motorcycle is dangerous than driving a car.   _____
6. I hope tomorrow's weather will be good than today.   _____

ANSWERS p.281, REVIEW TEST 11 p.234

UNIT
073

Grammar Gateway Basic

| Chris is **the tallest** person. *Superlatives*

🎧 074.mp3

①

JUSTIN AMY CHRIS

Amy is taller than Justin. Chris is taller than Amy.

Chris is **the tallest** person.

"tallest" is a *superlative*.

---

② We use **the** + **deepest**/**longest**/etc. *(superlatives)* to compare a person/thing with all the others in a group. We usually add **-est** at the end of *adjectives/adverbs* to make *superlatives*.

Adjective/Adverb	deep	long	new	bright
Superlative	the deep**est**	the long**est**	the new**est**	the bright**est**

- Lake Baikal is **the deepest** lake in Russia.
- Emily has worked here **the longest**. She started 20 years ago.
- That gym just opened. It's **the newest** gym in the city.
- Sirius is **the brightest** star in the night sky.

---

③ We add **-st**/**-iest**/etc. at the end of some *adjectives/adverbs*.

Adjective/Adverb	close	large	big	hot	early	easy
Superlative	the clos**est**	the larg**est**	the bi**ggest**	the ho**ttest**	the earl**iest**	the eas**iest**

We use **most** before long *adjectives/adverbs*.

Adjective/Adverb	popular	crowded	widely
Superlative	the **most** popular	the **most** crowded	the **most** widely

Some *superlatives* are irregular.

Adjective/Adverb	good	bad	far
Superlative	the **best**	the **worst**	the **farthest**

More about spelling rules: Appendix 3, p.250

- "Where is **the closest** bank from here?" "Just around the corner."
- That hotel has **the biggest** swimming pool in town.
- "Have you waited long?" "No, but Tina has. She arrived the **earliest**."
- This is **the most popular** song these days. Everyone listens to it.
- I had **the best** birthday! It was so fun.

   Note that we do not use **most** before *superlatives* that end with **est**.
   - The library is **the largest** building on campus. (*NOT* the most largest)

---

④ We can use *superlatives* without a *noun*.

- I'm **the youngest** in my family.
- "Do you have a cheaper camera?" "No. That's **the cheapest** in the store."

PRACTICE

A. Write the comparative and superlative of each adjective/adverb.

1. low   - *lower*   - *the lowest*
2. beautiful   -   -
3. good   -   -
4. clean   -   -

5. hot   -   -
6. happy   -   -
7. large   -   -
8. bad   -   -

B. Complete the sentences with the given words. Use the superlatives of the adjectives.

busy	creative	delicious	fresh	~~hard~~	strong

1. *(decision)* Choosing a college was *the hardest decision* of my life.
2. *(person)* Cindy has many good ideas. She is _____ on my team.
3. *(animals)* Elephants can lift heavy things. They're one of _____.
4. *(man)* Mr. Miller is _____ in our office. He always works late.
5. *(dish)* "Is the curry here good?" "Yes. It is _____ at this restaurant."
6. *(vegetables)* "That market sells _____ in town." "I should buy some carrots there, then."

C. Look at the pictures and complete the sentences with the comparatives and superlatives of the adjectives in the box.

expensive	~~fast~~	high	young

1. Victor is *the fastest* runner.
   He is *faster than* Leo.
2. A is _____ B.
   It is _____ dress.

3. Tina is _____ child.
   She is _____ Lucy.
4. Ronny's grade is _____ Martin's.
   His grade is _____.

D. Look at the three runners and complete the sentences about them with the superlatives of the adjectives in *italics*.

	JIMMY	STEVEN	KEVIN
Height	194 cm	190 cm	206 cm
Weight	81 kg	86 kg	92 kg
Age	23	25	19
Ranking	1st	3rd	2nd

1. *(tall)* Kevin *is the tallest* .
2. *(old)* Steven _____ .
3. *(good)* Jimmy _____ player.
4. *(heavy)* Kevin _____ .
5. *(short)* Steven _____ .

ANSWERS p.281, REVIEW TEST 11 p.234

Chris is **as** heavy **as** Paul.   as ... as

🎧 075.mp3

①

Chris is **as heavy as** Paul.
(Chris and Paul are the same weight.)

---

② **as** + *adjective/adverb* + **as**

We use **as ... as** to say that two people/things are the same in some way.

- I know Julie's sister. She's **as beautiful as** Julie.
- Mason speaks French **as well as** a native speaker.
- The film was **as interesting as** the book.
- Anita is 16 years old. She is **as old as** me.

---

③ **not as** + *adjective/adverb* + **as**

We use **not as ... as** to say that two people/things are not the same in some way.

- These cookies are **not as good as** Laura's.
- I don't watch the news **as often as** my dad.
- "It's very hot this summer."   "Yes, but it's **not as hot as** last year."
- William does**n't** jog **as regularly as** before. He's busy these days.

We can also use **comparative + than** instead of **not as ... as**.

- This lamp is **not as bright as** that one.
  OR That lamp is **brighter than** this one.
- Terry does**n't** eat **as quickly as** his brother.
  OR Terry's brother eats **more quickly than** Terry.

---

④ **as ... as possible**

| as soon as possible |
| as long as possible |
| as early as possible |

- Please come home **as soon as possible**.
- We'll wait for you **as long as possible**.
- "Let's leave **as early as possible** to avoid traffic."   "Good idea."

PRACTICE

A. Read the conversations and complete the sentences with **as . . . as** and the words in the box.

cheap	fast	heavy	~~long~~	new	tall

1 JENNY: I've lived in Seoul for two years.
TED: I've lived in Seoul for two years.

2 JIM: I can run 100 meters in 17 seconds.
ANNA: I can run 100 meters in 17 seconds.

3 HELEN: My shoes cost only $20.
SARAH: My shoes cost only $20.

4 ROBERT: I'm 175 cm tall.
FRED: I'm 175 cm tall.

5 JASON: My luggage weighs 30 kg.
JOY: My luggage weighs 30 kg.

6 NICK: I bought a new car yesterday.
PAULA: I bought a new car yesterday.

1. Ted has lived in Seoul _as long as_ Jenny.
2. Anna can run _____ Jim.
3. Helen's shoes are _____ Sarah's.
4. Robert is _____ Fred.
5. Jason's luggage is _____ Joy's.
6. Paula's car is _____ Nick's.

B. Read the sentences and complete the new ones with **not as . . . as** and the words in *italics*.

1. Katie was born in 1990. Tom was born in 1992.   (*old*) Tom _isn't as old as Katie_ OR _is not as old as Katie_ .
2. I can eat three donuts. Jim can eat five donuts.   (*much*) I _____ .
3. The park is 5 km away. The mall is 10 km away.   (*far*) The park _____ .
4. Sally goes to work at 9. Ian goes to work at 8.   (*early*) Sally _____ .
5. This tower is 5 m tall. That tower is 7 m tall.   (*high*) This tower _____ .
6. It's 3 degrees in Beijing. It's 9 degrees in Tokyo.   (*cold*) Tokyo _____ .

C. Rewrite the sentences above with **comparative + than**.

1. Katie _is older than Tom_ .
2. Jim _____ .
3. The mall _____ .
4. Ian _____ .
5. That tower _____ .
6. Beijing _____ .

D. Complete the sentences with **as . . . as possible** and the words in the box.

carefully	loud	often	quickly	~~soon~~

1. I can't talk now, but I'll call you back _as soon as possible_ .
2. There are glasses in those boxes, so carry them _____ .
3. This is our favorite restaurant. We come here _____ .
4. I still can't hear the music. Turn up the volume _____ .
5. The meeting won't take long. We'll finish _____ .

ANSWERS p.282, REVIEW TEST 11 p.234

I'll meet you **at** the bus stop.

Prepositions of place at, in, on (1)

🎧 076.mp3

at the bus stop

in the living room

on the floor

We use **at, in,** or **on** to talk about the place something happens or is located.

- I'll meet you **at the bus stop**.
- They're watching TV **in the living room**.
- My sister is doing yoga **on the floor**.

---

② **at** + *point* (mall, door/window, etc.)

| **at** the mall | **at** the door/window | **at** the desk | **at** the corner | **at** the traffic light |

- I bought this coat **at the mall**. It was on sale.
- "Who's **at the door**?" "It might be Ted."
- You can leave your room key **at the desk** in the hotel lobby.
- Go straight and turn right **at the corner**. Then you'll see the bookstore.
- All cars must stop **at the traffic light** when the light is red.

---

③ **in** + *area* (room, box, etc.)

| **in** the room | **in** the box | **in** the forest | **in** Paris | **in** the car |

- Tim is talking on the phone **in the room**.
- Please put these books **in the box**.
- I was hiking **in the forest**, and I saw a bear.
- Michelle will spend this summer **in Paris**.
- "I think I left my gloves **in the car**." "Should we go back?"

---

④ **on** + *surface* (wall, table, etc.)

| **on** the wall | **on** the table | **on** the ceiling | **on** the sofa | **on** the bench |

- The clock **on the wall** isn't working. It needs new batteries.
- "Have you seen my bag?" "Yes. It's **on the table**."
- Look! There's a bee **on the ceiling**!
- "Where's Tony?" "He's lying **on the sofa**."
- Don't sit **on the bench**. I just painted it.

PRACTICE

A. Look at the picture and write **at/in/on**.

1. There are three people _in_ the room.
2. A picture is hanging _____ the wall.
3. A dog is sleeping _____ the floor.
4. There are apples _____ the basket.
5. A man is sitting _____ the desk.

6. A woman is standing _____ the window.
7. There are flowers _____ the vase.
8. There are toys _____ the box.
9. A cat is sitting _____ the sofa.
10. A little boy is standing _____ the door.

B. Write **at/in/on**.

1. I studied English _in_ Canada four years ago.
2. "Why is Dad _____ the garage?" "He's fixing the car."
3. "Where did you see Nick?" "_____ the bus stop."
4. There was a lot of trash _____ the ground after the hurricane.
5. The people _____ the bench are eating sandwiches.
6. "Where are we getting off?" "_____ the next station."
7. "What's that _____ the shelf?" "It's raspberry jam. I made it yesterday."
8. "Is there any juice _____ the fridge?" "No. There's only water."

C. Complete the conversation with **at/in/on** and the words in *italics*.

JUSTIN: Dad, I'm bored. Where's Chris?
JAMES: ¹·He's _in his room_ . *(his room)*
       ²·He's studying _____. *(his desk)*
JUSTIN: Oh. Then where's Amy?
JAMES: ³·She's doing yoga _____. *(the living room)*
JUSTIN: Well, what about Mom?
JAMES: ⁴·She's _____. *(the mall)*
       If you're bored, you could read something.
       ⁵·There are some magazines _____. *(the table)*

JUSTIN

JAMES

ANSWERS p.282, REVIEW TEST 12 p.236

| I don't have to wear a suit **at** work. *Prepositions* of place at, in, on (2)

🎧 077.mp3

① We use **at** in the following expressions:

Everyday place	**at** work	**at** home	**at** school	**at** church
	at the doctor's (office)	**at** somebody's (house)		
Station/Airport	**at** the station	**at** the airport		
Event/Show	**at** a party	**at** a concert	**at** a baseball game	

- I don't have to wear a suit **at work**.
- "Can you wait for me **at the station**?"   "OK. I'll be there."
- I was **at a party** last night. I had a great time.
- Sally wasn't feeling well, so she stayed **at home**.
- Last night, we had dinner **at Laura's**.

② We use **in** in the following expressions:

Nature/Environment	**in** the world	**in** the sky	**in** the ocean
Printed material	**in** a book	**in** a picture	**in** a newspaper
Action/State	**in** bed (= "sleeping", "lying in bed")		
	in hospital (= "being hospitalized")	**in** prison/jail (= "being confined")	

- Mount Everest is the highest mountain **in the world**.
- "Have you ever heard of Isaac Newton?"   "Yes. I read about him **in a book**."
- "What were you doing this morning? I called you five times!"   "Sorry. I was **in bed**."
- Look! Can you see those stars **in the sky**?
- Jim is **in the hospital**. He's having surgery tomorrow.

③ We use **on** in the following expressions:

Street	**on** 2nd Avenue	**on** Main Street	
Floor	**on** the first floor	**on** the 3rd floor	
Transportation	**on** the train	**on** the bus	**on** the plane
	BUT: **in** the car	**in** the taxi	

- "Is your office **on 2nd Avenue**?"   "Yes. It's not far from here."
- "Excuse me. I'm looking for the restroom."   "It's **on the first floor**."
- I bought a newspaper to read **on the train**.
- I saw a famous actor **on the plane** yesterday.
- "Where is your luggage?"   "I put it **in the car**."

PRACTICE

A. Look at the pictures and complete the sentences with **at/in/on** and the words in the box.

2nd Avenue	a birthday party	~~school~~	the bus	the sky

1. The students are _at school_____.
2. The bookstore is _____.
3. They are _____.

4. There are birds _____.
5. They are _____.

B. Write **at/in/on**.

1. "I can't see you _in_____ the picture." "I'm there, at the back."
2. "Are you going out tonight?" "I might just watch TV _____ home."
3. Mr. Brown's house is _____ Oak Street.
4. Could you meet me _____ the airport? I'll arrive at 12 p.m.
5. "Is the cafeteria _____ the 2nd floor?" "No. The 3rd floor."
6. "Where's your brother?" "He's waiting _____ the car."

C. Complete the sentences with **at/in/on** and the words in the box.

a book	Ann's house	prison	the concert
the first floor	the train	~~the world~~	

1. Whales are the largest animals _in the world_____.
2. "What kind of music will the bands play _____?" "Jazz, I think."
3. Sorry I'm late. I fell asleep _____ and missed my stop.
4. I was _____ last night. Her room is so big.
5. "Where did you find that information?" "_____ from the library."
6. The thief was _____ for two years because he stole expensive jewelry.
7. "Excuse me. Where's customer service?" "It's _____ of this building."

D. Complete the conversation with **at/in/on** and the words in *italics*.

SANDY: Where's Justin today?
¹· I didn't see him _at school_____. *(school)*
AMY: ²· He's sick and needs to stay _____. *(bed)*
³· He was _____ this morning. *(the doctor's office)*
SANDY: ⁴· The one _____? *(Main Street)*
AMY: ⁵· Yes, but he is feeling better, and he's _____ now. *(home)*

SANDY

AMY

ANSWERS p.282, REVIEW TEST 12 p.236

The bus stop is **in front of** my house.

Other *prepositions* of place

🎧 078.mp3

---

①

in front of

- The bus stop is **in front of my house**.
- Daniel is waiting for you **in front of the station**.
- Jessica can speak well **in front of people**.

behind

- "Where is my scarf?" "It's **behind the chair**."
- I sit **behind Tate** in history class.
- "Can I park my car **behind the building**?" "Sorry, but you can't."

---

②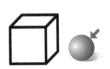

by, next to

- We had a picnic **by the lake** last weekend.
- "Who's the girl **next to Jake**?" "Angela. She's from Canada."
- "I'll meet you **by the elevator**." "OK. Sounds good."
- Philip is my neighbor. His house is **next to mine**.

---

③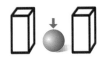

between

- That's my brother. He's standing **between Emily and Lynn**.
- The bank is **between the mall and the pharmacy**.
- I can't decide **between the cake, the donut, and the cookie** for dessert.

among

- Joan is the tallest girl **among the students** in her class.
- The children are hiding **among the trees**.
- Who is the best player **among the team members**?

---

④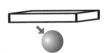

over

- A lamp is hanging **over the table**.
- It started raining, so Dave held an umbrella **over her head**.
- Can you see the rainbow **over that river**?

under

- I found a coin **under the sofa**.
- "My slippers are missing." "Did you look **under the bed**?"
- When we went to Paris, we took a picture **under the Eiffel Tower**.

PRACTICE

A. Look at the pictures and write **in front of / behind / by / next to**.

  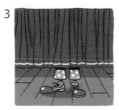  

1. Sarah is *in front of* _____ Ben.
2. Tom is standing _____ Mary.
3. There is someone _____ the curtain.

4. The kids are walking _____ the woman.
5. Nicolas is sitting _____ Nancy.

B. Look at the pictures and write **between/among/over/under**.

1. The bench is *between* _____ two large trees.
2. There are clouds _____ the mountains.
3. There is a cat _____ several dogs.

4. A man is sleeping _____ the tree.
5. Mike is sitting _____ the two men.

C. Choose the correct one.

1. "Who is Mr. Nelson?" "The man standing (between / among) Mr. Smith and Mr. Miller."
2. I can't see the professor. The man (behind / in front of) me is too tall.
3. "Can I sit (next to / over) you?" "Sorry. This seat is taken."
4. There is a police car (in front of / behind) us. Why is it following us?
5. In China, the Great Wall is the most popular place to visit (over / among) tourists.
6. There is a park (by / between) my house. I go there often.
7. There's a new exit sign (over / among) the door. We put it there yesterday.
8. I woke up on Christmas morning and found many presents (under / over) the Christmas tree.

D. Choose the correct one.

JAMES:

JAMES: Where are you going?
  1. Our car is (in front of / over) the supermarket.
LINDA: 2. No, we parked it (between / behind) the store.
JAMES: Wait! I found it. 3. It's (next to / among) that bank.
LINDA: Where? I don't see it.
JAMES: 4. There's a white car (under / between) the truck and the van.
LINDA: That's not ours. Oh, I just remembered! We took the subway!

LINDA

ANSWERS p.282, REVIEW TEST 12 p.236

UNIT
078

Grammar Gateway Basic

🎧 079.mp3

(1)

from 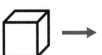 **to**

- Where is this letter **from**?
- I'm traveling **to Europe** next week.
- Susie's family came **from Vietnam**.
- We went **to the museum** last weekend.

up  **down**

- Jim went **up the ladder** to fix the roof.
- A rock is rolling **down the hill**.
- Look! A spider is climbing **up the wall**.
- Firefighters are coming **down the stairs**.

(2)

into   **out of**

- Ann poured soda **into the glasses**.
- Ken took his keys **out of his pocket**.
- Please come **into my office**.
- Can you take the bread **out of the oven**?

over   **under**

- We're flying **over the Grand Canyon**!
- I'm walking **under the bridge**.
- A cat jumped **over the chair**.
- The dolphins just passed **under the boat**.

(3)

through 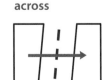 **across**

- The Nile flows **through Egypt**.
- Don't walk **across the road**.
- We carried the piano **through the door**.
- The actors danced **across the stage**.

along  **around**

- I jogged **along the beach** for an hour.
- The boats sail **around the island**.
- Flowers are growing **along the lake**.
- Jane rode her bicycle **around the track**.

(4)

on   **off**

- Can you put the bags **on the sofa**?
- Sam fell **off the bed** and woke up.
- I'll leave this report **on your desk**.
- We need to get **off the train** soon.

past   **toward**

- I drive **past the mall** every day.
- The bird flew **toward the tree**.
- We went **past the bus stop** by mistake.
- The children ran **toward their parents**.

PRACTICE

A. Look at the pictures and complete the sentences with the given words. Use the *present progressive*.

along	~~into~~	out of	over	up

1. *(dive)* She <u>'s diving into OR is diving into</u> the pool.
2. *(go)* The car _____ the bridge.
3. *(get)* They _____ school.
4. *(drive)* The car _____ the river.
5. *(walk)* She _____ the stairs.

across	around	off	past	through

6. *(pass)* The train _____ the tunnel.
7. *(go)* The car _____ the bank.
8. *(fall)* He _____ the table.
9. *(walk)* She _____ the street.
10. *(drive)* The car _____ the fountain.

B. Complete the sentences with the prepositions in the box.

~~around~~	down	into	over	to	under

1. "Where is the zoo?" "Go <u>around</u> that corner, and you'll find it on the left."
2. "The elevator is broken. We have to ride _____ the escalator." "Oh, no! We're on the top floor."
3. I found Andy. He was hiding _____ his desk!
4. The baseball player hit the ball _____ the fence! It's a home run!
5. "Did you spend your vacation in Hawaii?" "No, I went _____ Bali."
6. Ted read the letters and threw them _____ the trash can.

from	off	on	out of	through	toward

7. My neighbors moved here _____ Chicago last year. They lived there for a few years.
8. John is running _____ the finish line. I think he'll win the race!
9. "Ouch! You stepped _____ my foot." "Oh, I'm sorry."
10. Rachel didn't like the picture, so she took it _____ the wall.
11. A storm passed _____ the city last night. Many houses were damaged.
12. You should get _____ bed! You're late for school!

ANSWERS p.282, REVIEW TEST 12 p.236

UNIT 079

Grammar Gateway Basic

It arrives **at** 5:30.

Prepositions of time (1) **at**, **on**, **in**

 080.mp3

①

at 5:30 **on Monday** **in July**

We use **at, on,** or **in** to talk about the time something happens.

- "What time does the plane arrive?" "It arrives **at 5:30**."
- Do you want to go hiking **on Monday**?
- Angela is moving to Sydney **in July**.

② **at**

Specific time	**at** 10:30	**at** noon	**at** 3 o'clock
Meal time	**at** breakfast	**at** lunch	**at** dinner

- Every night, I go to sleep **at 10:30**.
- We can talk about our business trip **at lunch**.
- The library opens **at noon** on Sunday.
- "I had a good time **at dinner** last night." "I'm glad to hear that."

③ **on**

Day of the week	**on** Wednesday/Saturday	**on** Friday night / Sunday morning
Weekday/Weekend	**on** weekdays / a weekday	**on** weekends / the weekend
Date/Anniversary	**on** May 21 **on** my birthday	**on** our anniversary

- I have an interview **on Wednesday**.
- We work late **on weekdays**, so we sleep in **on weekends**.
- "My wedding is **on May 21**. Can you come?" "Of course I can!"
- I usually get a call from my parents **on my birthday**.

④ **in**

Month/Season	**in** January/June/December	**in** (the) spring/summer/fall/winter
Century/Year	**in** the 19th century	**in** 2018
Part of the day	**in** the morning/afternoon/evening	*BUT:* **at** night

- It often snows here **in January**.
- Cars were invented **in the 19th century**.
- I always go to the park for a walk early **in the morning**.
- The tennis court has lights, so we can play **at night**.

PRACTICE

A. Look at the pictures and complete the sentences with **at/on/in** and the appropriate nouns.

1  2  3  4  5

1. Patrick's birthday is _on Friday_____ .
2. Carol got the message _____ .
3. The building was built _____ .

4. He often exercises _____ .
5. Gina is having lunch with Greg _____ .

B. Write **at/on/in**.

1. I'll tell you about my plans _at_____ dinner tonight.
2. My parents are going to move into a new house _____ Saturday.
3. "I'm going to bed. I'll see you _____ breakfast." "OK. Good night."
4. "When are you leaving for London?" "_____ January 15."
5. New York is very beautiful _____ the fall.
6. "Kelly was born _____ 1975." "Wow, she looks so young."
7. We're going to a concert today. It starts _____ noon.
8. I can't watch TV _____ weekdays. I'm too busy.

C. Complete the sentences with **at/on/in** and the words in *italics*.

1. *(Sunday)* "I'm going to play baseball _on Sunday_____ ." "That will be fun."
2. *(February)* The new mall will open _____ .
3. *(lunch)* "Do you check your e-mails _____ ?" "No, not usually."
4. *(10 a.m.)* The meeting is _____ tomorrow morning.
5. *(our anniversary)* My husband gave me a necklace _____ .
6. *(the 20th century)* Christmas trees started becoming popular _____ .
7. *(the evening)* Amanda takes her dog for a walk _____ .
8. *(Saturday night)* We're going to a bar _____ . Can you join us?

D. Complete the conversation with **at/on/in** and the words in *italics*.

JUSTIN: 1. I'm having a party _on my birthday_____ . *(my birthday)*
SANDY: When is your birthday? 2. Is it _____ ? *(the weekend)*
JUSTIN: No. It's this Friday.
    3. The party starts _____ . *(11 o'clock)*
SANDY: 4. Sorry. I can't go _____ . *(the morning)*
    5. Can you meet me _____ or _____ ?
    (the afternoon) (night) I'll buy you dinner.

JUSTIN

SANDY

ANSWERS p.283, REVIEW TEST 12 p.236

UNIT

080

Grammar Gateway Basic

171

🎧 081.mp3

① **during** and **for**

We use **during** to say that something happens in a particular time period.

- Bats sleep **during the day**.
- Terry got hurt **during the basketball game**.
- I went to Italy **during the holidays**.
- "Did you visit many places **during your trip** to Ireland?" "Yes, we did."

We use **for** to say that something lasts over a particular time period.

- "Can I talk to you **for a second**?" "Sure."
- Holly has studied French **for three years**.
- I have known Kevin **for a long time**.
- We cleaned the house **for two hours**, but it's still dirty.

> Note that we use **during** and **for** in different ways.
>
> - I usually exercise **during lunch**. I feel refreshed.
>   (**during** is used to say that **exercise** happens at lunchtime.)
>
>   I usually exercise **for an hour**. I do yoga first, then I jog.
>   (**for** is used to say that **exercise** lasts over an hour.)
>
> - We are going to travel in Asia **during the summer**. I hope it's not too hot when we go.
>   We are going to travel in Asia **for two months**. We'll spend our whole vacation there.

② **in** and **within**

We use **in** to say that something happens after a particular time period has passed.

- "Are you ready?" "Not yet. I'll be ready **in 10 minutes**." (= I'll be ready after 10 minutes has passed.)
- The store will close **in two hours**. (= The store will close after two hours has passed.)
- Harry and Julie will get married **in one month**.
- It's my mom's birthday **in a few days**. I have to buy a gift for her.

We use **within** to say that something happens before a particular time period has passed.

- I can get there **within 15 minutes**, so I'll see you soon. (= I can get there before 15 minutes has passed.)
- Please pay this bill **within four days**. (= Please pay this bill before four days has passed.)
- You should return the book **within three weeks**. There is a fee if you're late.
- Tickets for the show were sold out **within a couple of hours**.

PRACTICE

A. Look at the tour group schedule and write **during/for**.

DAY 2 SCHEDULE	
09:00 ~ 11:00	Swimming at the beach
11:00 ~ 12:00	**[Free time]** - You can take pictures.
12:00 ~ 13:00	**[Lunch time]** - You can take a break.
13:00 ~ 15:00	Visiting the museum
15:00 ~ 18:00	Going to Central Park
18:00 ~ 20:00	**[Dinner time]** - You can go shopping.

1. Tourists will go swimming _for_ two hours.
2. They can take pictures _____ their free time.
3. They can take a break _____ lunch time.
4. They will visit the museum _____ two hours.
5. They will go to Central Park _____ three hours.
6. They can go shopping _____ dinner time.

B. Complete the conversations with **during/for** and the words in *italics*.

1. How long has Jimmy been asleep?
2. When did you get a haircut?
3. How long have you collected stamps?
4. When did Amber leave the office?
5. When were these pictures taken?
6. How long should I cook this sauce?
7. How long have you worked here?

(about 10 hours) _For about 10 hours_ .
(the weekend) _____ .
(eight years) _____ .
(our meeting) _____ .
(the winter) _____ .
(five minutes) _____ .
(about four months) _____ .

C. Choose the correct one.

1. The race lasted 50 minutes. All the runners finished (during / (within)) an hour.
2. "It's noon right now. Let's meet at 12:30." "OK. I'll see you (in / during) 30 minutes."
3. People cannot smoke (during / for) the flight.
4. I have played the flute (in / for) three years, but I can't play very well.
5. Frank was very nervous (within / during) his first job interview.
6. The winner of the contest will be announced (for / within) two weeks.
7. The lecture will begin (in / for) exactly 45 minutes. Please don't be late.

D. Find and change any mistakes in each sentence. Put ✓ if the sentence is correct.

1. The guests will come in an hour, so dinner should be ready by then. _____✓_____
2. I didn't sleep well yesterday. I woke up several times for the night. _____
3. It's Friday already! Our vacation starts next Friday, so it's within a week. _____
4. Sam wants to stay at my house during one night. _____
5. I've lived in this city for a month. I moved here four weeks ago. _____
6. We have a 60-minute lunch break, so we must eat in an hour. _____
7. I couldn't open my eyes during the horror movie. It was so scary! _____

ANSWERS p.283, REVIEW TEST 12 p.236

(1) We use **from . . . to** to say when something starts and ends.

- The café is open **from 2 to 9 p.m.**
- I work five days a week, **from Monday to Friday.**
- "How long will you stay in Africa?" "**From January to March.**"
- Mr. Chan was the president **from 2013 to last year.**

from 2 to 9 p.m.

> We can use **from** without **to** to say when something starts.
>
> - Call me in the afternoon. I'll be in my office **from 12 p.m.**
> - Our class will begin doing group projects **from November.**
>
> We can also use **from . . . until** instead of **from . . . to.**
>
> - It usually snows a lot here **from December until February.**
> - Dr. Kim sees patients **from 9 a.m. until 6 p.m.**

(2) We use **since** to say that something started at a certain point in time and continues until now.

- This museum has been open **since 1970.**
- Tom has been on vacation **since Tuesday.**
- I'm hungry. I haven't eaten anything **since breakfast.**
- Betty has had short hair **since high school.**

since 1970

(3) We use **by** to say that something happens before a certain point in time.

- You should drink this milk **by June 17.**
- I'm going to be late. I can't get there **by 8.**
- "Could you finish this work **by next Wednesday**?" "Sure. I can do it."
- "Have our guests arrived yet?" "No, but they will arrive **by noon.**"

by June 17

(4) We use **until** to say that something continues to a certain point in time.

- The road will be closed **until Friday.**
- I won't be home **until 9 p.m.** tonight.
- "Can I keep this book **until Saturday**?" "Yes, that's fine."
- "When can we meet?"
  "Is Friday OK? I won't have any time **until Thursday.**"

until Friday

PRACTICE

A. Look at the pictures and complete the sentences with **from . . . to.**

1  2  3  4  5

1. The class is _from 9 a.m. to 11 a.m._____ .
2. The road is closed _____ .
3. The store is open _____ .
4. Drivers cannot park _____ .
5. The tickets will be on sale _____ .

B. Complete the sentences about Brian with **since** and the verbs in *italics*. Use the *present perfect*.

BRIAN

1. I'm in Egypt. I came here last week.
2. I met Jason in high school.
3. I don't smoke anymore. I quit last year.
4. I got married in July.
5. I have a car. I bought it in 2014.

(be) He _has been in Egypt since last week_____ .
(know) He _____ .
(not smoke) He _____ .
(be married) He _____ .
(have) He _____ .

C. Write **by/until.**

1. I studied _until_____ 11 o'clock last night. I have an important test today.
2. This coupon must be used _____ August 3, and it can only be used once.
3. Some of my friends are coming to visit. They will stay with me _____ Friday.
4. "I have to write an essay _____ next Monday." "I'll help you with it."
5. The plane leaves at 3:30 p.m. We should arrive at the airport _____ 2 p.m.
6. The football game lasted _____ midnight. It was so long but exciting.

D. The following information is about The Rock Stars' concerts. Write **from . . . to / by / until.**

The Rock Stars Come to Springfield

THE ROCK STARS
COME TO SPRINGFIELD

From July 1st to July 7th

The Rock Stars are finally coming to town!
¹. Ticket sales began last month and will end _by_____ July 1.
The band will play five concerts.
². The concerts are _____ July 2 _____ July 6. They start at 8 p.m.
³. The concert hall will be very crowded, so if you want a good seat, you should arrive _____ 7:30.
⁴. Note: Please do not take any pictures _____ the end of the show.

ANSWERS p.283, REVIEW TEST 12 p.236

He is running **with** a dog. Other *prepositions* with, without, by

🎧 083.mp3

① We use **with** to mean "in the same place as someone or something" or "have something."

- He is running **with a dog**.
- The house **with the purple roof** is ours.
- "Would you like to have tea **with us**?" "Sure. I'd love to."

We also use **with** to talk about someone's physical characteristics.

- Patrick is the only boy **with green eyes** in his class.

We also use **with** to talk about a tool that is used to do something.

- You have to write your answers **with a pen**.

with a dog

② We use **without** to mean "not with."

- I can't imagine life **without the Internet**.
- You must not drive **without a license**.
- We have to start the meeting **without Jenny**. She's going to be late.

③ We use **by** + **taxi/bicycle**/etc. to talk about a method of transportation.

- "How did you get here?" "We came **by taxi**."
- I sometimes go to school **by bicycle**.
- "Are you driving to Chicago?" "No. I'm going **by train**."

But we usually use **on** before **foot**.

- I go to work **on foot**. It takes 20 minutes from my house.

on foot   **by taxi**

④

| about |
| for |
| like |
| of |

- "Can I help you?" "Yes. I'm looking for a book **about Peru**."
- "Thank you **for the advice**." "You're welcome."
- "What does Matt do?" "He's a doctor, **like his father**."
- "What's the name **of this band**?" "It's the White Tigers."

⑤ **without/about**/etc. *(prepositions)* + **-ing**

We can use **-ing** after *prepositions*.

- "Betty left **without saying** goodbye." "Oh, I'm surprised."
- "Please tell me **about working** at the gym." "It's interesting."
- Robert is very good **at singing**. I want him to sing at my wedding.

But we do not use **base form** after *prepositions*.

- Tourists asked me how to get to the station, so I helped them **by showing** them the way. *(NOT by show)*

PRACTICE

A. Look at the pictures and complete the sentences with **with/without** and the words in the box.

| a helmet | a knife | a swimming pool | his glasses |

1 2 3 4

1. He is cutting the bread _with a knife_ .
2. He is reading _____ .
3. She has a house _____ .
4. She is riding a motorcycle _____ .

B. Complete the sentences with **with/without/by/about/**etc. and the words in *italics*.

1. *(my brother)* "Do you live alone?"   "No. I live _with my brother_ ."
2. *(subway)* The best way to get to City Hall is _____ .
3. *(brown hair)* "Who is Teresa?"   "She's the girl _____ over there."
4. *(a ticket)* The concert is free. You can attend _____ .
5. *(plane)* We're going to Las Vegas _____ . It's the quickest way to get there.
6. *(this pair of jeans)* "What's the price _____ ?"   "It's $40."
7. *(foot)* "How far is the mall from here?"   "It's close enough to go _____ ."
8. *(my wallet)* Can I borrow a few dollars? I left home _____ this morning.
9. *(the meeting)* "Did you tell Matt _____ ?"   "Oh, no! I forgot."
10. *(a fish)* Carmen is a good swimmer. She swims _____ .

C. Read the sentences and complete the new ones with the prepositions in *italics*.

1. I feel sorry. I'm late.
    → *(for)* I feel sorry _for being late_ .

2. We drove for 10 hours. We didn't stop.
    → *(without)* We drove for 10 hours _____ .

3. Turn off the lights to save energy.
    → *(by)* We can save energy _____ .

4. I can't skate. I'm terrible at it.
    → *(at)* I'm terrible _____ .

5. Paula is going to get a promotion. She's happy.
    → *(about)* Paula is happy _____ .

6. You joined our book club. I'd like to thank you.
    → *(for)* I'd like to thank you _____ .

ANSWERS p.283, REVIEW TEST 12 p.236

① *adjective* + **about**/**at**/etc. *(prepositions)*

We can use *adjectives* and *prepositions* together in the following expressions:

about

excited about
sorry about
sure about

- We're **excited about** the trip.
- I'm **sorry about** the noise last night. I had a party.
- "Sally said she won't come back here." "Are you **sure about** that?"

at

angry/mad at
good at
surprised at

- "Why is Ryan **angry at** you?" "I broke his glasses."
- Michelle is very **good at** math.
- Everyone was **surprised at** my decision to move to another city.

for

famous for

- This bakery is **famous for** its apple pies.

from

different from

- How is the movie **different from** the book?

in

interested in

- Jay is **interested in** fashion. He dresses well. .

of

afraid of
full of
proud of
short of
tired of

- When I was young, I was **afraid of** spiders.
- "Why is the store **full of** people?" "There's a sale."
- You did a great job. I am very **proud of** you.
- I'm **short of** cash this week. Could I borrow $50?
- "I'm **tired of** the rain." "I know. It's been two weeks now."

to

married to
similar to

- Laura got **married to** Greg last month.
- Brad looks quite **similar to** his mother.

with

busy with
careful with
familiar with

- Darcy has been **busy with** his studies lately.
- You have to be **careful with** that knife. It's very sharp.
- "Have you heard this song?" "No. I'm not **familiar with** it."

More about adjective + preposition: Appendix 7, p.255

PRACTICE

A. Write the appropriate prepositions.

1. Frank is excited _about_ the football game today.
2. "Emily quit her job." "Yes. I was surprised _____ the news."
3. "You shouldn't bring food into the library." "I'm sorry _____ that. I didn't know."
4. I'm tired _____ pizza. Let's have Japanese food tonight.
5. Your shirt is similar _____ mine. Where did you buy it?
6. Jeremy doesn't want to come to the gallery with us. He's not interested _____ art.
7. Fifth Avenue in New York is famous _____ its shops.
8. Jake is afraid _____ the water, so he doesn't swim.

B. Look at the pictures and complete the sentences with the adjectives in the box and the appropriate prepositions.

| different | full | ~~good~~ | proud | sure |

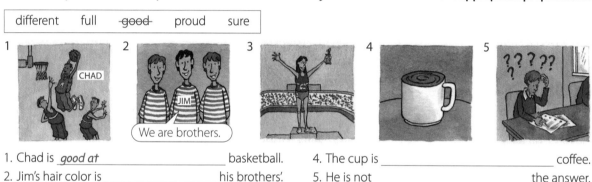

1. Chad is _good at_ _____ basketball.
2. Jim's hair color is _____ his brothers'.
3. She must be _____ herself.
4. The cup is _____ coffee.
5. He is not _____ the answer.

C. Complete the sentences with the words from each box and the appropriate prepositions.

| ~~angry~~ familiar married short similar | + | ~~himself~~ Italian food Julia money this city |

1. Adam was _angry at himself_ _____. He forgot to bring his homework to school.
2. "Is Greek food _____?" "No. They're very different."
3. Grace bought an expensive laptop, so she's _____ this month.
4. "Martin is getting _____ next week." "Are you going to their wedding?"
5. I'm not _____. I've never been here before.

D. Complete the conversation with the adjectives in *italics* and the appropriate prepositions.

LINDA

LINDA: Justin! Your room is so dirty.
JUSTIN: 1. I'm _sorry about_ that, Mom. *(sorry)*
2. But I'm so _____ my homework these days. *(busy)*
LINDA: 3. Are you _____ that? *(sure)*
You're always playing computer games.
JUSTIN: 4. Don't be _____ me, Mom. *(mad)*
I'll clean it tomorrow.

JUSTIN

ANSWERS p.283, REVIEW TEST 12 p.236

🎧 085.mp3

(1) *verb +* **about/at**/etc. *(prepositions)*

We can use *verbs* and *prepositions* together in the following expressions:

about

know about	● Did you **know about** the meeting?
talk about	● Julie often **talks about** her children.
think about	● "What do you **think about** Pam?" "She's very sweet."
worry about	● Don't **worry about** the interview. You'll do great.

at

look at	● **Look at** that baby. He's so cute.
shout at	● Ben **shouted at** us from across the street.
work at	● "How long have you **worked at** this company?" "For three years."

for

apply for	● I **applied for** a new job. Wish me luck!
ask for	● "I'm hungry." "I just **asked for** the menu."
look for	● "What are you **looking for**?" "My scarf. Have you seen it?"
search for	● The police are **searching for** the lost boy.
wait for	● "Who are you **waiting for**?" "Mr. Myers."

on

depend on	● Ian is my best friend. I always **depend on** him.
spend . . . on	● Don't **spend** too much money **on** clothes.

to

belong to	● "Is this your jacket?" "No. It **belongs to** Jerry."
happen to	● "What **happened to** Sam?" "I don't know."
listen to	● I often **listen to** the radio while I drive.
talk to	● Can I **talk to** you for a few minutes? It won't take long.
write to	● "Who are you **writing to**?" "My parents."

More about verb + preposition: Appendix 8, p.258

(2) We do not usually use *prepositions* after the following *verbs*:

answer	● Kathy didn't **answer** my question. (*NOT* answer to my question)
call	● Will you **call** me when you get home? (*NOT* call to me)
discuss	● We'll **discuss** the schedule tomorrow.
reach	● You can **reach** the airport easily from the train station.

PRACTICE

A. Look at the pictures and complete the sentences with the verbs in the box and the appropriate prepositions. Use the *present progressive*.

ask	look	~~talk~~	write

1. He _'s talking to OR is talking to_ a police officer.
2. They _____ the stars.
3. She _____ a salad.
4. She _____ a friend.

B. Complete the sentences with the verbs in *italics*. Add the appropriate prepositions if necessary.

1. *(shout)* You don't have to _shout at_ me. I can hear you.
2. *(apply)* "Did you _____ the job?" "Yes. They're going to call back next week."
3. *(answer)* "I called Betty, but she didn't _____ the phone." "Maybe she's busy."
4. *(depend)* "Will you be home before dinner time?" "Well, it _____ my work schedule."
5. *(belong)* Peter _____ a book club. The members meet once a month.
6. *(reach)* "Can you help me? I can't _____ the top shelf." "Sure."
7. *(worry)* "You look sad. What's wrong?" "I'm OK. Don't _____ me."
8. *(discuss)* Today, we're going to _____ the history of America.

C. Find and change any mistakes in each sentence. Put ✓ if the sentence is correct.

1. Students must listen the teacher carefully during class.   _listen → listen to_
2. We spent enough time on this matter. What should we discuss next? _____
3. Mr. Pond called to you while you were on vacation. _____
4. "What are you doing here?" "I'm waiting Sue." _____
5. What happened to you? You look terrible. _____
6. We reached to the top of the mountain by sunset. _____

D. Complete the conversation with the verbs in *italics* and the appropriate prepositions. Change the verb forms if necessary.

PAUL

CHRIS

PAUL: [1.] I'm _searching for_ a part-time job this summer. *(search)*
CHRIS: [2.] You should _____ a job at Tino's Restaurant. *(apply)*
     [3.] They are _____ a waiter. *(look)*
PAUL: Really? [4.] Who should I _____? *(talk)*
CHRIS: Mr. Tino is the owner. You can call the restaurant.
PAUL: How much is the pay?
CHRIS: I'm not sure. [5.] It _____ your working hours. *(depend)*

ANSWERS p.284, REVIEW TEST 12 p.236

She is **trying on** a hat. *Phrasal verbs*

🎧 086.mp3

①

She is **trying on** a hat.

"try on" is a *phrasal verb*.

---

② *Phrasal verbs* are *verb + preposition/adverb. Phrasal verbs* usually have different meanings from the original *verbs*.

on

get on (= "board")	
hold on (= "wait")	
try on (= "wear or use as a test")	
turn on (= "activate")	

- Passengers should **get on** the plane now.
- "We need to leave now." "**Hold on**. I'm almost ready."
- "Can I **try on** this jacket?" "Of course. Go ahead."
- Can you **turn on** the lights? It's getting dark.

out

eat out (= "dine at a restaurant")	
get out of (= "stop being in")	
go out (= "meet outside")	
hand out (= "give")	
take out (= "bring")	

- I don't want to cook dinner tonight. Can we **eat out**?
- I'll stop here, and you can **get out of** the car.
- "Let's **go out** tomorrow evening." "I can't. I have to work late."
- The teacher will **hand out** schedules before the class.
- Can you **take out** the dishes from the cupboard?

up

clean up (= "make neat or clean")	
get up (= "stop sleeping")	
wake up (= "stop sleeping")	
pick up (= "answer the phone")	
(= "get from somewhere")	

- Billy, please **clean up** your room.
- "What time do you usually **get up**?" "At 6:30."
- **Wake up**, Hector! It's time for school.
- "Did you call Esther?"
  "Well, someone **picked up** the phone, but they didn't say anything."

More about verb + preposition/adverb: Appendix 8, p.258

---

③ We can use an *object* before or after the *preposition/adverb*.

	object	
Cathy **put**	her socks	on.
Please **turn**	your phone	off.
Can you **slow**	the car	down?

OR

	object
Cathy **put on**	her socks.
Please **turn off**	your phone.
Can you **slow down**	the car?

But we do not use **it/them**/etc. *(pronouns)* after the *preposition/adverb*.

- "It's so hot." "Why are you wearing a sweater? **Take it off**." *(NOT Take off it)*
- The office desks are dirty. We need to **clean them up**. *(NOT clean up them)*

PRACTICE

A. Complete the sentences with the phrasal verbs in the box.

get up	go out	~~grow up~~	hold on	slow down	work on

1. "Where did you _grow up_?" "I was raised in Florida."
2. Erica can't come today. She has to _____ her essay.
3. "What are you going to do on weekends?" "I might _____ with Amanda on Sunday."
4. Can you _____? You're driving too fast.
5. I should go to bed now. I need to _____ early in the morning.
6. Can you _____ for a moment? I can't find my credit card.

come back	eat out	get on	get out of	hand out	take off

7. My parents are traveling in Europe now. They'll _____ home next Saturday.
8. I couldn't _____ the bus because it was full. I have to catch the next one.
9. "Do you _____ for lunch often?" "No. I always bring my lunch to work."
10. You have to pay before you _____ a taxi.
11. Could you _____ these menus to the customers, please?
12. Please _____ your shoes before coming inside the house.

B. Put the words in *italics* in the correct order.

1. *(wake / up / me)* "Can you _wake me up_ at 6 o'clock?" "OK."
2. *(this report / in / hand)* "When should I _____?" "By Friday."
3. *(away / take / them)* I've finished reading these magazines. You can _____.
4. *(up / it / clean)* The house is a mess! We need to _____ now.
5. *(turn / the oven / on)* Oh, no! I forgot to _____!
6. *(down / write / it)* Here's my address. You should _____ before you forget.
7. *(out / took / our trash)* My brother _____ this morning.
8. *(the light / on / switch)* It's dark inside. Can you please _____?
9. *(her / call / back)* Emma called and left a message. Are you going to _____?
10. *(the volume / up / turned)* I couldn't hear the radio, so I _____.

C. Put the words in *italics* in the correct order. Change the verb forms if necessary.

LINDA:

LINDA: [1.] James, I need to _pick up a hat_ OR _pick a hat up_.
(a hat / up / pick)
[2.] Can you _____ at the mall? *(off / me / drop)*
JAMES: Why are you buying the hat? You already have so many.
LINDA: [3.] Well, I _____ yesterday, and it was really nice. *(try / on / it)*
JAMES: But my favorite show is on TV now.
LINDA: Come on, James. [4.] _____, and let's go. *(the TV / turn / off)*

JAMES

ANSWERS p.284, REVIEW TEST 12 p.236

UNIT
086

Grammar Gateway Basic

🎧 087.mp3

The door opened.   He came in.

The door opened, **and** he came in.

② We use **and**, **but**, or **or** to connect two sentences.

We use **and** for two similar ideas.

- ⊙ I met Tony, **and** we had dinner.
- ⊙ Ms. Morris is a teacher, **and** her two sons are also teachers.

We use **but** for two contrasting ideas.

- ⊙ It was cloudy this morning, **but** the sky is clear now.
- ⊙ Michael can speak Spanish well, **but** he can't speak French.

We use **or** for two possibilities or choices.

- ⊙ Are you using this chair, **or** can I use it?
- ⊙ Have you been to Denmark before, **or** is it your first time?

  We can leave out repeated words after **and**, **but**, or **or**. In this case, we do not use a comma (,).

  - ⊙ I start work at 9 **and** finish at 6. (= , and I finish work at 6.)
  - ⊙ We can watch a comedy **or** an action movie. (= , or we can watch an action movie.)

③ We use **because** or **so** to connect a reason to a result.

We use **because** before reasons.	We use **so** before results.
⊙ Adam doesn't talk much **because** he is shy.	⊙ Adam is shy, **so** he doesn't talk much.
⊙ I tell my secrets to my sister **because** I trust her.	⊙ I forgot my wallet, **so** I went back home.

We can use **because** at the beginning of a sentence. In this case, we add a comma (,). Note that we do not use **so** at the beginning of a sentence.

- ⊙ **Because** we woke up late, we missed the train.
- ⊙ The opera was boring, **so** we didn't enjoy it. (*NOT* So we didn't enjoy the opera, it was boring.)

We can also use **because of** before reasons. We use **because** to connect sentences, but we use **because of** with *nouns*.

- ⊙ The flight was canceled **because there was a storm**. (*NOT* because of there was a storm)
  The flight was canceled **because of the storm**. (*NOT* because the storm)

PRACTICE

A. Complete the sentences with **and/but/or** and the words in the box.

do you need more time	do you want to drive yours	he couldn't attend
it hurt a lot	it tasted terrible	~~they won the game~~

1. The soccer team played well, _and they won the game_ .
2. Are you ready to order, _____ ?
3. I cut my finger, _____ .
4. Wendy invited John to the wedding, _____ .
5. The soup smelled delicious, _____ .
6. Should we take my car, _____ ?

B. Look at the pictures and complete the sentences with **so** and the words in the box. Then rewrite the sentences with **because**.

he was very tired	she bought a new one	she took some medicine	~~she washed it~~

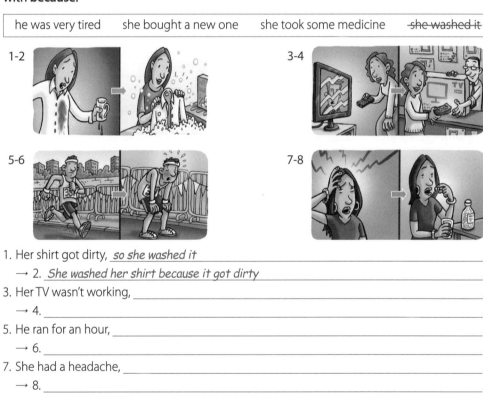

1-2

3-4

5-6

7-8

1. Her shirt got dirty, _so she washed it_ .
   → 2. _She washed her shirt because it got dirty_ .
3. Her TV wasn't working, _____ .
   → 4. _____ .
5. He ran for an hour, _____ .
   → 6. _____ .
7. She had a headache, _____ .
   → 8. _____ .

C. Write **because / because of**.

1. I like swimming _because_ it's fun and good for my health.
2. Leo is not going to come tonight _____ his another appointment.
3. Ben couldn't go to school _____ he was sick.
4. I need to leave now _____ I have a class in 30 minutes.
5. We couldn't sleep yesterday _____ the baby. She cried all night.
6. Megan is moving to China _____ her new job.

ANSWERS p.284, REVIEW TEST 13 p.238

She was watching TV **when** he came in. when and while

🎧 088.mp3

①

She was watching TV **when he came in**.

He fell asleep **while his boss was talking**.

② We use **when** to say that two actions happen or are in progress at the same time.

- My family moved to Arizona **when I was six years old**.
- Could you turn off all the lights **when you leave the house**?
- I was driving to work **when I saw an accident**.
- Emily and I were best friends **when she lived next door to me**.
- I always get nervous **when I have to speak in front of a lot of people**.

③ We can also use **while** to say that two actions happen or are in progress at the same time.

- Carol usually listens to music **while she's exercising**.
- "Did anyone call **while I was in the meeting**?" "Yes. Mr. Owens called."
- My parents met **while they were working at the same company**.
- "Can you mop the floor **while I'm doing the laundry**?" "Of course."
- Jennifer had a lot of visitors **while she was in the hospital**.

④ We can use **when** or **while** at the beginning of a sentence. In this case, we add a comma (,).

- **When I arrived,** nobody was at home.
  (= Nobody was at home when I arrived.)
- **While you're waiting for a table,** would you like to look at the menu first?
  (= Would you like to look at the menu first while you're waiting for a table?)
- **When we were in high school,** we joined the chess club.
- **While I'm away,** Matthew will take care of my dog.

⑤ Note that we use the *present simple* after **when** or **while** to talk about future events. We do not use **will**.

- What do you want to be **when** you **grow up**? (*NOT* when you'll grow up)
- It'll be warm and sunny **while** we **are** on vacation. (*NOT* while we'll be)
- I'll call you **when** I **have** time.
- Thomas will read the book **while** he**'s** on the train.

PRACTICE

A. Look at the pictures and complete the sentences with **when** and the words in the box.

he sat on the chair	~~he saw Daniel and Kelly~~	he woke up
it started to rain	they arrived at the theater	

1. _When he saw Daniel and Kelly_____, they were going to play tennis.
2. _____, it broke.
3. The movie was already playing _____.
4. Patty was running in the park _____.
5. It was 2 o'clock in the afternoon _____.

UNIT

088

Grammar Gateway Basic

B. Connect the two parts and rewrite them as one sentence.

1. While I was listening to the radio	he got injured
2. Do not use your cell phone	while you find a parking space
3. Can you set the table	while I make dinner
4. While I was taking a shower	I fell asleep
5. I'll get a shopping cart	Tom called me
6. While Matt was playing soccer	while you're driving

1. _While I was listening to the radio, I fell asleep_____.
2. _____.
3. _____?
4. _____.
5. _____.
6. _____.

C. Complete the sentences with the verbs in *italics*. Use the *present simple* or add **will**.

1. *(have)* I'm going to take a dance class when I _have_____ some free time.
2. *(meet)* We _____ Jane while we visit Seattle next week.
3. *(go)* When I _____ to the post office, I'll get you some stamps.
4. *(wait)* While you buy some groceries, I _____ in the car.
5. *(cook)* While Kevin _____ the steak, Laura will make the salad.
6. *(come)* Can you call me when you _____ home?
7. *(see)* Have a safe flight. I _____ you when you're back.
8. *(save)* When Molly _____ enough money, she'll travel to Greece.

ANSWERS p.284, REVIEW TEST 13 p.238

187

| The store closed **before** they arrived. before and after

🎧 089.mp3

(1)

The store closed **before they arrived**.

They arrived **after the store closed**.

---

(2) We use **before** to say that an action happens earlier than another action.
- Please come to my office **before you leave**.
- "What did you do **before you became a writer**?" "I was a teacher."
- Jess! You need to wake up **before it's too late**.
- That restaurant is very popular. We should make a reservation **before we go there**.
- "Should we get some drinks **before the concert starts**?" "Sure."

---

(3) We use **after** to say that an action happens later than another action.
- Let's go out to eat **after we do the cleaning**.
- We took a picture **after we reached the top of the mountain**.
- I'll finish the report **after I come back from lunch**.
- My sister moved to another city **after she got married**.
- "Turn off the TV **after you watch the movie**." "Don't worry. I will."

---

(4) We can use **before** or **after** at the beginning of a sentence. In this case, we add a comma (,).
- **Before David does something,** he always makes a plan first.
  (= David always makes a plan first before he does something.)
- **After I graduate from high school,** I'm going to get a job.
  (= I'm going to get a job after I graduate from high school.)
- **"Before you joined the team,** who was the leader?" "It was Tony."
- **After we finish this,** we should take a break.

---

(5) We can also use *nouns* or *-ing* after **before** or **after**.
- You should be home **before midnight**.
- Everyone was excited **after hearing** about the prize.
- Read the document very carefully **before signing** it.
- "How about taking a walk **after dinner**?" "That sounds like a good idea."

PRACTICE

A. Read the sentences and complete the new ones with **before/after**.

1. Andy goes to school. Then he goes to the library.
   → _Before Andy goes to the library_____, he goes to school.

2. I took a shower. Then I put on my clothes.
   → I put on my clothes _____.

3. I had to wait in line. Then I ordered a cup of coffee.
   → I had to wait in line _____.

4. I locked the door. Then I left home.
   → _____, I locked the door.

5. Diane entered the room. Then she turned on the light.
   → _____, she turned on the light.

6. The thieves ran away. Then the police arrived.
   → The thieves ran away _____.

7. My brother eats breakfast in the morning. Then he goes to the gym.
   → My brother goes to the gym _____.

8. The visitors checked out of the hotel. Then they went to the art museum.
   → _____, they went to the art museum.

B. Complete the sentences with **before/after** and the words in the box.

| drive | ~~go~~ | our wedding | read | the exam | the show |

1. Brush your teeth _before going_____ to bed.
2. I cried _____ the book. The ending was so sad.
3. I studied a lot _____, so I was prepared for it.
4. People should not drink alcohol _____ a car.
5. Dave is watching TV right now. He'll help me with my homework _____.
6. We're going to Hawaii _____. It will be a fun honeymoon.

C. The following is a recipe for Bella's Chocolate Chip Muffins. Complete the sentences with **before/after** and the words in *italics*.

> ### Bella's Chocolate Chip Muffins
> You'll need: Bella's Muffin Mix, 1 cup of water, 2 eggs, chocolate chips
>
> 1. Bella's muffins are the perfect dessert _after a meal_____. *(a meal)*
> 2. _____, heat the oven to 190 °C. *(baking the muffins)*
> 3. _____ into a bowl, add two eggs and a cup of water to the mix in the bowl. *(pouring the muffin mix)*
> 4. Finally, add chocolate chips _____ into the oven. *(putting the mixture)*
> 5. Your delicious muffins will be ready _____! *(25 minutes)*

ANSWERS p.284, REVIEW TEST 13 p.238

🎧 090.mp3

①

Past　　　Now

The city has changed **since she arrived**.

We use **since** to say that an action started at a certain point in time and continues until now.

- I've played cello **since I was 12 years old**.
- Many people have visited the zoo **since it opened**.
- Martin has been very busy **since he started his new job**.
- "How long has it been **since you quit smoking**?" "Three years."

We usually use the *present perfect* before **since**. In this case, we use the *past simple* after **since**.

- How have you been? It**'s been** a while **since** we **saw** each other.
- "Do you know Alice?" "Yes. I**'ve known** her **since** she **was** young."

②

We were waiting for you.

They didn't eat dinner **until he arrived**.

We use **until** to say that an action continues to a certain point in time.

- We won't start the class **until everyone gets here**.
- Mr. Simpson worked for our company **until he retired**.
- We stayed at the beach **until it started raining**.
- "Where is the library?" "Go straight **until you see the hospital**. Then turn left."

Note that we use the *present simple* after **until** to talk about future events. We do not use **will**.

- "When should I put the eggs in the water?" "Wait **until** it **boils**." (*NOT* until it'll boil)
- Please do not leave your seat **until** the bus **stops**. (*NOT* until the bus will stop)

③ We can also use *nouns* after **since** or **until**.

- I haven't seen Connor and Julie **since their wedding**.
- Mr. Brooks is on vacation now. He won't be back **until next Thursday**.

PRACTICE

A. Write **since/until**.

1. Please turn off your cell phones _until_ the test is over.
2. You have learned a lot _____ you joined Spanish class.
3. Can you wait for me here _____ I finish my meeting?
4. "Did you arrive late?" "No. I've been here _____ 8 o'clock."
5. I've been happier _____ I moved to my new apartment.
6. Ruth is going to stay with us _____ Sunday. She's leaving next Monday.

B. Complete the sentences with the words in *italics*. Use the *present perfect* or *past simple*.

1. *(meet at work)* Jerry and Karen have been good friends since they _met at work_.
2. *(not call me)* "Did you hear anything from Dad?" "No. He _____ since he left home."
3. *(open last month)* This restaurant has become popular since it _____.
4. *(break my leg)* I haven't gone to the gym since I _____.
5. *(not travel anywhere)* Since our son was born, we _____.
6. *(lose 10 pounds)* I _____ since I started exercising in June.

C. Complete the sentences with **until** and the words in the box.

she returned from vacation	it turns brown	she showed them the proof
the paint dries	~~the rain stops~~	we arrived at the theater

1. Don't play outside _until the rain stops_. You'll get wet.
2. Luckily, the movie didn't start _____.
3. The police didn't believe Ms. Wade _____.
4. You should leave the bread in the oven _____.
5. Matt had to do Sarah's job _____.
6. We've just painted the wall. Please do not touch it _____.

D. Look at the graphs and complete the sentences with **since/until**.

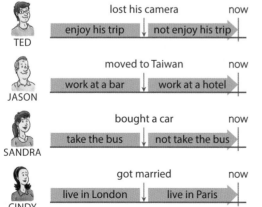

1. Ted enjoyed his trip _until he lost his camera_.
2. Ted hasn't enjoyed his trip _____.

3. Jason worked at a bar _____.
4. Jason has worked at a hotel _____.

5. Sandra took the bus _____.
6. Sandra hasn't taken the bus _____.

7. Cindy lived in London _____.
8. Cindy has lived in Paris _____.

ANSWERS p.285, REVIEW TEST 13 p.238

If it **rains**, she'll stay at home. *if (1)* **if** + *present simple*

🎧 091.mp3

(1)

If it rains, she'll stay at home.

If it doesn't rain, she'll go hiking.

If it rains, I'll stay at home.   If it doesn't rain, I'll go hiking.

---

(2) We use **if** + *present simple* to talk about things that are possible in the future. In this case, we use the following structure:

If . . . + *present simple*,	**. . . will/can/etc. +** base form

- **If you ask** the teacher, **he will answer** your question.
- **If you don't like** seafood, **we can eat** something else.
- **If Mr. Lewis calls, can you take** a message for me?
- **If I order** the clothes now, **the delivery will come** on Tuesday.
- **If Ms. Roy and Mr. Lee agree, I will cancel** today's meeting.

We can use **if** in the middle of a sentence. In this case, we do not use a comma (,).

- You can come to my house **if you get bored**. I'll be home all day.
- Sharon will miss the flight **if she doesn't leave** soon.
- You'll get your driver's license **if you pass** this test.
- We can go to the movies **if we're not busy** on Sunday.
- Should I take a taxi **if I want** to get there quickly?

---

(3) Note that we use the *present simple* after **if** to talk about future situations. We do not use **will**.

- Will you wake me up **if** you **get up** early tomorrow? *(NOT if you'll get up)*
- **If** Erin **helps** us, we'll finish the work quickly. *(NOT If Erin will help)*
- I'll let you know **if** I **hear** from Jess.
- **If** you **do** the laundry, I'll do the dishes.

PRACTICE

A. Complete the sentences with **if** and the words in the box.

I get this job	the guests arrive	the supermarket isn't closed
the traffic is bad	we are in the same class	~~we have enough time~~

1. *If we have enough time* _____, we can visit Olympic Park.
2. _____, we're going to be late.
3. _____, can I share your book? I forgot mine today.
4. _____, I'm going to work full-time.
5. _____, can you open the door for them?
6. _____, we should get some milk.

B. Judy is thinking about her future. Complete the sentences about her future. Add **if** if necessary.

JUDY

I'll go to a design school!

1. → study hard   *I'll study hard if I go to a design school* _____.
2. → become a famous designer   _____ if I study hard.
3. → make a lot of money   _____.
4. → help poor children   _____.
5. → feel happy   _____.

C. Complete the sentences with the words in *italics*. Use the *present simple* or add **will**.

1. *(I, take, you, to a game)* If you like football, *I'll take you to a game* _____.
2. *(Holly, forget, our appointment)* I'll be upset if _____ again.
3. *(You, feel, better)* _____ if you take this medicine.
4. *(Brandon, get, it)* If I send this letter today, _____ tomorrow.
5. *(your sister, come, to Toronto)* If _____, she can stay with me.
6. *(you, be, with me)* Everything will be fine if _____.

D. Complete the conversation with the words in *italics*.

KATE

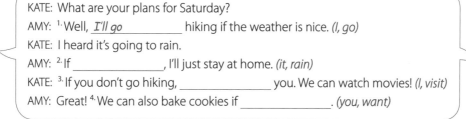

KATE: What are your plans for Saturday?
AMY: 1. Well, *I'll go* _____ hiking if the weather is nice. *(I, go)*
KATE: I heard it's going to rain.
AMY: 2. If _____, I'll just stay at home. *(it, rain)*
KATE: 3. If you don't go hiking, _____ you. We can watch movies! *(I, visit)*
AMY: Great! 4. We can also bake cookies if _____. *(you, want)*

AMY

ANSWERS p.285, REVIEW TEST 13 p.238

If he **had time**, he would eat breakfast. if (2)
if + *past simple*

092.mp3

①

Sorry, I have no time.

If he had time, **he would eat** breakfast.
(= He doesn't have time, so he's not able to eat breakfast.)

② We use **if** + *past simple* to talk about things that are not real or not possible now. In this case, we use the following structure:

If . . . + *past simple*,	. . . would(= 'd)/could/etc. + base form

- **If I knew** Harry's phone number, **I would call** him.
  (= I don't know Harry's phone number now, so I'm not able to call him.)
- **If we went** to Egypt, **we could see** the pyramids.
  (= We aren't in Egypt now, so we're not able to see the pyramids.)
- **If Donna was** here, **she'd enjoy** this meal.

  Note that we use the *past simple* after **if** to talk about present situations and not past situations.
  - **If you didn't own** a pet, **you could rent** that apartment.
  - **If I had** long hair like you, **I wouldn't cut** it.

We can use **if** in the middle of a sentence. Note that we do not use a comma (,).
- I could drive to work every day **if I had** a car.
- Aria would have more parties **if she didn't have** roommates.
- My life would be different **if I didn't meet** my best friend earlier.
- We could save money **if both of us worked**.

③ We usually use **were** instead of **was** after **if** when the *subject* is **I/he/she/it**.
- **If I were** rich, I'd open my own restaurant.
- **If Jerry were** taller, he could be a basketball player.
- **If Megan were** younger, she would go back to university.

④ We use **If I were/was you, I'd . . .** to give advice about present situations.
- **If I were/was you, I'd talk** to Benny about your problem.
- **If I were/was you, I wouldn't see** that movie. It's boring.
- "I'm going out for coffee." "**If I were/was you, I'd go** later. The café is usually crowded at this time."
- "What do you think about this jacket?" "**If I were/was you, I wouldn't buy** it."

PRACTICE

A. Complete the sentences with **if** and the words in the box.

| I am in Paris | ~~I have enough money~~ | I have more free time | it is sunny |

1. _If I had enough money_, I'd buy a new suit.

2. _____, I'd go to the park.

3. _____, I'd visit the Eiffel Tower.

4. _____, I'd play tennis often.

B. Complete the sentences with the words in *italics*. Add **would** if necessary.

1. *(the seminar, be)* I have meetings on Friday. If _the seminar were_ OR _the seminar was_ on Saturday, I'd go.
2. *(it, not be)* "Are you having fun at camp?" "_____ boring if you were here."
3. *(she, get up)* Ashley is late for class. If _____ earlier, she wouldn't be late.
4. *(Ryan, become)* _____ a lawyer if he weren't a journalist.
5. *(I, win)* I'd get a gold medal if _____ the race.
6. *(we, not wear)* If it wasn't cold, _____ jackets.

C. Complete the conversations with **If I were you, I'd . . .** and the words in the box.

| ~~be excited~~ | not drink it | not drive | say sorry to her |

1. I'm nervous about moving to a new city.
2. The traffic seems very bad today.
3. I had a fight with my girlfriend.
4. I bought this juice three weeks ago.

If I were you, I'd be excited _____.

_____.

_____.

_____.

D. Rewrite the sentences with **if**.

1. My parents don't live near here, so I don't see them on weekends.
   → _If my parents lived near here, I'd see them on weekends_ .
2. Ted works in the afternoons, so he doesn't get up early.
   → _____ .
3. Brenna isn't busy, so she can meet us.
   → _____ .
4. Dan has a knee injury, so he can't play soccer.
   → _____ .

ANSWERS p.285, REVIEW TEST 13 p.238

UNIT
092

Grammar Gateway Basic

if | do vs. **if | did**

if (3) **if** + *present simple* vs. **if** + *past simple*

🎧 093.mp3

①

If she **is** here, he**'ll be** happy.

(It is possible that she is here.)

If she **was** here, he**'d be** happy.

(She is not here.)

② **if I do** and **if I did**

We use **if** + *present simple* to talk about things that are possible in the future.

- **If** the weather **is** warm, I**'ll go** for a walk.
  (It is possible that the weather will be warm.)

- **If** Eric **exercises** every day, he**'ll be** healthier.
  (It is possible that Eric will exercise every day.)

- **If** we **decide** to go to the party, we**'ll let** you know.

- **If** the store **is closed**, we **can park** our car in front of it.

- Jim **will wear** the pants **if** they **aren't** too big.

- We **can walk** to the station together **if** you **take** the subway home.

- **Can** you **bring** the letter to my office **if** it **arrives**?

- You **can ask** me for advice **if** you **have** any problems.

We use **if** + *past simple* to talk about things that are not real or not possible now.

- **If** the weather **was** warm, I**'d go** for a walk.
  (The weather isn't warm now.)

- **If** Eric **exercised** every day, he**'d be** healthier.
  (Eric doesn't exercise every day now.)

- **If** today **were** a holiday, we **could go** on a picnic.

- **If** Anna **studied** harder, she **could get** a good grade on the test.

- I**'d buy** that bag **if** it **weren't** sold out.

- The room **would look** better **if** this wall **was** a different color.

- We **could leave** work early **if** we **didn't have** a meeting today.

- I**'d take** a trip to China alone **if** I **spoke** Chinese well.

PRACTICE

A. Complete the conversations with **if** and the words in the box. Use the *present simple* or *past simple*.

Ashley isn't so tired	I find it	the mall is open	~~we leave now~~

1. A: What time is it?
   B: It's 6:30. *If we leave now*, we'll catch the train.

2. A: _____,
   we could go shopping.
   B: I know! But it closed early today.

3. A: I think I left my ring at your house yesterday.
   B: OK. _____, I'll give it back to you.

4. A: _____ tonight,
   she would go to the movies with us.
   B: That's OK. She can join us next time.

I see him	she doesn't sleep late	the restaurant isn't full	we take 4th Avenue

5. A: _____, we could eat there.
   B: Do you know any other place to have dinner?

6. A: _____,
   we'd come home earlier.
   B: You're right. Let's use that road next time.

7. A: Where's Max? I've waited here for an hour.
   B: _____, I'll tell him you are here.

8. A: I hope Sarah won't be late tomorrow.
   B: _____,
   she will be on time.

B. Complete the sentences with the words in *italics*. Add **will/would** if necessary.

1. *(help you)* If you ask Mike, he *'ll help you* OR *will help you* with your essay.
2. *(be fresh)* Those vegetables look old. I would buy some if they _____.
3. *(attend)* If the wedding wasn't on Friday, I _____. I have an appointment that day.
4. *(pick you up)* If you call me at the airport, I _____.
5. *(have a car)* I wouldn't take the bus if I _____. The bus is always crowded.
6. *(not like coffee)* If Hannah _____, she can have tea.
7. *(be healthier)* I don't go to the gym regularly. If I exercised every day, I _____.
8. *(not take an umbrella)* If you _____ with you, you'll get wet.

C. The following is an e-mail from Amy to Sandra. Choose the correct one.

Subject	Hi, Sandra
To	sandra77@gotmail.com
From	amy318@gotmail.com

Hi, Sandra. How are you doing in Seattle?
I'm going to a music festival today. [1.] If you were here, it (will /(would)) be more fun.
The concert is at the park. I am glad the weather is nice.
[2.] If it (rains / rained) during the concert, the show can be canceled.
Many bands are going to play, but my favorite one is not coming.
[3.] If it (performs / performed), I would be happier.
I heard it might play next year. [4.] If that is true, I (will come / would come) again.

Love, Amy

ANSWERS p.285, REVIEW TEST 13 p.238

🎧 094.mp3

①

*I know the girl **who** won the race.*

He knows **the girl**. <u>She</u> won the race.
subject

He knows **the girl <u>who</u>** won the race.
relative pronoun

---

② We use **who/which/that** *(relative pronouns)* after a *noun* to identify it.

	noun	*who/which/that*	
•	Do you know **the woman**	who	**is standing there?** (**the woman** is standing there.)
•	**The flight**	which	**goes to Boston** was canceled. (**The flight** goes to Boston.)
•	I always eat **chocolate**	that	**is from Italy.**

---

③ We use **who** to talk about people.

	person	*who*	
•	Peter is married to **a woman**	who	**is a lawyer.** (**a woman** is a lawyer.)
•	Do you know **anyone**	who	**can speak German?**

	person	*who*	
•	**My uncle**	who	**lives in Dallas** is coming to visit. (**My uncle** lives in Dallas.)
•	**The man**	who	**is sitting next to Jamie** is my brother.

We use **which** to talk about things.

	thing	*which*	
•	This is **the sweater**	which	**was made by my mother.** (**the sweater** was made by my mother.)
•	Easy Film is **a company**	which	**is famous for its digital cameras.**

	thing	*which*	
•	**The bus**	which	**goes to 10th Avenue** has just left. (**The bus** goes to 10th Avenue.)
•	**The keys**	which	**are on the table** are mine.

We can use **that** to talk about people/things.

	person/thing	*that*	
•	I bought **an apartment**	that	**is close to a park.** (**an apartment** is close to a park.)
•	Do you know **anyone**	that	**knows about computers?**

	person/thing	*that*	
•	**The tour group**	that	**visited the museum** had a great time. (**The tour group** visited the museum.)
•	**The toys**	that	**are on sale** are on this shelf.

PRACTICE

A. Bill has met a lot of people during his trip. Look at the pictures and complete the sentences about them with **who**.

1
(I can speak English.)

2
(I have six children.)

3
(I play the violin.)

4
(We are very famous.)

5
(I fix cars.)

6
(I am 99 years old.)

1. Bill met a man *who can speak English* _____ .
2. He sat next to a woman _____ .
3. He saw a man _____ .

4. He saw two women _____ .
5. He met a man _____ .
6. He visited a woman _____ .

B. Write **who/which**.

1. Do you know the girl _who_____ has red hair over there?
2. The name of the person _____ called yesterday was Samantha Smith.
3. The books _____ were newly published are in the New Arrivals section.
4. Patrick has a friend _____ comes from Spain.
5. I went to a restaurant _____ makes excellent soups.
6. Hanna is a person _____ cares about others.
7. Have you seen my bag _____ has green and blue stripes?
8. The pictures _____ were taken by Eric are hanging on the wall.

C. Rewrite the two sentences as one with **who/which/that**.

1. That building is really tall. It was built recently. → *That building which (OR that) was built recently is really tall* .
2. I bought a new sofa. It was on sale. → _____ .
3. The store sells magazines. It's around the corner. → _____ .
4. The people are very nice. They live downstairs. → _____ .
5. I found a suitcase. It belongs to Mr. Harris. → _____ .
6. Sarah taught the students. They graduated last year.

   → _____ .

7. A man just waved to us. He is standing across the street.

   → _____ .

8. We're excited about the festival. It will begin next week.

   → _____ .

ANSWERS p.285, REVIEW TEST 13 p.238

(1)

We really loved the food, James!

They love **the food**. **He made** <u>it</u>.
object

They love **the food which** he made.
relative pronoun

---

(2) We can use **who/which/that** *(relative pronouns)* as the *object*.

	who/that		
○ Jane is **the girl**	who/that	**Harry likes.**	*(Harry likes **the girl**.)*
○ My father is **the person**	who/that	**I respect the most.**	

	who/that		
○ **The man**	who/that	**you met in the lobby**	is my boss. *(You met **the man** in the lobby.)*
○ **The employees**	who/that	**I worked with**	were helpful.

	which/that		
○ Dave likes **the new phone**	which/that	**Alice bought for him.**	*(Alice bought **the new phone** for him.)*
○ Anna often buys **clothes**	which/that	**she never wears.**	

	which/that		
○ **The earrings**	which/that	**I lost yesterday**	were expensive. *(I lost **the earrings** yesterday.)*
○ **The book**	which/that	**my friend lent me**	was really interesting.

Note that we can also use **who/which/that** as the *subject*.

	who/that		
○ **The lady**	who/that	**lives next door**	is friendly. *(**The lady** lives next door.)*
○ **The student**	who/that	**won the contest**	will receive $100.

	which/that		
○ We visited **an old church**	which/that	**was built** in 1650.	*(**an old church** was built in 1650.)*
○ I bought **a camera**	which/that	**works** under water.	

---

(3) We can leave out **who/which/that** when it is the *object*.

- **Most people** (who/that) **I know** are from Las Vegas.
- Can I use **the scissors** (which/that) **you have**?
- I can't remember **the dream** (which/that) **I had last night**.

But we cannot leave out **who/which/that** when it is the *subject*.

- I have **a friend** who/that **works at the hospital**. *(NOT a friend works at the hospital)*
- **The café** which/that **is on Pine Street** is always crowded. *(NOT The café is on Pine Street)*
- This is **a song** which/that **is very popular these days**.

PRACTICE

A. Complete the sentences with **who/which** and the words from each box.

the book	~~the boy~~	the cake		Brian Smith wrote	~~I met~~	I wore
the dress	the show		+	you're baking		you were watching

1. "Did I tell you about _the boy who I met_____ during the trip?" "No. Tell me about him."
2. _____ to the party was too tight. It wasn't comfortable.
3. I can't wait to taste _____. It smells so good.
4. "_____ is over. Can I change the channel?" "OK."
5. _____ was great. I finished reading it last night.

B. Rewrite the two sentences as one with **that**. Leave out **that** if possible.

1. Jamie gave me some shoes. She didn't want them. → Jamie _gave me some shoes she didn't want_____.
2. I used to have a friend. I trusted him. → I _____.
3. I know a neighbor. He has many pets. → I _____.
4. The girl drove us to school. She isn't my sister. → The girl _____.
5. Paul ate all of the chocolate. He bought it in Belgium.
   → Paul _____.
6. I saw the art exhibit last night. It is open until next week.
   → The art exhibit _____.
7. We went to a restaurant. It's famous for its dessert.
   → We _____.
8. The boss introduced that man to us today. He's going to attend the next meeting.
   → That man _____.

C. Find and change any mistakes in each sentence. Put ✓ if the sentence is correct.

1. I've talked to the man owns that store.   _____ _owns → who (OR that) owns_____
2. The house was sold last week is empty right now. _____
3. We stayed at the hotel many tourists recommended. _____
4. People exercise regularly live longer.   _____
5. Where is the book was on the table?   _____
6. Is that the train that you're waiting for?   _____

D. Complete the conversation with **who/which** and the words in *italics*. Leave out **who/which** if possible.

Neighbor: ¹·We loved the food _you made_____, James. *(you, made)*
JAMES: Thanks! ²·Next time, let's go to a restaurant _____
        recently. *(open)*
        ³·My friend _____ cooking in Italy owns it. *(studied)*
Neighbor: ⁴·Is that the restaurant _____ last week? *(you, visited)*
JAMES: Yes. I had pasta there and it was very good.

Neighbor

JAMES

ANSWERS p.286, REVIEW TEST 13 p.238

UNIT
095

Grammar Gateway Basic

🎧 096.mp3

(1)

There is a boat in the ocean.

There are a lot of people on the beach.

---

(2) We can use **there is/are** to say that someone or something exists.

there	is / are	(not)		Is / Are	there ...?

- **There is** a new shopping mall in town.
- I can't make a cake. **There aren't** any eggs.
- "**Are there** any shirts you want to buy?" "That green one."

---

(3) **there is** + *singular/uncountable noun*

- **There is a package** for you at the front desk.
- We can't buy that sofa because **there isn't enough space** in our apartment.

there are + *plural noun*

- **There are lots of parties** during the holidays.
- "**Are there any direct flights** from Seoul to Madrid?" "Let me check."

---

(4) We use **there was/were** to talk about the past in the following ways:

there	was / were	(not)		Was / Were	there ...?

- **There was** a bookstore here, but it moved to Main Street.
- The class finished early because **there weren't** any questions.

---

(5) We use **there have/has been** (*present perfect*) in the following ways:

there	have / has	(not)	been		Have / Has	there	been ...?

- "**Have there been** any calls for me?" "Yes. The manager called."
- "Where is the train?" "**There has been** a delay. It'll be here soon."

PRACTICE

A. Look at the pictures and complete the sentences with **there is/are** and the words in the box.

a lake	a̶ ̶m̶a̶n̶	some fish	some people

 1    2    3    4

1. _There is a man_ _____ at the door.
2. _____ on the bridge.
3. _____ in the water.
4. _____ in the park.

B. Complete the sentences with **there is/are** or **there was/were**. Write negative sentences if necessary.

1. " _Is there_ _____ anybody at home?" "Rick might be back from work."
2. _____ an empty seat near the door, so I sat there.
3. I want to check my e-mail, but _____ any computers in this hotel.
4. _____ any bread to make sandwiches, so I had to go to the store.
5. Can you help me? _____ some problems with my new cell phone.
6. I want to see a movie tonight, but _____ anything to watch.
7. _____ any questions before we start today?

C. Complete the sentences with **there have/has been** and the words in *italics*.

1. *(two storms)* _There have been two storms_ _____ since Monday.
2. *(any visitors)* "_____ here recently?" "Yes, but not many."
3. *(a lot of accidents)* _____ on the road these days. Drive slowly.
4. *(a change)* "_____ to my schedule?" "No. It's still the same."
5. *(not, many tourists)* _____ in the city this year.
6. *(not, any rain)* _____ this month. The weather is very dry.

D. Complete the conversation with **there is/are** or **there was/were** and the words in *italics*.

PAUL

PAUL: 1. _There are a lot of people_ _____ on the beach today. *(a lot of people)*
CHRIS: I know. 2. _____ here yesterday. *(not many people)*
PAUL: Well, the weather is very nice today.
     3. _____ in the sky. *(not a cloud)*
CHRIS: Look! There is a boat there. It's a perfect day for a boat ride.
     4. _____ around here? *(a rental shop)*
PAUL: 5. _____ before, but I'm not sure if it's still here. *(one)*
CHRIS: OK. Let's check.

CHRIS

ANSWERS p.286, REVIEW TEST 14 p.240

①

Happy birthday!

He gave **his wife a ring**.
　　　　person　　*thing*

OR He gave **a ring** to **his wife**.
　　　　　thing　　　　*person*

---

② We use *person + thing* after the following *verbs*:

give	make	send	show	buy	teach

- I **gave Kathy my phone number**. We'll talk about the project over the phone.
- Josh **made me an omelet** this morning. It was very good.
- Richard **sent us a wedding invitation**. He's getting married next month.
- "Can you **show me your ticket**, please?" "Sure. Here you go."
- Fiona **will buy her boyfriend a box of chocolates** on Valentine's Day.
- My father **taught me French** when I was young. He's from France.

---

③ We can use **to** or **for** to talk about a thing first.

give/send/show/teach + *thing* + **to** + *person*

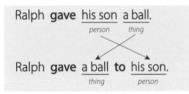

Ralph **gave** his son a ball.
　　　　　person　*thing*

Ralph **gave** a ball **to** his son.
　　　　　thing　　　*person*

- I **sent** my friends gifts. → I **sent** gifts to my friends.
- Could you **show** me the city map? → Could you **show** the city map to me?
- Ms. Brown **teaches** us science. → Ms. Brown **teaches** science to us.

make/buy + *thing* + **for** + *person*

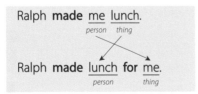

Ralph **made** me lunch.
　　　　　person *thing*

Ralph **made** lunch **for** me.
　　　　　person　　　*thing*

- Will you **buy** me a cup of coffee? → Will you **buy** a cup of coffee **for** me?
- Joan **will make** Rick a sandwich. → Joan **will make** a sandwich **for** Rick.
- We **bought** Mr. Lee some fruit. → We **bought** some fruit **for** Mr. Lee.

PRACTICE

A. Look at the pictures and complete the sentences with the given words. Use the *past simple*.

a doll	his room	~~some flowers~~	some coffee

1 These are for you.

2 JEN Thank you, mom!

3 KIM This is my room.

4 JAKE Here you are.

1. *(give)* He _gave Lucy some flowers_ .
2. *(buy)* She _____ .

3. *(show)* He _____ .
4. *(make)* He _____ .

B. Complete the sentences with **to/for** and the given words.

buy an apartment	~~give her address~~	make breakfast
send Christmas cards	show my new car	teach music

1. *(me)* Victoria _gave her address to me_ . You don't have to ask her again.
2. *(him)* "Does your son still live with you?" "No. We _____."
3. *(students)* Mr. Franks had another job before he was a banker. He _____ .
4. *(you)* "Did I _____?" "No. Is it the one in front of the house?"
5. *(me)* My husband _____ last weekend. It was good.
6. *(his friends)* "Does Paul _____ every year?" "Yes. He makes them himself."

C. Rewrite the sentences. Add or leave out **to/for**.

1. The doctor gave Ryan some medicine.   _The doctor gave some medicine to Ryan_ .
2. Did Tim send those gifts to you?   _____ ?
3. Money can't buy happiness for us.   _____ .
4. Laura teaches students yoga.   _____ .
5. Can you show me your passport?   _____ ?
6. My mother made me a sweater.   _____ ?

D. Put the words in *italics* in the correct order.

AMY

AMY: Mom, did Dad do anything special for your birthday?
LINDA: Yes! 1. He _bought me dinner_ at a nice hotel. *(dinner / me / bought)*
　　　　2. And he _____ . *(me / a ring / to / gave)*
AMY: A ring? Wow!
LINDA: Well, it's also for our 30th wedding anniversary.
AMY: I forgot about that! We should have a party.
　　　　3. I'll _____ . *(send / invitations / your friends)*
　　　　4. I can _____ too! *(you / a cake / make / for)*

LINDA

ANSWERS p.286, REVIEW TEST 14 p.240

Come here. Orders, suggestions, etc.

(1) We use **come/be**/etc. at the beginning of a sentence to give orders.

- **Come** here.
- The knife is really sharp. **Be** careful.
- "Where is the bank?"
  "**Go** straight and **turn** right at the next corner."
- **Hurry** up! We'll be late for class!

Come here!

Don't + touch/leave/etc. *(negative)*

- The wall was just painted. **Don't touch** it.
- **Don't leave** your bag there. Someone might take it.
- It's warm enough in here. **Don't turn** on the heater.
- **Don't forget**. It's Mom's birthday tomorrow.

(2) We use **Let's** + **go/take**/etc. to suggest doing something together.

- **Let's go** inside.
- **Let's take** a break for a few minutes.
- "I'm really hungry. **Let's order** something."
  "OK. How about Thai food?"
- "Where is Brian right now? Is he coming soon?"
  "I don't know. **Let's call** him."

Let's go inside!

Let's not + **waste/wash**/etc. *(negative)*

- We have a lot to do. **Let's not waste** time.
- It's going to rain this afternoon. **Let's not wash** the car today.
- **Let's not discuss** this now. We can do it later.
- I'm tired. **Let's not stay** too long at the party.

(3) We use **How** + **wonderful/kind**/etc. *(adjectives)* to express strong emotions.

- Look at the view. **How wonderful!**
- "Dad, I made this card for you. Happy Father's Day!"
  "**How kind!**"
- "Emily lost her grandmother last Saturday."
  "**How sad!** Is she OK?"
- This soup is great. **How delicious!**

How wonderful!

We can also use **What (+ a/an)** + *adjective* + *noun* to express strong emotions.

- I have four meetings today. **What a busy day!**
- "I got a promotion yesterday!" "**What great news!**"
- "Have you heard? Jim won the lottery." "Really? **What a lucky guy!**"
- **What an interesting painting!** Who is the artist?

PRACTICE

A. Complete the sentences with the appropriate verb for each situation.

be	~~close~~	do	slow	wake

1. The window is open. You feel cold.
2. Your friend is driving too fast.
3. It's already noon, but your brother is still in bed.
4. Your sister wants to play games, but she has homework.
5. Your friends are talking loudly in the library.

> _Close_ _____ the window.
> _____ down.
> _____ up.
> _____ your homework.
> _____ quiet.

B. Look at the pictures and complete the sentences with **don't** and the verbs in the box.

~~sit~~	smoke	swim	take

1. _Don't sit_ _____ on the bench!
2. _____ pictures here.
3. _____ in the river.
4. Please _____ _____ here.

C. Complete the conversations with **Let's / Let's not** and the verbs in the box.

ask	~~buy~~	go	listen	start	watch

1. A: This lamp doesn't work.
   B: It's old. _Let's buy_ _____ a new one.

2. A: _____ to some music.
   B: Good idea. I'll turn on the radio.

3. A: This movie doesn't look interesting.
   B: _____ it then.

4. A: When are we having the meeting?
   B: _____ at 3:30.

5. A: _____ jogging today. I'm tired.
   B: OK. Let's relax at home.

6. A: Do you know the answer to this question?
   B: No. _____ Philip. He might know.

D. Write expressions with **How** for 1-3 and **What** for 4-6 for each situation.

1. Your friend told you a funny joke.
2. You saw a very expensive bag.
3. You watched an exciting baseball game on TV.
4. Your friend has a nice car.
5. You just received lovely flowers from someone.
6. You're in a hotel room, and it has a great view.

> _How funny_ _____ !
> _____ !
> _____ !
> _____ !
> _____ !
> _____ !

ANSWERS p.286, REVIEW TEST 14 p.240

①

He said that I could use his car.

"**You can** use my car."

He **said that I could** use his car.

"**said that**" is used to report what James said.

---

② We use **said that** to report what someone said. We change the *subject* and use the *past simple*.

	Yesterday			*Today*		
●	Katie:	"I am	so excited."	→	Katie **said that**	she was	so excited.
●	John:	"I want	to play outside."	→	John **said that**	he wanted	to play outside.
●	Chris:	"I will	lend you my camera."	→	Chris **said that**	he would	lend me his camera.
●	Mom:	"You have to	be home by 11."	→	Mom **said that**	I had to	be home by 11.
●	The boss:	"You can	leave early."	→	The boss **said that**	we could	leave early.

We can leave out **that**.

- ● Gino just called. He **said** his flight was delayed. (= He said that his flight was . . .)
- ● The news **said** it snowed heavily in Seattle today. (= The news said that it snowed . . .)

---

③ We can also use **told** to report what someone said. We use *person + that* after **told**.

		person + that	
●	I **told**	Dad that	I was ready for school.
●	Matt **told**	me that	he made some pasta for me.
●	Tom **told**	us that	he didn't need our help.
●	"You **told**	me that	you wouldn't be late again." "I'm sorry."
●	Ella and Dan **told**	you that	it was their wedding anniversary yesterday, didn't they?

We can also leave out **that**.

- ● The doctor **told me** I should exercise twice a week. (= The doctor told me that I should . . .)
- ● Wendy **told her friends** she was going to leave. (= Wendy told her friends that she was . . .)

---

④ We always use a *person* after **told**. But we do not use a *person* after **said**.

- ● Lisa **told me** she couldn't come to work this morning. (*NOT* Lisa told she couldn't . . .)
  Lisa **said** she couldn't come to work this morning. (*NOT* Lisa said me she couldn't . . .)
- ● You **told me** everything would be fine.
  You **said** everything would be fine.

PRACTICE

A. Look at the pictures and report what each person says with **said**.

1  I have a headache.

2  We're getting married.

3  I am on vacation.

4  We're going out.

5  BETTY — I'll call later.

6  I can't find my dog. MARK

1. *He said (that) he had a headache* .
2. _____ .
3. _____ .
4. _____ .
5. _____ .
6. _____ .

B. Rewrite the sentences above with **told**. Use **me** for 1-4.

1. *He told me (that) he had a headache* .
2. _____ .
3. _____ .
4. _____ .
5. _____ .
6. _____ .

C. Write **said/told**.

1. Nicole _said_ she didn't know Kim's phone number.
2. "Kevin _____ me that he could spend Christmas with us." "Really? That's great!"
3. Ms. Hill _____ that she worked at a museum.
4. "How are you getting to the airport?" "Todd _____ he would take me."
5. "I liked the book that you gave me." "I _____ you it was good."
6. Larry _____ me he could take care of our children this weekend.
7. Kelly _____ she was busy. Let's just go to the bar without her.
8. "How long do we have to wait?" "The waiter _____ me 10 minutes would be enough."

ANSWERS p.287, REVIEW TEST 14 p.240

| I like it **too**. I don't like them **either**. too and either, so and neither

🎧 100.mp3

①

I like pizza. | I like it **too**.

I like it too.

I don't like onions. | I **don't** like them **either**.

I don't like them either.

---

② We use **too** to mean "also" in positive sentences.

- Kenneth is from Canada. His wife **is too**.
  (= His wife is also from Canada.)
- "I want to go to Europe this summer."
  "**I do too.**" (= I also want to go to Europe.)
- "I'm going to have coffee. What about you?"
  "**I'll** have coffee **too**."
- "I've met Stacy."
  "**I have too**. She's very nice."

We use **either** to mean "also" in negative sentences.

- "John and Jane weren't at the party."
  "Bob **wasn't either**." (= Bob also wasn't at the party.)
- We didn't have any wine, and we **didn't** have any beer **either**. (= we also didn't have any beer)
- "I shouldn't spend too much money today."
  "**I shouldn't either**."
- "I've never run in a marathon before."
  "**I haven't either**. This is my first time."

---

③ We can use **so** to mean "also."

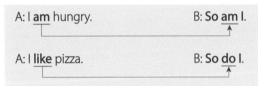

A: I **am** hungry.   B: **So am I.**

A: I **like** pizza.   B: **So do I.**

- "I **was** angry with Nate yesterday."
  "**So was I.**" (= I was also angry with Nate.)
- "We **watched** the Olympics this year."
  "**So did we.**" (= We also watched the Olympics.)
- "Bill **can** speak Japanese."
  "**So can his brother**. They lived in Japan."

Note that **So I am, Neither I do,** etc. are incorrect.

- "I'm 21 years old." "**So am I.**" (*NOT* So I am)
- "I don't like vegetables." "**Neither do I.**" (*NOT* Neither I do)

We can use **neither** to mean "also not."

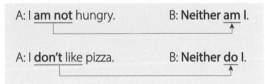

A: I **am not** hungry.   B: **Neither am I.**

A: I **don't** like pizza.   B: **Neither do I.**

- "I **don't** exercise often."
  "**Neither do I.**" (= I also don't exercise.)
- "Grace **won't** be ready until 7 o'clock."
  "**Neither will Leo.**" (= Leo also won't be ready.)
- "I **haven't** seen Ross for a long time."
  "**Neither have I**. He has been very busy."

PRACTICE

A. Write **too/either**.

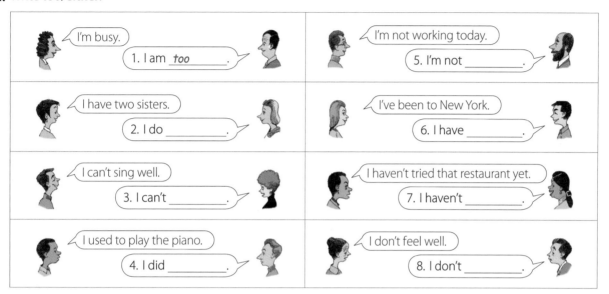

I'm busy.
1. I am *too* _____.

I have two sisters.
2. I do _____.

I can't sing well.
3. I can't _____.

I used to play the piano.
4. I did _____.

I'm not working today.
5. I'm not _____.

I've been to New York.
6. I have _____.

I haven't tried that restaurant yet.
7. I haven't _____.

I don't feel well.
8. I don't _____.

B. Complete the conversations with **so/neither** and the words in *italics*.

1. I'm sleepy.
2. I haven't gone skiing before.
3. I can ride a motorcycle.
4. Fred isn't married.
5. Sue and I are British.
6. My roommate doesn't talk a lot.
7. The soup wasn't very good.
8. Alice and Ron live in San Diego.

(I) *So am I* _____.
(I) _____.
(Brian) _____.
(Maria) _____.
(we) _____.
(mine) _____.
(the salad) _____.
(Jim and Emily) _____.

C. Write **too/either** or **so/neither**.

1. "That was a very funny movie." "I enjoyed it *too* _____."
2. Erica doesn't like dogs, and she doesn't like cats _____.
3. "I should get up early tomorrow." "_____ should I."
4. This bread smells great. I hope it tastes good _____.
5. "We're going to have a Halloween party tonight." "_____ are we."
6. We don't have a TV, and we don't have a computer _____.
7. "I haven't talked to Ms. Williams lately." "_____ have I."
8. We visited a zoo last weekend. We went to an art museum _____.
9. "Mark isn't good at sports." "_____ is Roy."
10. "Martin can fall asleep in noisy places." "I know! _____ can Harry."

ANSWERS p.287, REVIEW TEST 14 p.240

211

GRAMMAR GATEWAY
BASIC

REVIEW TEST

The Review Test can help you check what you learned in the units. If you are not sure about the answer to a question, go back to the units and review them.

Look at the pictures and complete the sentences with the verbs in *italics*. Use the *present simple* or *present progressive*.

Name: ALBERT
Job: Writer

Name: ANGELA
Job: Chef

Name: KEVIN
Job: Teacher

Name: SIMONE
Job: Nurse

1. *(write, drink)* Albert __writes__ novels. He __'s drinking OR is drinking__ coffee.
2. *(work, listen)* Angela _____ at a restaurant. She _____ to music.
3. *(read, teach)* Kevin _____ a newspaper. He _____ at a high school.
4. *(shop, help)* Simone _____ . She _____ sick people.

Put the words in *italics* in the correct order.

5. *(is / he / busy)*
   Tom is working hard. __He's busy OR He is busy__ today.

6. *(Mom / is / pancakes / making)*
   " _____ ?" "No, Dad is making them."

7. *(do / not / we / use / it)*
   Let's give Eric our camera. _____ anymore.

8. *(you / know / him / do)*
   "Why is that man waving at us? _____ ?" "Yes. He's my neighbor."

9. *(are / Lisa and Anton / from England / not)*
   _____ . They are French.

10. *(not / wear / Julia / does / glasses)*
    "Are these glasses Julia's?" "No, they're Nick's. _____ ."

Complete the questions with the words in *italics*. Use the *present simple* or *present progressive*.

11. *(I, late)* __Am I late__ for the party?   No, you're not.
12. *(you, practice)* _____ the violin every day?   Yes, I do.
13. *(birds, eat)* _____ worms?   Yes, they do.
14. *(it, rain)* _____ right now?   Yes, it is.
15. *(Brian, take)* _____ the bus to school?   No, he doesn't.
16. *(you, watch)* Why is the TV on? _____ it?   Yes, I am.
17. *(she, work)* Who is that woman? _____ here?   No, she doesn't.
18. *(you, ready)* _____ for the meeting?   No, I'm not.

Choose the correct one.

19. "You look tired. Are you OK ?" "I _____ sick."
   a) am   b) is   c) are

20. Sally _____ a good singer. I like her songs very much.
   a) am   b) is   c) are

21. It's rainy today, but it _____ cold.
   a) am not   b) is not   c) are not

22. I _____ tall, but I'm good at basketball.
   a) am not   b) is not   c) are not

23. "I like those pants. _____ they expensive?" "No, they're not."
   a) Is   b) Are   c) Am

24. "I lost my eraser." " _____ one in my pencil case. You can use mine."
   a) I'm having   b) I'm have   c) I have

25. Andrew doesn't have a car. He _____ the subway every day.
   a) take   b) takes   c) don't take

26. In Fiji, it _____ in the winter.
   a) is not snowing   b) don't snow   c) doesn't snow

27. " _____ fish for dinner tonight?" "No, I don't like fish."
   a) Do you want   b) Are you wanting   c) You are want

28. Emma _____. Her husband makes their meals.
   a) is not cook   b) doesn't cook   c) don't cook

29. I don't want to go out today. _____ too much.
   a) It's snowing   b) It's not snow   c) It's snow

30. "What are you and Mark doing?" " _____ a game."
   a) We're playing   b) We're play   c) We play

31. Is that Bill? He _____ his glasses today.
   a) is not wearing   b) is not wear   c) doesn't wear

32. My parents _____ well. They both have a cold.
   a) are feel   b) aren't feel   c) aren't feeling

33. " _____ right now?" "No, she's reading a book."
   a) Is Margaret studying   b) Is Margaret study   c) Does Margaret study

ANSWERS **p.288**

If you are not sure about some answers, go back to the following units:

QUESTION	1	2	3	4	5	6	7	8	9	10	11	12	13	14	15	16
UNIT	10	10	10	10	1	5	8	9	2	8	3	9	9	5	9	5
	17	18	19	20	21	22	23	24	25	26	27	28	29	30	31	32	33
	9	3	1	1	2	2	3	10	6	8	9	8	4	4	5	5	5

Jenny sent a postcard to Brian with some pictures. Complete the sentences with the verbs in the box using the *past simple*.

| ~~arrive~~ | buy | see | take | visit | walk |

Dear Brian,

How are you? I'm in France!

1. I _arrived_ in Paris last Saturday.
2. On Sunday, I _____ along the river.
3. The next day, I _____ an art museum with my friend.
4. I _____ many beautiful paintings.
5. I _____ lots of photos.
6. This morning, I _____ some gifts for you.

Best wishes,
Jenny

Complete the conversations with the words in *italics*. Use the *present simple* or *past simple*.

7. (*I, make*) _I made_ spaghetti for you.
8. (*I, not see*) _____ you yesterday.
9. (*Susie, be*) _____ your friend in college?
10. (*I, have*) _____ a headache.
11. (*you, go*) _____ to the concert last weekend?
12. (*he, be*) Who is that handsome man? _____ a freshman?
13. (*I, not know*) _____ the way to City Hall. Can you give me directions?

Thanks, Grace!
I was sick.
Yes, she was.
Take this medicine.
No. I stayed at home.
He's my brother!
Sure, follow me.

Put the words in *italics* in the correct order.

14. (*was / he / not*)
Jacob didn't eat dinner. _He wasn't_ OR _He was not_ hungry.

15. (*did / Lucy / go / not*)
_____ to school yesterday. It was Sunday.

16. (*Ben / clean / did*)
"_____ the bathroom yesterday?" "Yes, he did."

17. (*you / were / studying*)
"I saw you at the library yesterday. _____?" "Yes. I had an exam today."

18. (*waiting / were / we*)
"Why were you and Joseph at the airport last night?" "_____ for Jenna."

Choose the correct one.

19. "What were you doing at 6 yesterday?" "I _____ ."
   a) am worked   (b) was working   c) am working

20. Last Tuesday _____ Tracy's birthday. She's 20 years old now.
   a) was   b) were   c) is

21. Sally _____ at home this morning. She didn't answer the door.
   a) wasn't   b) weren't   c) isn't

22. " _____ jogging when you saw them last week?" "Yes, they were."
   a) Was Tom and Jane   b) Were Tom and Jane   c) Are Tom and Jane

23. "This sandwich is amazing! Did you make it?" "No, I _____ it at a store."
   a) bought   b) was buying   c) buy

24. Kyle and I _____ butterflies every day, but we're too busy these days.
   a) used to catching   b) were catching   c) used to catch

25. Jason _____ to school yesterday. He took the bus.
   a) didn't walk   b) walks   c) doesn't walk

26. _____ in Taiwan?" "Yes. I was there for two years."
   a) Did you use to live   b) Do you used to live   c) Are you living

27. "Sorry I called you so late last night." "That's OK. I _____ when you called."
   a) wasn't sleeping   b) was sleeping   c) am sleeping

28. "Was your team playing soccer at 2 this afternoon?" "No, we _____ lunch."
   a) used to have   b) are having   c) were having

29. Last night at 11, Andrew and Rachel _____ TV. They were playing video games.
   a) aren't watching   b) watched   c) weren't watching

30. " _____ you this afternoon?" "No, she didn't."
   a) Was Jennifer call   b) Did Jennifer call   c) Does Jennifer call

31. " _____ when you saw him?" "Yes, he was."
   a) Was Thomas exercising   b) Were Thomas exercising   c) Is Thomas exercising

32. I _____ swimming lessons on Tuesdays, but I quit.
   a) take   b) used to take   c) am taking

33. The store _____ on weekends. Now it opens on Saturdays.
   a) didn't use to open   b) use not to open   c) don't use to open

ANSWERS p.288

If you are not sure about some answers, go back to the following units:

QUESTION	1	2	3	4	5	6	7	8	9	10	11	12	13	14	15	16
UNIT	13	13	13	13	13	13	13	14	12	6	14	3	8	12	14	14
17	18	19	20	21	22	23	24	25	26	27	28	29	30	31	32	33
16	15	15	11	12	16	13	17	14	17	16	15	16	14	16	17	17

Put the words in *italics* in the correct order.

1. *(owned / a dog / you / have / ever)*
   <u>Have you ever owned a dog</u> ?

2. *(we / not / yet / eaten dinner / have)*
   _____ .

3. *(many concerts / has / Mark / been to)*
   _____ .

4. *(the snow / stopped / has / just)*
   _____ ?

5. *(made / some muffins / Aaron and Nick / have)*
   _____ .

6. *(not / Mandy / a roller coaster / ridden / has)*
   _____ before.

 Look at the pictures and complete the sentences with the words in the box. Write negative sentences if necessary.

be sick	~~have this camera~~	know each other	rain

7. I *'ve had this camera* since 2012.

8. We _____ for 10 years.

9. It _____ since last month.

10. He _____ for two days.

 Complete the conversations with the verbs in *italics*. Use the *past simple* or *present perfect*.

11. Do you speak French?
12. Have you talked to Cindy lately?
13. Do your parents like that TV show?
14. How long have you been in China?
15. Why are you late?
16. Your son is so tall now.
17. Where's your car?
18. When did Susan come to this company?

(study) A little. I *ve studied* since March.
(call) Yes. She _____ me two days ago.
(watch) Yes. They _____ it for many years.
(come) I _____ here in 2009.
(get) I _____ up late this morning.
(grow) He _____ a lot since last year.
(break) My car _____ down last week.
(work) She _____ here for three months.

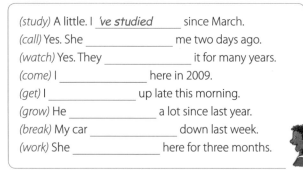

Choose the correct one.

19. "_____ Tim and Lisa arrived at the party?" "Yes. They're dancing now."
   a) Have   b) Did   c) Do

20. "Have you already finished college?" "Yes. I _____ two years ago."
   a) have graduated   b) graduated   c) graduate

21. My baseball team lost again. We _____ a game since last year.
   a) haven't won   b) don't won   c) didn't win

22. I haven't seen my sister _____ five years. I miss her so much.
   a) since   b) ago   c) for

23. My daughter is at the hospital. She _____ her arm yesterday.
   a) has hurt   b) hurts   c) hurt

24. "What's wrong with the lamp?" "Jack _____ it."
   a) has broken   b) have broken   c) doesn't break

25. Jason and I _____ to the museum last Thursday.
   a) have gone   b) went   c) go

26. "Have you ever been to New Zealand?" "No. I _____ abroad."
   a) have traveled   b) haven't traveled   c) hasn't traveled

27. "_____ your homework yet?" "I'll do it tomorrow."
   a) You done have   b) Have you done   c) Have done you

28. "Is Dad still at home?" "No. He _____ to work."
   a) has gone   b) has been   c) doesn't go

29. "How long have you been married?" "We've been married _____ 1998."
   a) since   b) ago   c) for

30. Martin is so smart. He _____ an exam.
   a) have never failed   b) has never failed   c) hasn't never failed

31. "_____ come yet?" "Yes. It's on your desk."
   a) The mail did   b) Have the mail   c) Has the mail

32. "Am I late?" "No. The movie _____ yet."
   a) has started   b) hasn't started   c) haven't started

33. "Jessica looks upset." "_____ her watch."
   a) She has lost   b) She hasn't lost   c) Has she lost

ANSWERS **p.288**

If you are not sure about some answers, go back to the following units:

QUESTION	1	2	3	4	5	6	7	8	9	10	11	12	13	14	15	16
UNIT	20	22	20	22	18	20	19	19	19	19	21	21	21	21	21	21
17	18	19	20	21	22	23	24	25	26	27	28	29	30	31	32	33
21	21	18	21	19	19	21	18	21	20	22	20	19	20	22	22	18

Put the words in *italics* in the correct order.

1. *(like / Lisa / this ring / will)*
   <u>Will Lisa like this ring</u> ?

2. *(going / marry her / he / to / is)*
   Jake loves his girlfriend so much. _____.

3. *(you / are / speaking)*
   _____ at the seminar? I saw your name on the list.

4. *(going / are / to / watch the fireworks / you)*
   " _____ tonight?" "No. I'm tired."

5. *(not / will / it / I / forget)*
   "The password is 0922." "OK. _____."

6. *(playing soccer / are / Alex and I / not)*
   _____ this weekend. We're going to the beach instead.

 Look at the pictures and complete the sentences with **be going to** and the words in the box.

drink some wine	~~fall~~	get on the train	stop at the light

7. The tree <u>is going to fall</u> .
8. She _____.
9. The car _____.
10. They _____.

 Complete the conversations with **will** and the verbs in the box. Write negative sentences if necessary.

cook	meet	~~open~~	stay	tell	touch	turn on	write

11. These gifts are for Janice.
12. Can I have your phone number?
13. You have to get up early tomorrow.
14. It's so cold.
15. I just painted that wall. It's still wet.
16. It's a secret.
17. I'm so hungry.
18. Let's see a movie tonight.

OK. I <u>won't open</u> them.
Sure. I _____ it down for you.
I know. I _____ up late.
You're right. I _____ the heater.
All right. I _____ it.
Don't worry. I _____ anyone.
I _____ something for you.
Sure. I _____ you at the theater.

Choose the correct one.

19. Take this medicine. You _____ better.
    a) are going to get   b) were going to get   c) got

20. "You can get a 10 percent discount on this coat." "Really? _____ it!"
    a) I took   b) I take   c) I'll take

21. "Do you have any plans for this Sunday?" "_____ my grandparents."
    a) I visited   b) I visit   c) I'm going to visit

22. "_____ busy tomorrow?" "I'm not sure. Why?"
    a) Do you and Nate be   b) Will you and Nate be   c) You and Nate will be

23. We need to hurry. The bank _____ in 10 minutes.
    a) close   b) closes   c) closed

24. "This steak tastes awful." "Does it? I _____ it, then."
    a) won't eat   b) don't eat   c) didn't eat

25. "Did you book a ticket for Tokyo?" "Yes. _____ next Wednesday."
    a) I leave   b) I won't leave   c) I'm leaving

26. "Hurry up!" "Don't worry. We _____ late."
    a) will be   b) won't be   c) are

27. _____ the meeting this afternoon. She's sick.
    a) Jenny's attending   b) Jenny doesn't attend   c) Jenny's not attending

28. "_____ soon?" "I don't think so."
    a) Is the rain going to stop   b) Is the rain stop   c) Does the rain stop

29. Tina _____ the exam next week because she studied very hard.
    a) will pass   b) passes   c) passed

30. "We _____ to Seattle next month." "I'm glad you're staying here."
    a) don't move   b) aren't going to move   c) didn't move

31. I _____ with Kim next Sunday. Do you want to go with us?
    a) am going shopping   b) am not going shopping   c) was going shopping

32. "_____ to my birthday party?" "Of course. When is it?"
    a) Did you come   b) Do you come   c) Will you come

33. "_____ the car today?" "No. You can use it."
    a) Are you going to use   b) Are you use   c) Did you use

ANSWERS **p.288**

If you are not sure about some answers, go back to the following units:

QUESTION	1	2	3	4	5	6	7	8	9	10	11	12	13	14	15	16
UNIT	23	24	25	24	23	25	24	24	24	24	23	23	23	23	23	23
17	18	19	20	21	22	23	24	25	26	27	28	29	30	31	32	33
23	23	24	23	24	23	25	23	25	23	25	24	23	24	25	23	24

Put the words in *italics* in the correct order.

1. *(can / teach / you / me)*
   "I want to learn Spanish. *Can you teach me*_____?" "OK."

2. *(not / might / he / come)*
   "Is Tom coming to the beach with us?" "I'm not sure. _____."

3. *(think / get / should / he / I)*
   Fred's hair is very long. _____ a haircut.

4. *(would / like / you / to / dance)*
   "_____ with me?" "Sure."

5. *(do / have to / not / I / go)*
   _____ to the hospital. I'm feeling much better.

 Look at the pictures and complete the sentences with the given words. Write negative sentences if necessary.

| be scared | call the police | fall down the stairs |
| fix the roof | ~~turn off the stove~~ | use the car |

6. *(should)* You *should turn off the stove*_____.

7. *(can)* We _____.

8. *(have to)* We _____.

9. *(might)* Watch out! You _____!

10. *(have to)* You _____.

 I'm nervous.

11. *(must)* We _____.

 Complete the sentences with the verbs in *italics* using the *present simple* or *past simple*. Write negative sentences if necessary.

12. *(must)* "It's very cold today. You *must*_____ wear a jacket!" "OK, I will."
13. *(can)* The view from the tower was amazing. We _____ see the entire city.
14. *(have to)* Hank _____ get up early yesterday. He didn't go to work.
15. *(should)* You _____ drive so fast. You could get in an accident.
16. *(must)* "That's the last train! We _____ miss it." "Let's run."
17. *(have to)* My new sweater was too big for me. I _____ return it last weekend.
18. *(can)* The teacher spoke too quickly. I _____ understand him.

Choose the correct one.

19. "_____ David play the guitar?" "Yes, he can."
   a) Must   b) Should   c) Can

20. Phillip's car is very dirty. He _____ clean it often.
   a) must not   b) shouldn't   c) might

21. "_____ get a soda, please?" "Sure, here you go."
   a) Can I   b) Would I   c) Should I

22. "_____ use your pen?" "Of course. Go ahead."
   a) May I   b) Would you like to   c) Could you

23. "Western Hotel, how can I help you?" "_____ a reservation for two nights, please."
   a) I'd like make   b) Would you to make   c) I'd like to make

24. Sarah _____ do the laundry last night. She was too tired.
   a) can't   b) couldn't   c) might not

25. The plane will land now. All passengers _____ wear seatbelts.
   a) must   b) had to   c) shouldn't

26. Gary failed his driving test. He _____ take it again.
   a) have to   b) has to   c) doesn't have to

27. "Can you finish your homework tonight?" "I don't know. I _____ finish it."
   a) shouldn't   b) must not   c) might not

28. "_____ order some food for us?" "Yes! I'm hungry."
   a) Would you like   b) Would I   c) Should I

29. I _____ wash the dishes. My sister has done it already.
   a) must not   b) don't have to   c) doesn't have to

30. "_____ fix my computer for me, please?" "Sure."
   a) You would   b) Could you   c) Should you

31. Sam broke Melinda's cup. He _____ apologize.
   a) should   b) can   c) could

32. I'm new here. _____ show me around the office?
   a) Would you   b) May I   c) I'd like to

33. "_____ more wine?" "No, thank you. I've had enough."
   a) Would you like   b) Would you like to   c) Should I

ANSWERS p.289

If you are not sure about some answers, go back to the following units:

QUESTION	1	2	3	4	5	6	7	8	9	10	11	12	13	14	15	16
UNIT	26	27	31	32	30	31	26	30	27	30	29	29	26	30	31	29
	17	18	19	20	21	22	23	24	25	26	27	28	29	30	31	32	33
	30	26	26	29	28	28	32	26	29	30	27	31	30	28	31	32	32

Look at the pictures and complete the sentences with the verbs in the box using the passive. Use the *past simple*.

| ~~catch~~ | make | steal | take | write |

1   2   3   4   5

1. The thieves *were caught* _____ by the policeman.
2. The scarves _____ in Italy.
3. The letter _____ by Jackie.
4. The pictures _____ in New York.
5. The painting _____ by someone.

Put the words in *italics* in the correct order.

6. *(it / visited / is)*
   Michael's town is famous. *It is visited* _____ by many tourists each year.

7. *(pets / allowed / not / are)*
   "Can we take our dog with us?"   "No, _____ in the museum."

8. *(the house / not / was / sold)*
   _____ yesterday. It's still for sale.

9. *(the Mona Lisa / painted / was / Leonardo da Vinci / by)*
   _____.

10. *(These dishes / not / can / used / be)*
    _____ in a microwave.

Complete the sentences with the verbs in *italics* using the active or passive. Use the *past simple*.

11. *(prepare)* "This pasta is amazing. Who made it?"   "All the dishes *were prepared* _____ by Chef Antonio."
12. *(cancel)* "Did you go to the meeting yesterday?"   "No, it _____."
13. *(have)* "Were you with Susie this morning?"   "Yes, I _____ coffee with her."
14. *(break)* The window _____ by the storm last night.
15. *(not finish)* "Did you do your homework?"   "I _____ it. I was too busy."
16. *(invent)* The light bulb _____ by Thomas Edison.
17. *(watch)* "What did Frank do on Saturday?"   "He _____ movies all day."
18. *(not wash)* "Has Bruce washed the car yet?"   "It _____ when I saw it this morning."

Choose the correct one.

19. The apple pies in this bakery are fresh. They _____ every morning.
    a) baked   (b) are baked   c) are bake

20. I can't read this book. It _____ in German.
    a) is written   b) was writing   c) wrote

21. I sent flowers to my friend, but they _____.
    a) were delivered   b) weren't delivered   c) don't deliver

22. "What instrument does Jane play?" "She _____ the flute."
    a) plays   b) is played   c) was played

23. Fred _____ tomatoes. He doesn't like them.
    a) isn't eaten   b) wasn't eaten   c) doesn't eat

24. "What's George's phone number?" "Sorry, I _____."
    a) don't know   b) am not known   c) wasn't known

25. "Thirty people _____ to the party, but only 10 people came." "That's too bad."
    a) invited   b) were invited   c) weren't invited

26. "Why was Jack crying this morning?" "He _____ for the soccer team."
    a) wasn't chosen   b) chose   c) isn't chosen

27. Thomas Neilson's books are very famous. They _____ every year.
    a) are read many people   b) read by many people   c) are read by many people

28. Samantha's house is very old. It _____ in 1964.
    a) was built   b) were built   c) built

29. "Where's your phone?" "I _____ it last night."
    a) am lost   b) was lost   c) lost

30. An office party _____ by Ms. Harper.
    a) will plan   b) is planning   c) will be planned

31. "Why were you late to work this morning?" "The road _____ by snow."
    a) blocked   b) was blocked   c) is blocked

32. "Where did you get that car?" "Tony _____ it to me."
    a) was lent   b) lent   c) is lent

33. "Who taught you math in high school?" "I _____."
    a) was taught by Mr. Adams   b) was taught Mr. Adams   c) taught by Mr. Adams

ANSWERS **p.289**

If you are not sure about some answers, go back to the following units:

QUESTION	1	2	3	4	5	6	7	8	9	10	11	12	13	14	15	16
UNIT	34	33	34	33	34	34	33	33	34	33	34	34	34	34	34	34
17	18	19	20	21	22	23	24	25	26	27	28	29	30	31	32	33
34	34	34	34	34	34	34	34	34	34	34	34	34	34	34	34	34

Write **Who/What/Where/When**.

1. _Where_ are you from?
2. _____ does your brother do?
3. _____ is your favorite singer?
4. _____ did you meet your wife?
5. _____ does the next bus arrive?
6. _____ are those people in the picture?
7. _____ can I see the doctor?
8. _____ time does your plane leave?

I'm from Thailand.
He's a scientist.
Tracy Swift. Her songs are really good.
At our university. We were classmates.
In 10 minutes.
They are my neighbors.
At 11 o'clock tomorrow morning.
At 9 p.m.

 Read what each person thinks and complete the indirect questions.

9. Do you know _who that man is_ ?

Who is that man?

10. Can you tell me _____ ?

Where can I put this?

Why did you buy this hat?

When will Erica get here?

11. I wonder _____ .

12. Do you know _____ ?

 Put the words in *italics* in the correct order.

13. (*you / tried / have / Mexican food*)
    Have you tried Mexican food before? It's really good.

14. (*this necklace / much / does / cost / how*)
    "_____?" "$70."

15. (*many / here / work / people / how*)
    "_____?" "Around a hundred."

16. (*will / busy / whether / you / be*)
    Can you tell me _____ next Saturday?

17. (*go / when / Cindy / did*)
    "_____ to Hong Kong?" "Last Friday."

18. (*this / from / where / is / wine*)
    "_____?" "It was made in Italy."

Choose the correct one.

19. "_____ mine?" "This one."
    a) Cup which is   b) Which is cup   c) Which cup is

20. "_____ will you arrive?" "At about 4 o'clock."
    a) When   b) Where   c) Why

21. "That was a very long flight, _____?" "Yes. Nearly 10 hours!"
    a) isn't it   b) wasn't it   c) was it

22. "_____ do I turn on this machine?" "Press the green button."
    a) When   b) Who   c) How

23. "_____ would you like, beef or pork?" "Beef, please."
    a) Which   b) How   c) Who

24. I don't know _____ to school today.
    a) if Chris went   b) did Chris go   c) Chris went

25. "_____ are you calling?" "My boyfriend."
    a) What   b) Who   c) How

26. "Josh and Sharon just arrived." "_____ together?"
    a) They did came   b) Did they come   c) Did they came

27. _____ is my bag? I can't find it.
    a) Where   b) When   c) Why

28. "_____ from your house?" "About two miles away."
    a) How far is your school   b) How far your school is   c) How your school is far

29. "_____ did Catherine go back to the store?" "She left her purse there."
    a) When   b) Where   c) Why

30. "Can you tell me _____ for dessert?" "I want something sweet."
    a) what do you want   b) you want what   c) what you want

31. "I can't leave my car here, _____?" "No. You have to park over there."
    a) can I   b) can you   c) can't I

32. "_____ lived in Sydney?" "For 20 years."
    a) How long you have   b) How have you long   c) How long have you

33. "_____ the piano?" "No, but she can play the guitar."
    a) Jamie can play   b) Can Jamie play   c) Can play Jamie

ANSWERS **p.289**

If you are not sure about some answers, go back to the following units:

QUESTION	1	2	3	4	5	6	7	8	9	10	11	12	13	14	15	16
UNIT	37	36	36	37	37	36	37	36	40	40	40	40	35	38	38	40
17	18	19	20	21	22	23	24	25	26	27	28	29	30	31	32	33
37	37	36	37	39	38	36	40	36	35	37	38	37	40	39	38	35

TEST 8 -ing and to . . . (UNIT 41-45)

Look at the pictures and complete the sentences with the words in the box.

| cook | go to the museum | ~~play soccer~~ | read books | sing | wait in line |

1. I love *playing soccer*
   OR *to play soccer* .

2. I hate _____
   _____ .

3. I practice _____
   _____ every day.

4. I enjoy _____
   _____ .

5. I plan _____
   _____ .

6. I like _____
   _____ at cafés.

Complete the sentences with the verbs in *italics*. Use **-ing** or **to . . .** if necessary.

7. *(play)* "Do you go to the golf course every week?" "Yes. *Playing* _____ golf is my hobby."
8. *(send)* "Where are you going?" "I'm going to the bank _____ some money."
9. *(make)* "When will you return home?" "At about 6. I'll help you _____ dinner tonight."
10. *(eat)* "I want to lose weight." "You should avoid _____ snacks."
11. *(stay)* "Why didn't you come to the party?" "My dad made me _____ at home."
12. *(move)* "There is no space for the new printer." "Let's try _____ it to the other room."
13. *(learn)* "I'm studying Japanese these days." "Why did you decide _____ a foreign language?"

Put the words in *italics* in the correct order.

14. *(writing / finished / I / my report)*
    " *I finished writing my report* ." "Great. Can I see it?"

15. *(me / use / Aaron / let / his)*
    My mobile phone wasn't working, so _____ .

16. *(to / buy / does / need / Kim)*
    " _____ a new computer?" "Yes, hers is very old."

17. *(taught / Nicole / to dance / me)*
    "You're a great dancer." "Thank you. _____ ."

18. *(good / swimming / is)*
    _____ for your health.

Choose the correct one.

19. "When did you decide _____ a book?" "About three years ago."
    a) to write   b) writing   c) write

20. "Jenna made Dale _____ yesterday." "What did she do?"
    a) to cry   b) crying   c) cry

21. "Mr. Smith offered _____ me chess." "That's great. You're going to enjoy it."
    a) to teach   b) teaching   c) teach

22. "Can you _____ these plants, please?" "Sure. Where should they go?"
    a) help me moving   b) help me move   c) help moving me

23. Why are you still watching TV? I told you _____ to bed an hour ago.
    a) to go   b) going   c) go

24. Sophie keeps _____ me text messages during class. I want her to stop.
    a) to send   b) sending   c) send

25. "What are you going to do next Saturday?" "I'm planning _____ Chad."
    a) visit   b) visiting   c) to visit

26. "_____ a cheesecake takes about an hour." "Really? It doesn't take very long."
    a) Bake   b) Baking   c) Baked

27. "Anna and Joe want me _____ their tennis club." "That sounds like fun."
    a) join   b) joining   c) to join

28. I don't enjoy _____ basketball outside when it's hot.
    a) to play   b) playing   c) play

29. _____ a taxi isn't easy on Fridays. Let's take a bus.
    a) Get   b) Got   c) Getting

30. "Why did you go to the supermarket in the morning?" "Emily had me _____ some milk."
    a) to buy   a) buying   c) buy

31. "I went to the library _____ a book." "What book did you borrow?"
    a) borrowing   b) borrow   c) to borrow

32. "Why did you stop _____ to the fitness center?" "I hurt my back."
    a) to go   b) going   c) go

33. "Do you have time _____ every day?" "Yes. I usually go to the gym after work."
    a) to exercise   b) exercising   c) exercise

ANSWERS p.289

If you are not sure about some answers, go back to the following units:

QUESTION	1	2	3	4	5	6	7	8	9	10	11	12	13	14	15	16
UNIT	43	43	42	42	42	43	41	45	44	42	44	43	42	42	44	42
17	18	19	20	21	22	23	24	25	26	27	28	29	30	31	32	33
44	41	42	44	42	44	44	42	42	41	44	42	41	44	45	43	45

Put the words in *italics* in the correct order. Use the plural form of the nouns if necessary.

1. (*dog / has / he / five*)

   "Does Brian have any pets?" " _He has five dogs_____."

2. (*many / attend / student / the concert*)

   "Did _____ yesterday?" "No, not very many."

3. (*snow / some / on / the road*)

   There's _____ . Please drive carefully.

4. (*get / a / of / orange juice / glass*)

   "Could I _____ , please?" "Sure."

5. (*ones / buy / new*)

   "Your shoes are old!" "I know, I'm going to _____ tomorrow."

 Look at the pictures and complete the sentences with -' or -'s and the nouns in the box.

| ~~book~~   house   office   seat   suitcases |

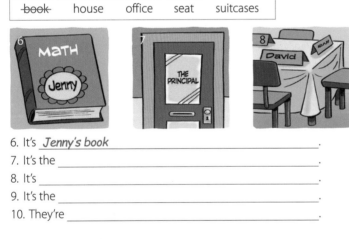

6. It's _Jenny's book_____ .
7. It's the _____ .
8. It's _____ .
9. It's the _____ .
10. They're _____ .

 Complete the sentences with the nouns in the box. Add **a/an** or **the** if necessary.

| airport   ~~computer~~   drums   information   money   salt   taxi   umbrella |

11. I'd like to buy _a computer_____ . Could you help me choose a model?
12. "Did Clara take _____ with her? It's raining outside." "Yes, I gave her one."
13. "This soup needs some _____ . Do we have any?" "Yes, we do. Here you are."
14. "We're going to be late. We should catch _____ ." "There's one over there."
15. "Can you play _____ ?" "No, I can't."
16. Mary's flight arrives in four hours. Let's wait for her at _____ .
17. Can you lend me some _____ ? I want to get a soda.
18. "Could you give me some _____ about the test next Monday?" "Of course."

Choose the correct one.

19. "I think my eyesight is getting worse." "You should get _____."
    a) new glasses   b) a new glasses   c) a new glass

20. "Do we have an exam tomorrow?" "No, _____ is next Friday."
    a) exam   b) an exam   c) the exam

21. Michael raises many _____ on his farm for their wool.
    a) a sheep   b) sheep   c) sheeps

22. "Do you need help with your bag?" "No, thanks. I can lift it by _____."
    a) me   b) mine   c) myself

23. "Have you seen _____ in my garden?" "Yes, they're beautiful!"
    a) the flowers   b) a flower   c) flowers

24. "Is there _____ nearby?" "Yes, there's one across the street."
    a) a bank machine   b) the bank machine   c) bank machine

25. "What's the highest mountain in _____?" "Mount Everest."
    a) world   b) a world   c) the world

26. "What were you doing when I called?" "I was having _____ with Jason."
    a) dinners   b) dinner   c) the dinner

27. "Where's Lisa?" "She _____."
    a) went to a work   b) went to work   c) went to the work

28. Eric is going to the airport too. You should get a ride with _____.
    a) him   b) his   c) he

29. "How's the weather in Chicago these days?" "_____ has rained for five days."
    a) The weather   b) Chicago   c) It

30. This letter has your name on it. It must be _____.
    a) your   b) you   c) yours

31. "Are you wearing my earrings?" "No. _____ are mine."
    a) This   b) Those   c) These

32. Matt's company is on _____.
    a) the fifth floor of the building   b) the fifth floor's building   c) the building of the fifth floor

33. "Can I borrow one of your hats today?" "Sure. _____?"
    a) Which ones   b) Which one   c) The ones

ANSWERS **p.290**

If you are not sure about some answers, go back to the following units:

QUESTION	1	2	3	4	5	6	7	8	9	10	11	12	13	14	15	16
UNIT	46	46	47	48	57	54	54	54	54	54	49	49	47	49	50	50
17	18	19	20	21	22	23	24	25	26	27	28	29	30	31	32	33
47	47	48	49	48	55	49	49	50	50	50	51	52	53	56	54	57

Look at the pictures and write **some/any/no**.

1. She took _some_____ photos.
2. There aren't _____ people in the park.
3. There are _____ apples on the table.
4. He didn't receive _____ mail today.
5. There is _____ water in the swimming pool.

 Choose the correct one.

6. Have you had dinner?
7. Was traffic slow this morning?
8. Did you go to bed early last night?
9. Do you read many books?
10. How's the soup?
11. Let's go to Europe together!
12. How was the beach yesterday?
13. Have you finished fixing the car?

Yes, but I didn't eat (*much* / *many*) food.
No, there were (*few* / *little*) cars on the road.
No, I had (*much* / *many*) things to do.
Yes, I usually read six books (*all* / *every*) month.
It needs (*a little* / *a few*) salt.
I can't. I haven't saved (*much* / *many*) money.
Terrible. It rained (*all* / *every*) day.
I couldn't. I had (*little* / *a little*) time today.

Put the words in *italics* in the correct order. Add **of** if necessary.

14. *(friends / my / day / all)*
   "What are you going to do tomorrow?" "I'm meeting with _my friends all day_____."

15. *(them / are / both)*
   "What color are Kate's cats?" "_____ white."

16. *(my / live / cousins / most)*
   _____ in New York. Only one lives in Boston.

17. *(has / none / he)*
   "Does Brandon have any brothers?" "No, _____."

18. *(mine / them / is / neither)*
   "Which ball is yours, the red or blue one?" "_____. Mine is at home."

Choose the correct one.

19. "Would you like _____ cookies?" "Yes, please. I love cookies."
    a) none   b) some   c) no

20. "Do you have any bananas? I'd like to buy some." "I'm sorry, we have _____."
    a) no   b) none bananas   c) none

21. I haven't seen _____ movies this month. I've been too busy.
    a) any   b) some   c) no

22. _____ is knocking on the door. It might be John.
    a) Someone   b) Anything   c) Nowhere

23. "I think someone is crying. Do you hear _____?" "No, I don't."
    a) somewhere   b) anything   c) nothing

24. Jessica is popular. She has _____.
    a) many friends   b) much friends   c) all friends

25. "Do you have any rooms available?" "Yes, we have _____. Would you like to check in?"
    a) few   b) a little   c) a few

26. "How much milk do we have?" "Very _____. We should buy a carton tomorrow."
    a) a little   b) little   c) few

27. "Do you have any items on sale?" "Yes, _____ item is on sale."
    a) all of   b) all   c) every

28. Clark is very tired. He played soccer _____ day today.
    a) all   b) every   c) all of

29. I don't have to do much homework tonight. I have finished _____ it already.
    a) lot of   b) a lot   c) a lot of

30. "Did you do well on your history test?" "I think so, but _____ the questions were difficult."
    a) some   b) some of   c) most

31. I went to two different bakeries, but _____ them had bagels.
    a) neither   b) neither of   c) either of

32. "Do you want to go out for dinner or eat at home?" "_____ is fine."
    a) Both   b) Neither   c) Either

33. "Are any banks open at 6 p.m.?" "I'm not sure. _____ banks close before 5 p.m."
    a) Most   b) Most of   c) None

ANSWERS **p.290**

If you are not sure about some answers, go back to the following units:

QUESTION	1	2	3	4	5	6	7	8	9	10	11	12	13	14	15	16
UNIT	58	58	58	58	59	60	61	60	62	61	60	62	61	62	64	64
17	**18**	**19**	**20**	**21**	**22**	**23**	**24**	**25**	**26**	**27**	**28**	**29**	**30**	**31**	**32**	**33**
59	64	58	59	58	58	58	60	61	61	62	62	60	64	64	63	64

TEST 11 Adjectives and Adverbs (UNIT 65-75)

Look at the pictures and complete the sentences with the words from each box. Change the adjectives into adverbs.

| ~~laugh~~ | shout | sit | think | + | angry | hard | ~~loud~~ | uncomfortable |

Ha ha ha ha

You did! No, you did!

1. They _'re laughing loudly_ .
2. He _____ .
3. She _____ .
4. They _____ .

Put the words in *italics* in the correct order.

5. *(are / for / small / me / too)*
   My old shirts _are too small for me_ . I need to buy new ones.

6. *(rarely / is / crowded)*
   "That café _____." "You're right. I often go there to study."

7. *(to / tall / enough / not / ride)*
   Thomas wanted to ride the roller coaster, but he was _____ it.

8. *(tired / too / to / go)*
   "I am _____ to the movies." "Let's stay at home, then."

9. *(for / everyone / enough)*
   "How many tickets did you buy?" "I bought _____."

10. *(always / my car / can / use)*
    You _____ if you need it.

Complete the sentences with the words in *italics*. Use the comparatives or superlatives of the adjectives/adverbs if necessary.

11. *(heavy)* Can you help me carry these bags? They are too _heavy_ for me.
12. *(good)* Something smells _____! What are we having for dinner?
13. *(large)* This skirt is too small for me. Do you have a _____ size?
14. *(beautiful)* I think roses are _____ than tulips.
15. *(high)* Mount Everest is the _____ mountain in the world.
16. *(hot)* "When is the _____ time of the day?" "Around 2 p.m."
17. *(fast)* "Can you run _____ than Nathan?" "No. He's the fastest in my school."
18. *(strong)* Susan is very strong, but she's not as _____ as her brother.

Choose the correct one.

19. "Did you enjoy the movie?" "Yes, it was _____ the one we saw yesterday."
a) the most interesting   (b) more interesting than   c) interesting

20. "Did you make _____?" "Of course."
a) pizza enough for the guests   b) pizza for the guests enough   c) enough pizza for the guests

21. I _____ in the ocean, but I want to try one day.
a) never have swum   b) have never swum   c) have swum never

22. "Your shoes are so _____." "I know. I'm going to wash them tomorrow."
a) dirty   b) dirtiest   c) dirtier

23. "Why are _____ at the shopping mall?" "It is having a sale."
a) so much people   b) so many people   c) so many person

24. Ashley's house is _____ to school, so she always arrives at class first.
a) the most close   b) more closer   c) the closest

25. My dad loves fishing. _____ me fishing on weekends.
a) He takes often   b) Often takes he   c) He often takes

26. I'm telling you a _____ story. You have to believe me.
a) true   b) truer   c) truly

27. Today is _____ yesterday. Let's go to the park.
a) not as cold as   b) as not cold as   c) as cold as not

28. Troy has a stomachache. He ate dinner _____.
a) too quickly   b) quickly too   c) too quicker

29. I finished work late yesterday. I was _____ usual.
a) busier   b) busier than   c) the busiest

30. Did you do your homework _____ to get a good grade?
a) enough good   b) well enough   c) enough well

31. It snowed a lot last night. You should drive _____.
a) careful   b) carefully   c) more careful

32. "Please finish your work _____." "OK. I'll try my best."
a) as sooner as possible   b) as soon as possible   c) as possible as soon

33. "That ring has a really big diamond." "It's _____ ring in the store."
a) expensive   b) more expensive   c) the most expensive

ANSWERS **p.290**

If you are not sure about some answers, go back to the following units:

QUESTION	1	2	3	4	5	6	7	8	9	10	11	12	13	14	15	16
UNIT	66	66	67	66	69	68	70	69	70	68	69	65	73	73	74	74
17	18	19	20	21	22	23	24	25	26	27	28	29	30	31	32	33
72	75	73	70	68	71	71	74	68	65	75	69	73	70	66	75	74

TEST 12   Prepositions and Phrasal Verbs (UNIT 76-86)

Look at the pictures and complete the sentences with **at/in/on** and the words in the box.

| ~~a bench~~   home   the 4th floor   the bathroom   work |

1. They are sitting _on a bench_____ .
2. They are _____ .
3. The hair salon is _____ .
4. He just arrived _____ .
5. He is changing his clothes _____ .

Complete the conversations with the given words.

| behind   by   down   for   from   in   ~~next to~~   to |

6. Is City Hall near here?
7. When can you return my book?
8. How long have you known Tim?
9. When does the movie start?
10. Are you Chinese?
11. Where are you going for vacation?
12. Where is Scott?
13. Is there a bathroom on this floor?

(that building) It's right _next to that building_____ .
(this Friday) I'll return it _____ .
(five years) _____ .
(10 minutes) It starts _____ .
(Korea) No, I'm _____ .
(Germany) I'm going _____ .
(the curtains) He's hiding _____ .
(the stairs) No. It's _____ .

Put the words in *italics* in the correct order.

14. *(drinking / without / water)*
    Kate is very thirsty. She ran for three hours _without drinking water_____ .

15. *(on / the / turn / air conditioner)*
    "This room is hot." "Maybe you can _____ ."

16. *(about / the trip / excited)*
    We're going to Disneyland next week. We're very _____ .

17. *(spends / on / unnecessary things / money)*
    Robert likes to save money. He never _____ .

18. *(the / up / clean / trash)*
    All visitors to the park have to _____ before they leave.

Choose the correct one.

19. "Where is your brother?" "He's standing _____ Colin and Ian."
    a) among   (b) between   c) under

20. "Do you know where the parking lot is?" "It's _____ the white building."
    a) behind   b) from   c) to

21. "Thank you _____ me home last night." "No problem."
    a) for drive   b) for driving   c) for drive to

22. It was raining, so we got _____ of the taxi and ran.
    a) in   b) off   c) out

23. I finished fixing your computer. You can _____ now.
    a) turn on it   b) turn it on   c) it turn on

24. "Where were you _____ 3 o'clock yesterday?" "I was at the shopping mall with Jake."
    a) in   b) on   c) at

25. The guests are coming soon. We need to finish cleaning the house _____ 20 minutes.
    a) within   b) during   c) at

26. "Are you good _____ swimming?" "No. What about you?"
    a) in   b) of   c) at

27. I went to school _____ my pencil case yesterday. I had to borrow a pen.
    a) with   b) by   c) without

28. "This question is so difficult." "How _____ Ms. Brown for help?"
    a) about ask   b) about to ask   c) about asking

29. "Can you hand _____ these free samples to the customers?" "Of course."
    a) on   b) out   c) to

30. The theater is famous _____ its comfortable seats, but the tickets are too expensive.
    a) at   b) for   c) to

31. "I might be late for our appointment." "OK. I'll wait _____ 8 p.m."
    a) by   b) during   c) until

32. "What is Jennifer doing?" "She's talking _____ Mr. Silver."
    a) for   b) to   c) at

33. I forgot to get the mail. Can you go to the mailbox and _____?
    a) pick it up   b) pick up it   c) it pick up

ANSWERS **p.290**

If you are not sure about some answers, go back to the following units:

QUESTION	1	2	3	4	5	6	7	8	9	10	11	12	13	14	15	16
UNIT	76	77	77	77	76	78	82	81	81	79	79	78	79	83	86	84
17	18	19	20	21	22	23	24	25	26	27	28	29	30	31	32	33
85	86	78	78	83	86	86	80	81	84	83	83	86	84	82	85	86

TEST 13 Conjunctions and Clauses (UNIT 87-95)

Complete the sentences with **and/but/or/so/because** and the words in *italics*.

1. *(they went to a café)* Chris and Judy saw a movie, *and they went to a café* .
2. *(should we take a bus)* Do you want to drive, _____ ?
3. *(I drank too much wine last night)* I feel sick today _____ .
4. *(she couldn't come)* Matt invited Cindy to his house, _____ .
5. *(she took some medicine)* Christina had a headache, _____ .

Put the words in *italics* in the correct order. Use the *present simple* or *past simple*.

6. *(sunny / if / it / be)*
   If it is sunny OR *If it's sunny* _____ today, Ben will wash his car.

7. *(work / finish / I / if)*
   "Are you coming to the party tonight?" "I'll go _____ early."

8. *(I / you / be / if)*
   "My tooth hurts too much." "I'd see a dentist _____ ."

9. *(she / since / leave / the company)*
   I haven't seen Amanda _____ .

10. *(Martin / it / open / when)*
    "What happened to our front door?" "It broke _____ ."

11. *(while / she / on vacation / be)*
    Rachel is going to stay at a resort _____ next month.

Look at the pictures and complete the sentences with **who/which**.

12. She is wearing a hat *which cost $120* .
13. He's pointing at the woman _____ .
14. He's the man _____ .
15. They're standing in front of a house _____ .

This hat cost $120 dollars.

She was on TV last night.

I met him during the trip.

Ted's dad built that house.

Choose the correct one.

16. On weekends, Evan goes to the library _____ reads some magazines.
    a) and   b) because   c) so

17. My new computer is expensive, _____ it's not very fast.
    a) so   b) but   c) while

18. "Why are you late?" "It was rush hour, _____ there were a lot of cars on the road."
    a) but   b) or   c) so

19. The girl _____ the race is my sister. I'm so proud of her.
    a) who she won   b) which won   c) who won

20. _____ I woke up, someone was knocking on the door.
    a) While   b) When   c) Since

21. Marvin is going to call Susie _____ work today.
    a) when he will finish   b) when he finish   c) when he finishes

22. He's the man _____ at Sophie's shop last week.
    a) that saw   b) which I saw   c) I saw

23. "Dad, will you buy me a new phone _____ a high score on my next exam?" "Yes, of course."
    a) if I get   b) if I'll get   c) if I got

24. _____ you if you don't finish cleaning the kitchen by noon.
    a) I help   b) I'll help   c) I would help

25. Nick _____ his friend's wedding if he weren't on a business trip.
    a) will attend   b) would attend   c) attends

26. Please turn down the music. I can't sleep _____ the noise.
    a) and   b) because   c) because of

27. Bill wanted to eat at a restaurant _____ Mexican food, but he couldn't find one.
    a) served   b) who served   c) that served

28. My uncle has taught English at this school _____ he was 25 years old.
    a) since   b) while   c) when

29. The picture _____ is great. I'll hang it on the wall in my living room.
    a) which drew   b) you drew   c) who you drew

30. You should brush your teeth _____ you go to bed.
    a) before   b) after   c) since

ANSWERS **p.291**

If you are not sure about some answers, go back to the following units:

QUESTION	1	2	3	4	5	6	7	8	9	10	11	12	13	14	15	16
UNIT	87	87	87	87	87	91	91	92	90	88	88	94	94	95	95	87
17	18	19	20	21	22	23	24	25	26	27	28	29	30			
87	87	94	88	88	95	93	93	93	87	94	90	95	89			

Look at the picture and complete the sentences with **There is a** or **There are two/three**/etc. and the nouns in the box. Use the plural form if necessary.

| bird | boy | glass | table | ~~woman~~ |

1. _There is a woman_ on the chair.
2. _____ in the tree.
3. _____ under the tree.
4. _____ on the table.
5. _____ in the water.

 Put the words in *italics* in the correct order.

6. (*me / that pencil / give*)
   "Could you _give me that pencil_ ?" "Sure. Here you are."

7. (*wanted / he / told / me*)
   Mark _____ to go to the beach yesterday. Did he go?

8. (*not / dinner / let's / cook*)
   _____ tonight. I want to go to the Italian restaurant downtown.

9. (*said / she / sleeping / that / was*)
   Julia _____ when I called her.

10. (*a / what / lunch / delicious*)
    _____ ! Everything tasted great.

 Complete the conversations with **too/either** or **so/neither**.

11. I love classical music.	Ian does _too_ .
12. I haven't been to Japan before.	I haven't been there _____ .
13. We'll visit our parents on Christmas.	_____ will Sarah and I.
14. Kim doesn't like beer.	I don't like it _____ . I prefer wine.
15. We've just had lunch.	_____ have we. Let's get some tea.
16. I wasn't good at math when I was young.	_____ was my son.
17. I didn't enjoy the movie.	_____ did I. It was boring.
18. Melvin and I watched the soccer game yesterday.	Really? I did _____ .

Choose the correct one.

19. It is busy at the museum today. _____ a lot of visitors.
    a) There haven't been   b) There have been   c) There is

20. I _____ from Boston. Did you get it?
    a) sent a postcard you   b) sent you to a postcard   c) sent you a postcard

21. "I tried calling Tim many times, but there is no answer." "_____!"
    a) How strange   b) How a stranger   b) What strange

22. "_____ many people at Molly's party?" "Yes. I had a good time with them."
    a) Were there   b) Was there   c) Is there

23. Cathy will _____ . Tomorrow is his birthday.
    a) buy a cake to her father   b) buy a cake her father   c) buy a cake for her father

24. Sharon likes sushi, and her husband does _____ .
    a) either   b) too   c) so

25. _____! Sue looks very cute in it.
    a) This picture look   b) This picture look at   c) Look at this picture

26. Tom said you speak Chinese well. Could you _____ ?
    a) teach Chinese to me   b) Chinese teach me   c) teach Chinese me

27. "I can't cook very well." "_____."
    a) I can either   b) Neither can I   c) Neither I can

28. I'm worried about Mike. He _____ a cold.
    a) he has said   b) had he said   c) said he had

29. _____ the pot! It's still hot.
    a) Do touch   b) Don't touch   c) Not touch

30. Lynn _____ to her house last night, but I was too busy.
    a) said I can come   b) said I could come   c) say I could come

31. "_____ a break." "OK. Let's sit on that bench for a minute."
    a) Let's take   b) Let's taking   c) Let's not take

32. _____ any onions in the grocery store, so I couldn't make onion soup.
    a) There were   b) There weren't   c) There wasn't

33. Steve _____ the meeting was canceled, so I stayed home.
    a) said me   b) told to me   c) told me

ANSWERS p.291

If you are not sure about some answers, go back to the following units:

QUESTION	1	2	3	4	5	6	7	8	9	10	11	12	13	14	15	16
UNIT	96	96	96	96	96	97	99	98	99	98	100	100	100	100	100	100
17	18	19	20	21	22	23	24	25	26	27	28	29	30	31	32	33
100	100	96	97	98	96	97	100	98	97	100	99	98	99	98	96	99

GRAMMAR GATEWAY
BASIC

APPENDIX

The appendix can help you understand basic essentials for learning English and organize what you have learned in the units. It also introduces helpful phrases.

Parts of Sentences and Parts of Speech

Knowing the basic elements of grammar will help you understand English better. Let's take a look at which elements make up sentences and what parts of speech you need to know.

A Parts of Sentences

Subject and verb

She runs.
<u>subject</u> <u>verb</u>

Every English sentence needs a subject (**She**) and a verb (**runs**). The subject is the person/thing that does the action of the verb in the sentence. The verb expresses the action or state of the person/thing.

Object

He drives **the bus**.
<u>subject</u> <u>verb</u> <u>object</u>

Some sentences have a subject (**He**), a verb (**drives**), and an object (**the bus**). The object is the person/thing that is affected by the action of the verb.

Complement

We are **hungry**.
<u>subject verb complement</u>

Some sentences have a subject (**We**), a verb (**are**), and a complement (**hungry**). A complement is used to describe or identify the subject or object.

Modifier

They hike **every weekend**.
<u>subject</u> <u>verb</u> <u>modifier</u>

In addition to the basic elements of a sentence (**They hike**), there are also modifiers (**every weekend**). A modifier is an additional element that is not necessary in the sentence. However, it adds more details to a sentence.

B Parts of Speech

Noun Name of a person/place/thing

girl　**desk**　**music**

The name of everything around us, like **girl**, **desk**, and **music**, is a noun.

Pronoun Words used instead of nouns

Jack is my brother.
He is a doctor.
pronoun

The pronoun (**He**) is used instead of the noun (**Jack**). We use pronouns when it is not necessary to repeat nouns.

Verb Words that describe an action or state

She **plays** the piano.
verb
She **likes** music.
verb

Verbs (**plays**, **likes**) describe the action or state of someone or something.

Adjective Words that describe nouns

It's a **red** car.
adjective

An adjective (**black**) describes a noun (**car**). Adjectives show the condition or characteristic of a noun.

Adverb Words that modify verbs, adjectives, other adverbs, or the entire sentence

It runs **fast**.
adverb

An adverb (**fast**) adds more information to a verb (*runs*), an adjective, an adverb, or a sentence.

Conjunction Words that connect other words or sentences

She has a dog **and** a cat.
conjunction

A conjunction (**and**) connects two or more words (**a dog**, **a cat**) or sentences.

Preposition Words used before nouns or pronouns

The telephone is **on** the table.
preposition

A preposition (**on**) is used before a noun (**table**) or pronoun. Prepositions indicate places, locations, time, and more.

Interjection Words that express emotions

Wow!
interjection

An interjection (**Wow**) is a word that we use to express our emotions, like when we are happy, angry, surprised, and more.

2 | **Irregular Verbs** (UNIT 13, 18, 33)

 In English, some verbs change forms in an irregular way. Let's take a look at the list of common irregular verbs.

Present	Past	Past Participle
am/is/are	was/were	been
awake	awoke	awoken
beat	beat	beaten
become	became	become
begin	began	begun
bite	bit	bitten
blow	blew	blown
break	broke	broken
bring	brought	brought
build	built	built
burn	burned/burnt	burned/burnt
buy	bought	bought
catch	caught	caught
choose	chose	chosen
come	came	come
cost	cost	cost
cut	cut	cut
dive	dived/dove	dived
do	did	done
draw	drew	drawn
dream	dreamed/dreamt	dreamed/dreamt
drink	drank	drunk

Present	Past	Past Participle
drive	drove	driven
eat	ate	eaten
fall	fell	fallen
feel	felt	felt
fight	fought	fought
find	found	found
fly	flew	flown
forget	forgot	forgotten
forgive	forgave	forgiven
freeze	froze	frozen
get	got	got/gotten
give	gave	given
go	went	gone
grow	grew	grown
hang	hung	hung
have	had	had
hear	heard	heard
hide	hid	hidden
hit	hit	hit
hold	held	held
hurt	hurt	hurt
keep	kept	kept

Present	Past	Past Participle	Present	Past	Past Participle
know	knew	known	set	set	set
lay	laid	laid	shine	shone	shone
lead	led	led	shoot	shot	shot
learn	learned/learnt	learned/learnt	show	showed	shown/showed
leave	left	left	shut	shut	shut
lend	lent	lent	sing	sang	sung
let	let	let	sit	sat	sat
lie	lay	lain	sleep	slept	slept
light	lit	lit	speak	spoke	spoken
lose	lost	lost	spend	spent	spent
make	made	made	stand	stood	stood
mean	meant	meant	steal	stole	stolen
meet	met	met	swim	swam	swum
pay	paid	paid	take	took	taken
put	put	put	teach	taught	taught
quit	quit	quit	tear	tore	torn
read [riːd]	read [red]	read [red]	tell	told	told
ride	rode	ridden	think	thought	thought
ring	rang	rung	throw	threw	thrown
rise	rose	risen	understand	understood	understood
run	ran	run	upset	upset	upset
say	said	said	wake	woke	woken
see	saw	seen	wear	wore	worn
sell	sold	sold	win	won	won
send	sent	sent	write	wrote	written

3 Spelling Rules (UNIT 4, 6, 13, 18, 33, 41, 46, 66, 73, 74)

English verbs, nouns, adjectives, and adverbs can change forms. Let's take a look at the following charts to see how they change.

A Spelling rules for verbs

Adding -(e)s (When the subject is **he/she/it**/etc. in the present simple)

+ -s	bring → brings make → makes sleep → sleeps	eat → eats sing → sings meet → meets	walk → walks drink → drinks live → lives
-ss/-sh/-ch/-x + -es	pass → passes miss → misses kiss → kisses wash → washes wish → wishes	finish → finishes brush → brushes watch → watches catch → catches teach → teaches	reach → reaches search → searches fix → fixes mix → mixes relax → relaxes
-o + -es	go → goes	do → does	
Consonant + -y →change **y** to **i** + -es	study → studies carry → carries worry → worries reply → replies	copy → copies marry → marries bury → buries fly → flies	cry → cries hurry → hurries apply → applies try → tries
Vowel + -y →+ -s	play → plays say → says	stay → stays pay → pays	buy → buys enjoy → enjoys

Adding -ing

+ -ing	go → going	be → being	know → knowing
-e →remove e + -ing	come → coming dance → dancing have → having make → making write → writing	take → taking leave → leaving live → living ride → riding shine → shining	smile → smiling prepare → preparing give → giving choose → choosing drive → driving
-ee + -ing	agree → agreeing	see → seeing	
-ie →change ie to y + -ing	die → dying	lie → lying	tie → tying
Words ending with single vowel + single consonant →add the same consonant + -ing	run → running sit → sitting cut → cutting set → setting	put → putting hit → hitting stop → stopping swim → swimming	plan → planning shop → shopping begin → beginning refer → referring

Adding -(e)d

+ -ed	answer → answer**ed** want → want**ed**	help → help**ed** watch → watch**ed**	clean → clean**ed** work → work**ed**
-e/-ee/-ie + -d	create → create**d** believe → believe**d**	agree → agree**d** die → die**d**	tie → tie**d** lie → lie**d**
Consonant + -y →change **y** to **i** + **-ed**	try → tr**ied** study → stud**ied**	cry → cr**ied** rely → rel**ied**	marry → marr**ied** apply → appl**ied**
Vowel + -y → + -ed	enj**oy** → enjoy**ed**	del**ay** → delay**ed**	pl**ay** → play**ed**
Words ending with single vowel + single consonant →add the same consonant + -ed	prefer → prefer**red**	st**op** → stop**ped**	pl**an** → plan**ned**

B Spelling rules for nouns

Adding -(e)s (Plural nouns)

+ -s	hat → hat**s** flower → flower**s**	dog → dog**s** girl → girl**s**	book → book**s** tree → tree**s**
-s/-ss/-sh/-ch/-x + -es	bus → bus**es** glass → glass**es**	dish → dish**es** brush → brush**es**	sandwich → sandwich**es** box → box**es**
-f(e) →change f to v + -es	shelf → shel**ves** leaf → lea**ves**	wolf → wol**ves** wife → wi**ves**	knife → kni**ves** life → li**ves**
Consonant + -y →change **y** to **i** + **-es**	baby → bab**ies** city → cit**ies**	lady → lad**ies** family → famil**ies**	berry → berr**ies** story → stor**ies**
Consonant + -o → + -es	potato → potato**es** *BUT:* kilo → kilo**s**	tomato → tomato**es** piano → piano**s**	hero → hero**es** photo → photo**s**
Vowel + -y → + -s	b**oy** → boy**s**	d**ay** → day**s**	monk**ey** → monkey**s**

C Spelling rules for adjectives/adverbs

Adding -ly to adjectives (Adverbs)

+ -ly	careful → careful**ly**	quick → quick**ly**	slow → slow**ly**
-y →change y to i + -ly	angry → angr**ily** lazy → laz**ily**	noisy → nois**ily** busy → bus**ily**	sleepy → sleep**ily** lucky → luck**ily**
-le →-ly	probab**le** → probab**ly**	incredib**le** → incredib**ly**	

Adding -(e)r to adjectives/adverbs (Comparatives)

1-syllable adj./adv. + -er	fast → fast**er**	cheap → cheap**er**	high → high**er**
1-syllable adj./adv. ending with e →+ -r	nic**e** → nic**er**	clos**e** → clos**er**	wid**e** → wid**er**
1-syllable adj./adv. ending with single vowel + single consonant →add the same consonant + -er	big → big**ger**	hot → hot**ter**	thin → thin**ner**
2 or more syllable adj./adv. ending with y →change y to i + -er	eas**y** → eas**ier** early → earl**ier**	heav**y** → heav**ier** happ**y** → happ**ier**	hungr**y** → hungr**ier** prett**y** → prett**ier**

Adding **more** before adjectives/adverbs (Comparatives)

more + 2 or more syllable adj./adv.	beautiful → **more** beautiful	recently → **more** recently

Adding **the** + -(e)st to adjectives/adverbs (Superlatives)

1-syllable adj./adv. + -est	fast → the fast**est**	cheap → the cheap**est**	high → the high**est**
1-syllable adj./adv. ending with e →+ -st	nic**e** → the nic**est**	clos**e** → the clos**est**	wid**e** → the wid**est**
1-syllable adj./adv. ending with single vowel + single consonant →add the same consonant + -est	big → the big**gest**	hot → the hot**test**	thin → the thin**nest**
2 or more syllable adj./adv. ending with y →change y to i + -est	eas**y** → the eas**iest** early → the earl**iest**	heav**y** → the heav**iest** happ**y** → the happ**iest**	hungr**y** → the hungr**iest** prett**y** → the prett**iest**

Adding **the most** to adjectives/adverbs (Superlatives)

most + 2 or more syllable adj./adv.	beautiful → the **most** beautiful	recently → the **most** recently

* Consonant: **b, c, g, y**, etc. / Vowel: **a, e, i, o, u**
* Syllable: a unit of sound with one vowel sound. (**cheap** = one syllable, **mar·ket** = two syllables)

4 | **Short Forms** (UNIT 1, 2, 3, 8, 12, 14, 18, 23, 26, 31, 32)

In everyday conversation, we use short forms such as **I'm**, **she's**, etc. more often than **I am**, **she is**, etc. Let's take a look at the following ways to make short forms.

A Short forms

	be (am/is/are)	have (have/has)	will	would
I	I'm	I've	I'll	I'd
he	he's	he's	he'll	he'd
she	she's	she's	she'll	she'd
it	it's	it's	it'll	it'd
we	we're	we've	we'll	we'd
you	you're	you've	you'll	you'd
they	they're	they've	they'll	they'd

B Short forms (Negative)

be	do	have	will, would, etc.
is not → **isn't** / **'s not** are not → **aren't** / **'re not** was not → **wasn't** were not → **weren't**	do not → **don't** does not → **doesn't** did not → **didn't**	have not → **haven't** / **'ve not** has not → **hasn't** / **'s not**	will not → **won't** / **'ll not** would not → **wouldn't** / **'d not** cannot → **can't** could not → **couldn't** should not → **shouldn't**

C Exceptions in short forms

's is the short form of **is** or **has**.
- "Where is David?" "He**'s** in the garage. He**'s** fixing his car." (= He is in the garage. He is fixing his car.)
- My brother loves traveling. He**'s** been to almost every country in South Asia. (= He has been to . . .)

We do not use short forms in short answers with **yes**.
- "Are you Mr. Jones?" "Yes, **I am**." (*NOT* Yes, I'm.)
- "Is he a professor?" "Yes, **he is**." (*NOT* Yes, he's.)

5 | **Nouns and *the*** (UNIT 47, 50)

Some nouns look like countable nouns, but they are actually uncountable nouns. Some nouns are used with or without **the**. Let's take a look at the list of common nouns that can be confusing.

A Nouns we cannot count

bread	cheese	chocolate	food	fruit	meat
paper	money	wood	furniture	luggage	ice
information	advice	news	work	cash	

- "Do you want some **bread**?" "Yes, please."
- We need to order some **paper**. We don't have any for the copy machine.
- I asked Tony for **information** about the seminar.

B Nouns without *the*

home	go home	(be) at home		
work	go to work	(be) at work	start work	finish work
school	go to school	(be) at school	start school	finish school
college	go to college	(be) in college		
bed	go to bed	(be) in bed		
church	go to church	(be) in church	(be) at church	
prison	go to prison	(be) in prison		

- Ms. Smith was very sick, so she had to **go home** early.
- Please call me after 3 p.m. I won't **be at work** until then.
- "When did your child **start school**?" "Last September."
- I **was in college** two years ago. I graduated last year.
- "I'm getting sleepy. I think I'll **go to bed**." "OK. Good night."
- The Morgans **are at church** now. They will come back in an hour.

C Names with or without *the*

Names we use with **the**

Ocean/Sea	the Pacific	the Atlantic	the Black Sea	the Mediterranean Sea
River	the Amazon	the Nile	the Thames	the Mississippi River

- **The Mediterranean Sea** is north of Africa.
- **The Amazon** is the second longest river in the world.

Names we use without **the**

Mountain	**Mount Fuji** **Mount Everest** **Mount St. Helens** **Mount Kilimanjaro** *BUT*: We use **the** with mountain ranges. **the** Himalayas **the** Alps **the** Andes **the** Rocky Mountains
Lake	**Lake Michigan** **Lake Victoria** **Lake Superior** **Lake Titicaca**
Continent	**Asia** **Africa** **Europe** **North/South America** **Australia** **Antarctica**
Country	**Italy** **France** **Korea** **Germany** *BUT*: We use **the** with countries that contain States, Kingdom, or Republic. **the** United States of America **the** United Kingdom **the** Czech Republic

- **Mount Fuji** is the highest mountain in Japan.
- I want to take a trip to **the Himalayas**.
- My family visited **Lake Michigan** during our vacation.
- People in **Asia** eat a lot of rice.
- "How long does it take to fly to **Italy**?" "I can check for you."
- Washington, D.C. is the capital of **the United States of America**.

6 | **Pronouns** (UNIT 51, 53)

 In English, pronouns change form when they are the subject or the object, or when they show possession. Let's take a look at the different forms of pronouns.

	Subjective pronouns	Objective pronouns	Possessive adjectives	Possessive pronouns
Singular	I	me	my	mine
	you	you	your	yours
	he	him	his	his
	she	her	her	hers
	it	it	its	-
Plural	we	us	our	ours
	you	you	your	yours
	they	them	their	theirs

Subjective pronouns
We use **I/we/you**/etc. *(pronouns)* as the subject of a sentence.

Objective pronouns
We use **me/us/you**/etc. *(pronouns)* as the object of a sentence.

Possessive adjectives
We use **my/our/your**/etc. *(adjectives)* before nouns to talk about possession.

Possessive pronouns
We use **mine/ours/yours**/etc. *(pronouns)* to talk about something that belongs to someone.

7 | Adjective + Preposition Phrases (UNIT 84)

In English, there are many adjective + preposition phrases, such as **sorry about** and **good at**. Let's take a look at the following list of common phrases along with examples.

about	**angry about**	
	● Mr. Meyer is **angry about** the mistakes in the report.	
	excited about	
	● Brian is **excited about** the football game today.	
	nervous about	
	● "Are you **nervous about** your first day at work?" "Not really."	
	sad about	
	● Kristy is **sad about** moving. She'll miss her friends.	
	sorry about	
	● I'm **sorry about** being late. It won't happen again.	
	sure about	
	● I asked how much the car was, but the salesperson wasn't **sure about** the price.	
	upset about	
	● We had a party, and our neighbors were **upset about** the noise.	
	worried about	
	● "I'm so **worried about** tomorrow's exam." "I'm sure you'll do great."	
at	**angry at**	
	● I'm **angry at** Betty for losing my cell phone.	
	good at	
	● Christine is really **good at** mathematics.	
	mad at	
	● My wife is **mad at** me for forgetting our anniversary.	
	surprised at	
	● John was **surprised at** his high score on the test.	
for	**bad for**	
	● Coffee isn't **bad for** your health if you don't drink too much.	
	crazy for	
	● Monica is **crazy for** romance novels.	
	famous for	
	● This restaurant is **famous for** its pasta.	

from	**different from** ● "How is this apartment **different from** the other one?" "This one has an extra bathroom."
in	**dressed in** ● Edward is usually **dressed in** a suit at his office. **interested in** ● I'm **interested in** art, so I often go to galleries.
of	**afraid of** ● You don't have to be **afraid of** my dog. He won't bite. **certain of** ● Erica loves me. I'm **certain of** it. **full of** ● "Why is the store **full of** people?" "There's a sale today." **jealous of** ● A lot of people are **jealous of** Kenny because he's so popular. **proud of** ● My sister won a prize. I am very **proud of** her. **sick of** ● I'm **sick of** eating the same thing every day. Let's try a new restaurant. **tired of** ● Brent was **tired of** waiting for his friend, so he went home.
to	**clear to** ● The instructions for my new camera aren't **clear to** me. **identical to** ● "What do you think of my new laptop?" "It looks **identical to** Jeremy's." **married to** ● Jeff has been **married to** his wife for six years. **nice to** ● Matt, you should be **nice to** your younger sister. **similar to** ● Your shoes look **similar to** mine.
with	**angry with** ● I'm sorry I broke your glasses. Please don't be **angry with** me. **busy with** ● Brenda had to quit the softball team. She was too **busy with** work.

careful with

- Be **careful with** that plate. It's hot.

familiar with

- I'm **familiar with** this neighborhood. I've lived here for a long time.

happy with

- Thomas is very **happy with** his new bicycle.

pleased with

- "Are you **pleased with** your birthday gifts?" "Yes! I love them."

wrong with

- What's **wrong with** the TV? It doesn't work.

8 | Phrasal Verbs (UNIT 85, 86)

In English, there are many phrasal verbs, such as **talk about** and **look at**. Let's take a look at the following list of common phrasal verbs along with examples.

about	**care about** ● I don't **care about** music much. **hear about** ● "Have you watched the movie *Titan*?" "No, but I **heard about** it from my friend." **talk about** ● Everyone was **talking about** Clara's new car. **think about** ● Donna **thought about** changing jobs, but she decided to stay. **worry about** ● "I'm sorry I'm late." "Don't **worry about** it. I didn't wait long."
at	**arrive at** ● We **arrived at** the station on time. **laugh at** ● I **laughed at** my friend's funny story. **look at** ● The visitors are **looking at** paintings in the gallery. **smile at** ● Look! The baby is **smiling at** us.
around	**go around** ● **Go around** the corner and you'll see the bank. **look around** ● "How can I help you?" "I'm just **looking around**." **pass around** (= "offer") ● Andy, could you **pass around** the snacks to the guests? **show around** (= "guide") ● Could you **show** me **around** the city? **take around** (= "guide") ● Follow me, and I will **take** you **around** the museum. **turn around** ● We're driving the wrong way! We have to **turn around**.
away	**go away** ● I want to **go away** for my vacation. **keep away** ● Please **keep away** from that wall. The paint is still wet.

	pass away (="die")	
	● My grandmother **passed away** last year.	
	put away (="return something to where it belongs")	
	● Could you **put away** your books?	
	run away (="leave quickly")	
	● The dog jumped over the fence and **ran away**.	
	take away (="remove")	
	● The medicine will **take away** the pain.	
	throw away (="put in a trash can")	
	● I **threw away** my old furniture before I moved here.	
back	**call back**	
	● Tim will **call** you **back** in one hour.	
	come back	
	● "When will you **come back**?" "In two hours."	
	get back	
	● We **got back** from our trip to Rome this morning.	
	go back	
	● Can we **go back** home to get my bag?	
	look back	
	● I **looked back**, but nobody was there.	
	pay back (="return money that was borrowed")	
	● Can I borrow $50? I can **pay** you **back** tomorrow.	
	take back (="return something", "receive again")	
	● This hair dryer isn't working. I'm going to **take** it **back** to the store.	
	turn back (="stop and return")	
	● The traffic was bad, so we had to **turn back**.	
down	**break down** (="stop working")	
	● The photocopier **broke down**, so I couldn't copy the report.	
	calm down	
	● Ms. Ling told her children to **calm down** and be quiet.	
	fall down	
	● Thomas **fell down** and hurt his leg.	
	lie down	
	● I'm not feeling well. I'm going to **lie down** for an hour.	
	look down	
	● **Look down** there! There are ducks under the bridge.	
	pass down (="give to a younger person")	
	● My older sister's clothes were **passed down** to me.	
	put down	
	● **Put down** that vase! You will break it.	

shut down (="stop", "close")
● Make sure to **shut down** the computer before you leave.

slow down
● You need to **slow down**. You're driving too fast.

sit down
● Please **sit down** and wait for a few minutes.

take down (="write down")
● "Did you **take down** the salesperson's phone number?" "Yes."

turn down
● "Dan, the music is too loud." "Sorry, I'll **turn** it **down**."

write down
● I'll **write down** some directions for you.

for

apply for
● Ms. Miller **applied for** the bank job, but she didn't get it.

care for (="protect", "have affection for")
● My mom **cares for** me when I'm sick.

look for (="search for")
● "What are you **looking for**?" "My wallet."

search for
● I **searched for** my keys all morning, but I couldn't find them.

wait for
● Don't **wait for** me. I'm going to be late.

work for
● Mr. Donald **works for** the restaurant.

in

bring in
● "It's raining now." "Really? We have to **bring in** the laundry!"

check in (="report someone's arrival")
● Please **check in** at least an hour before your flight.

fill in
● You need to **fill in** the blanks with your name and address.

get in
● Hurry up and **get in** the car. It's getting late.

hand in (="submit")
● Students must **hand in** their homework after class.

stay in
● It was snowing too hard, so we **stayed in**.

off

call off (="cancel")
● Derek **called off** the party because he was sick.

drop off
● Can you **drop** me **off** at the mall? I need to buy some clothes.

	fall off	
	● Cindy **fell off** the bicycle and hurt her knees.	
	get off	
	● Daniel **got off** the train at Central Station.	
	put off (= "delay")	
	● Mr. Jenkins **put off** the meeting. He changed it to next Monday.	
	switch off	
	● Please **switch off** your phones during the flight.	
	take off (= "remove clothing", "begin to fly")	
	● Please **take off** your shoes at the front door.	
	turn off	
	● Did you **turn off** the heater when you left home?	
on	**carry on** (= "continue")	
	● The teacher told Jenny to be quiet, but she **carried on** talking.	
	get on	
	● That's our bus. Let's **get on**.	
	go on (= "continue")	
	● "Is my story too long?" "No. It's very interesting. Please **go on**."	
	hold on (= "wait")	
	● "May I speak to Mr. Grey, please?" "**Hold on** and I'll connect you."	
	keep on (= "continue")	
	● "Where's the bank?" "**Keep on** walking straight ahead."	
	put on (= "wear")	
	● Don't forget to **put on** your coat. It's very cold outside.	
	switch on	
	● Don't **switch on** the light. I'm trying to sleep.	
	try on (= "wear or use as a test")	
	● "Can I **try on** this shirt?" "Sure."	
	turn on	
	● Dad **turned on** the TV to watch the news.	
	work on	
	● I'll **work on** my science report after school today.	
out	**bring out**	
	● The company will **bring out** a new product next month.	
	eat out	
	● "Shall we **eat out** tonight?" "That sounds good. What about Italian?"	
	find out (= "discover")	
	● Did you **find out** what happened to Sammy?	
	give out	
	● My parents **give out** gifts every Christmas.	

	go out (= "meet outside")	
	● "What are you doing tonight?" "I'm **going out** with some friends."	
	hand out (= "give")	
	● We'll **hand out** the party gifts after the dinner.	
	look out (= "be careful")	
	● **Look out**! There's a car coming!	
	put out (= "stop")	
	● The men **put out** the fire at the office building.	
	run out	
	● We need to go to the gas station. We might **run out** of gas.	
	take out (= "bring")	
	● Would you **take out** the dishes from the dishwasher?	
	watch out (= "be careful")	
	● **Watch out**! There's a bee by your head.	
	work out (= "exercise")	
	● Todd **works out** at the gym every evening.	
over	**get over** (= "overcome")	
	● Andrew **got over** his cold after only two days.	
	go over (= "review")	
	● Kimberly **went over** her notes before the test.	
	read over (= "read carefully")	
	● We **read over** your report. It was very good.	
	turn over	
	● The pancake was cooked on one side, so Judy **turned** it **over**.	
through	**get through** (= "pass", "contact on the phone", "complete")	
	● Traffic was bad, so it took 20 minutes to **get through** the tunnel.	
	go through (= "pass", "experience")	
	● This train **goes through** Boston.	
to	**belong to**	
	● "Whose car is that?" "It **belongs to** Tim."	
	reply to	
	● I asked Brenda a question, but she didn't **reply to** me.	
	talk to	
	● I **talked to** the neighbors about the noise.	
up	**break up** (= "end a relationship")	
	● Did you hear? Chad and Lisa **broke up**!	
	bring up (= "mention", "raise from childhood")	
	● You **brought up** a good point at the meeting.	
	clean up (= "make neat or clean")	
	● Marina **cleaned up** the kitchen this morning.	

get up (= "stop sleeping")

- When do you usually **get up** in the morning?

give up (= "stop trying")

- I want to **give up** smoking soon.

grow up

- When Timmy **grows up**, he wants to be a singer.

hang up (= "end a phone call")

- Randy **hung up** the phone without saying goodbye.

hurry up

- Bob, you need to **hurry up**. The train leaves in 10 minutes.

look up (= "search")

- "What does this word mean?" "**Look** it **up** in the dictionary."

pick up (= "answer a telephone", "get from somewhere")

- I called Joey three times, but he didn't **pick up**.

speak up (= "speak loudly")

- You need to **speak up**. I can't hear you well.

stand up

- At the wedding, everyone **stood up** when the bride entered the room.

stay up (= "continue to be awake")

- I never **stay up** late on weekdays.

turn up

- I like this song! Could you **turn up** the volume, please?

wake up (= "stop sleeping")

- Tony, **wake up**! It's time for breakfast.

GRAMMAR GATEWAY
BASIC

ANSWERS

PRACTICE Answers

REVIEW TEST Answers

PRACTICE Answers

UNIT 001

A

2. are; we're
3. am; I'm
4. is; it's
5. are; they're
6. is; he's

B

2. is a photographer
3. are in their car
4. are on the stage
5. is a repairman

C

2. I'm *OR* I am
3. It's *OR* It is
4. we're *OR* we are
5. You're *OR* You are
6. It's *OR* It is
7. I'm *OR* I am
8. She's *OR* She is

D

2. 'm 21 years old *OR* am 21 years old
3. is swimming
4. is a high school student
5. are my parents

UNIT 002

A

2. This water isn't
   OR This water is not
3. you're not *OR* you aren't
   OR you are not
4. Mark isn't *OR* Mark is not
5. we're not *OR* we aren't
   OR we are not
6. I'm not *OR* I am not
7. Sharon isn't *OR* Sharon is not
8. My books aren't
   OR My books are not

B

2. Richard isn't 23 years old
   OR Richard is not 23 years old
3. Sally and Alex aren't from Brazil
   OR Sally and Alex are not from
   Brazil
4. I'm not a nurse
   OR I am not a nurse
5. Tomorrow isn't Thursday
   OR Tomorrow is not Thursday

C

2. 're
3. 're
4. 'm
5. 's
6. 'm not
7. isn't
8. 'm not

D

2. isn't *OR* is not
3. are
4. 're not *OR* aren't *OR* are not

UNIT 003

A

2. Is
3. Are
4. Am
5. Is
6. Are
7. Are

B

2. Is it
3. Am I
4. Are you
5. Is today
6. Are Joel and Mary
7. Is she
8. Are we

C

2. No, I'm not

3. No, he's not *OR* No, he isn't
4. Yes, I am
5. No, they're not *OR* No, they aren't
6. No, it's not *OR* No, it isn't
7. Yes, she is

D

2. My name is Chun
3. Are you from China
4. I'm Chinese *OR* I am Chinese
5. Are you in this class
6. we're in the same class *OR* we are
   in the same class

UNIT 004

A

2. sitting
3. writing
4. having
5. coming
6. shopping
7. waiting
8. dying

B

2. 're eating popcorn
   OR are eating popcorn;
   're crying *OR* are crying
3. 's driving *OR* is driving;
   is ringing

C

2. is playing the violin
3. is entering the bank
4. are flying in the sky
5. is standing at the bus stop

D

2. He's having *OR* He is having
3. The children are helping
4. Mitchell is preparing
5. They're jogging
   OR They are jogging
6. I'm tying *OR* I am tying
7. We're selling *OR* We are selling

8. She's getting *OR* She is getting

UNIT 005

A

2. isn't moving *OR* is not moving
3. 're enjoying *OR* are enjoying
4. 're not wearing *OR* aren't wearing
   OR are not wearing
5. is teaching
6. 'm not swimming
   OR am not swimming

B

2. my sister is listening
3. Are you crying
4. Am I singing
5. Are you and Vicky baking
6. The wind is blowing
7. Are your brothers riding
8. Kyle is wearing

C

2. Yes, I am
3. No, I'm not
4. No, he's not *OR* No, he isn't
5. Yes, they are
6. Yes, it is

D

2. I'm having *OR* I am having
3. You're not *OR* You aren't drinking
   OR You are not drinking
4. we're selling *OR* we are selling

UNIT 006

A

2. shines
3. walk
4. ride
5. calls
6. work
7. costs
8. gets

B

2. carries
3. does

4. flies
5. has
6. reaches
7. goes
8. passes

C

2. does
3. has
4. speak
5. plays
6. cry
7. buy

D

2. Your father likes
3. we have
4. I prepare
5. Mom wants

UNIT 007

A

2. leaves home
3. starts work
4. goes to lunch
5. finishes work

B

2. Hannah washes
3. The post office opens
4. Pandas eat
5. My husband and I make
6. Water covers

C

2. collects
3. likes
4. bakes
5. need
6. close
7. jogs

D

2. has
3. live
4. cut
5. hunt
6. needs

UNIT 008

A

2. doesn't understand Chinese *OR*
   does not understand Chinese
3. don't look well
   OR do not look well
4. don't have a lot of homework *OR*
   do not have a lot of homework
5. doesn't watch TV
   OR does not watch TV
6. don't make any noise
   OR do not make any noise
7. doesn't clean *OR* does not clean

B

2. doesn't know *OR* does not know
3. remembers
4. don't want *OR* do not want
5. doesn't like *OR* does not like

C

2. work
3. shows
4. doesn't bite *OR* does not bite
5. don't buy *OR* do not buy
6. snows

D

2. don't eat *OR* do not eat
3. doesn't smell *OR* does not smell
4. hate
5. tastes

UNIT 009

A

2. Does Rosa have a boyfriend
3. Does Mr. Gill need more time
4. Do we know your phone number
5. Do you own a bicycle
6. Does the bus usually arrive
7. Do your kids like dogs

B

2. Do we know
3. Do your children go
4. Does Janet drive
5. Does Ted play
6. Does George work

7. Do you talk

C

2. Yes, I do
3. No, he doesn't
4. Yes, I do
5. No, she doesn't
6. Yes, we do

D

2. I want some mangoes
3. we don't have mangoes
4. Does it taste good

UNIT 010

A

2. is riding; works
3. is playing; designs
4. paints; 's sleeping OR is sleeping

B

2. Angela goes
3. I'm looking OR I am looking
4. The post office doesn't deliver OR
   The post office does not deliver
5. We buy
6. Jason and Fred aren't studying
   OR Jason and Fred are not
   studying
7. Mr. Smith's phone is ringing

C

2. 're swimming OR are swimming
3. spends
4. Do; remember
5. 's attending OR is attending
6. hates

D

2. ✓
3. shop → 're shopping
   OR are shopping
4. ✓
5. isn't having → doesn't have
   OR does not have
6. don't do → 'm not doing
   OR am not doing

UNIT 011

A

2. was at school
3. were at a restaurant
4. was at a store

B

2. The stars were
3. He was
4. These gloves were
5. My friends and I were
6. It was

C

2. was; 'm OR am
3. were; was
4. was; Is
5. are; were
6. was; 's OR is; 's OR is

D

2. was
3. were
4. was
5. is
6. are

UNIT 012

A

2. was asleep
3. wasn't on time
   OR was not on time
4. was angry
5. wasn't happy OR was not happy

B

2. weren't
3. wasn't
4. were
5. was
6. weren't

C

2. Was Howard at the meeting
3. Were you with Jessica
4. Kim and Lucy were there
5. The baseball game was exciting
6. Was your mom a cook

7. I was in Lisbon
8. Were you at the gym

D

2. I wasn't at school
   OR I was not at school
3. you were fine
4. The window was open
5. Were you cold

UNIT 013

A

2. played
3. invited
4. cried
5. went
6. worked

B

2. It closes
3. Laura and Nick got
4. Earth travels
5. We laughed
6. I forgot
7. Jeff flies
8. I need

C

2. ✓
3. meets → met
4. ✓
5. rains → rained
6. wins → won
7. ✓

D

2. took the bus
3. went to bed late
4. studied for our test

UNIT 014

A

2. She didn't read the newspaper OR
   She did not read the newspaper
3. She went to the gym
4. She didn't wash the car
   OR She did not wash the car

5. She attended a cooking class
6. She had lunch with Jackie

B

2. Did Sarah pass
3. Did you read
4. Did someone knock
5. Did you get
6. Did we miss
7. Did Dave grow up
8. Did the Smiths buy

C

2. Did you buy
3. My friends and I didn't visit
   OR My friends and I did not visit
4. Elena met
5. we didn't lock *OR* we did not lock
6. Jake found

D

2. I didn't like *OR* I did not like
3. Did you see
4. Paul watched

A

2. were dancing
3. was carrying
4. were eating
5. was waving

B

2. was listening
3. were attending
4. were playing
5. was crossing

C

2. They're watching
   OR They are watching
3. Alice was lying
4. I was visiting
5. We were standing
6. He's holding *OR* He is holding

D

2. We were practicing

3. I was worrying
4. We were performing

A

2. A woman wasn't sitting here
   OR A woman was not sitting here
3. I was meeting them outside
4. He wasn't carrying a bag
   OR He was not carrying a bag

B

2. Joe and I were enjoying the party
3. Evan was writing an e-mail
4. We were waiting for the bus
5. Was it snowing there
6. Was Sally going to the bank

C

2. Was Victor practicing
3. Eric and I weren't working
   OR Eric and I were not working
4. I was buying
5. Were you walking
6. We were cooking
7. I wasn't talking
   OR I was not talking
8. Was Clara swimming
9. I was sitting
10. Were you and Pete visiting

A

2. used to be
3. used to like
4. used to live

B

2. didn't use to drink
   OR did not use to drink
3. used to eat
4. used to own
5. used to sell
6. didn't use to speak
   OR did not use to speak
7. used to be

C

2. exercises
3. used to listen
4. remember
5. used to go
6. used to take

D

2. used to have
3. used to come
4. used to be

A

2. 's broken *OR* has broken
3. 's eaten *OR* has eaten
4. 's painted *OR* has painted
5. 've made *OR* have made
6. 's taken *OR* has taken

B

2. went; gone
3. bought; bought
4. ran; run
5. played; played
6. wrote; written
7. drove; driven
8. knew; known
9. sent; sent

C

2. hasn't eaten *OR* has not eaten
3. has grown
4. hasn't spoken *OR* has not spoken
5. 've ridden *OR* have ridden
6. haven't seen *OR* have not seen

D

2. Have you studied
3. Has Ben finished the report
4. Have you read
5. Has Amanda called you
6. Have the guests arrived

A

2. 's stayed *OR* has stayed

3. 's driven OR has driven
4. 's grown OR has grown
5. 've lived OR have lived
6. 's caught OR has caught

B

2. have been married for
3. hasn't rained since
   OR has not rained since
4. has driven his car for
5. haven't talked to Ben for
   OR have not talked to Ben for
6. hasn't eaten anything since
   OR has not eaten anything since
7. 've known them for
   OR have known them for

C

2. How long has she played
3. How long have they attended
4. How long has she taken
5. How long has he been
6. How long have you had

UNIT 020

A

2. I've (never) played chess before
3. I've (never) lived in the country
4. I've (never) ridden a roller coaster
5. I've (never) seen a kangaroo
6. I've (never) had a pet

B

2. Have you ever watched an opera
3. Have you ever gone bungee
   jumping
4. Have you ever swum in the ocean
5. Have you ever been to Paris
6. Have you ever run a marathon

C

2. has been
3. 's gone OR has gone
4. 's gone OR has gone
5. 've been OR have been

D

2. Have you watched

3. Have you ever been
4. haven't been OR have not been
5. Have you eaten
6. 've never tried OR have never tried

UNIT 021

A

2. 've been OR have been
3. invented
4. saw
5. has grown

B

2. ✓
3. didn't use → haven't used
   OR have not used
4. knew → has known
5. ✓
6. have visited → visited

C

2. I haven't seen OR I have not seen;
   Brenna talked
3. Ms. Conner spoke; She's taken
   OR She has taken
4. I joined; We've worked
   OR We have worked
5. My plane hasn't arrived
   OR My plane has not arrived;
   It departed

D

2. My parents moved
3. How long have you been
4. I came
5. I've lived OR I have lived

UNIT 022

A

2. 's just dived OR has just dived
3. has just opened
4. 've just met OR have just met

B

2. We've already had
   OR We have already had

3. He's already read
   OR He has already read
4. I've already sent
   OR I have already sent

C

2. Have you visited him yet
3. He hasn't started it yet
   OR He has not started it yet
4. I haven't seen him yet
   OR I have not seen him yet
5. Has Lily called you back yet

D

2. I've already paid the money
   OR I have already paid the money
3. You haven't used it yet
   OR You have not used it yet
4. I've just given that one
   OR I have just given that one

UNIT 023

A

2. You'll find OR You will find
3. They'll win OR They will win
4. She'll return OR She will return
5. We'll need OR We will need
6. It'll help OR It will help

B

2. I'll drive
3. I'll lend you
4. I'll take it

C

2. won't take OR will not take
3. won't forget OR will not forget
4. 'll explain OR will explain
5. won't stop OR will not stop
6. won't sleep OR will not sleep
7. 'll call OR will call

D

2. We'll miss the train
   OR We will miss the train
3. Will you meet me at the airport
4. She'll be here in a minute
   OR She will be here in a minute

5. I'll have the chicken salad
   OR I will have the chicken salad
6. Will your family travel this fall
7. Will Jonathan pass the exam
8. I'll change it OR I will change it

UNIT 024

A

2. 're going to take
   OR are going to take
3. is going to leave
4. 's not going to graduate
   OR isn't going to graduate
   OR is not going to graduate
5. 're not going to be
   OR aren't going to be
   OR are not going to be
6. 'm going to relax
   OR am going to relax
7. 'm not going to rent
   OR am not going to rent

B

2. 's going to watch a movie
   OR is going to watch a movie
3. 're going to have a sale
   OR are going to have a sale
4. 's going to take an exam
   OR is going to take an exam

C

2. Is Tina going to meet
3. I'm going to see
   OR I am going to see
4. Are you going to buy
5. Brian is going to join
6. They're going to get
   OR They are going to get
7. Is it going to hurt

D

2. I'm going to cook
   OR I am going to cook
3. It's going to be OR It is going to be
4. Are you going to need
5. I'm not going to need
   OR I am not going to need

UNIT 025

A

2. 's seeing a movie
   OR is seeing a movie
3. 's taking a swimming lesson
   OR is taking a swimming lesson
4. 's visiting her grandparents
   OR is visiting her grandparents
5. 's attending Karen's wedding
   OR is attending Karen's wedding
6. 's leaving for Brazil
   OR is leaving for Brazil

B

2. leaves at 2:15
3. arrives at 2:00
4. begins at 9:00

C

2. Are you staying
3. The plane departs
4. Brenda is moving
5. It begins
6. The meeting finishes
7. I'm meeting OR I am meeting

D

2. leaves
3. 'm visiting OR am visiting
4. starts

UNIT 026

A

2. can fix
3. can talk
4. can't join OR cannot join
5. can't wear OR cannot wear
6. can stay
7. can't understand
   OR cannot understand

B

2. Can your parrot talk
3. Can Karen help
4. Can you attend
5. Can your husband drive
6. Can you tell

C

2. can't see OR cannot see
3. can walk
4. could buy
5. can't remember
   OR cannot remember
6. couldn't ride OR could not ride
7. can have
8. couldn't answer
   OR could not answer

D

2. he could understand
3. I could speak
4. I can't remember
   OR I cannot remember
5. Can I join
6. You can come

UNIT 027

A

2. might travel by train
3. might go to Martin's wedding
4. might move next month

B

2. might help
3. might not come
4. might try
5. might not fit
6. might not like
7. might invite
8. might not buy
9. might be
10. might rain

C

2. might not have
3. might go
4. might not be

UNIT 028

A

2. Can I take this seat
3. Can I get some water
4. Can I close the window

B

2. May I help
3. Can you call
4. May I look
5. May I borrow
6. Can you check
7. Can you buy

C

2. Could you come to my office
3. Could you sign this form
4. Could you read me another story
5. Could you move your car
6. Could you tell me your name

D

2. can you tell me
3. Can you say the number
4. Can I see it

UNIT 029

A

2. must stop
3. must not smoke
4. must not take
5. must turn off

B

2. had to
3. had to
4. must
5. had to
6. must

C

2. must not feel
3. must miss
4. must not know
5. must hurt
6. must not have
7. must read

D

2. must not forget
3. must check
4. must not go

UNIT 030

A

2. have to see
3. have to wait
4. have to use

B

2. have to teach
3. doesn't have to take
4. doesn't have to call
5. have to ask
6. don't have to pay
7. has to attend

C

2. doesn't have to write
3. don't have to run
4. have to be *OR* must be
5. must not park
6. have to pack *OR* must pack
7. don't have to bring
8. has to leave *OR* must leave

D

2. We had to stop at the gas station
3. I didn't have to tell John
4. Allan didn't have to buy a ticket
5. I had to change my clothes

UNIT 031

A

2. should buy
3. should speak
4. should wash

B

2. Children shouldn't watch
   OR Children should not watch
3. you should return
4. We should take
5. I shouldn't go *OR* I should not go
6. We shouldn't make
   OR We should not make

C

2. Should I find a new job
3. should I go to the airport
4. Should I change the channel?

5. Should I invite

D

2. I think she should stay at home
   OR I don't think she should stay at
   home
3. I think he should sell his computer
   OR I don't think he should sell his
   computer
4. I think she should go out for
   dinner *OR* I don't think she should
   go out for dinner

UNIT 032

A

2. Would you turn off
3. Would you bring
4. would you answer
5. Would you drive
6. Would you show

B

2. Would you like some wine
3. Would you like some ice cream
4. Would you like an orange

C

2. Would you like to go shopping
3. Would you like some bread
4. Would you like a map
5. Would you like to see the menu
6. Would you like to play golf

D

2. I'd like to study biology
   OR I would like to study biology
3. I'd like a ticket
   OR I would like a ticket
4. I'd like to invite you
   OR I would like to invite you
5. I'd like that blue sweater
   OR I would like that blue sweater
6. I'd like to visit Europe
   OR I would like to visit Europe

UNIT 033

A

2. 's written *OR* is written
3. aren't required
   OR are not required
4. Are; made
5. 's delivered *OR* is delivered
6. isn't used *OR* is not used
7. Are; baked

B

2. It was built
3. My dog is washed
4. It was canceled
5. His paintings are displayed
6. These photos were taken

C

2. can be worn
3. can't be shown
   OR cannot be shown
4. won't be announced
   OR will not be announced
5. must be paid

D

2. needs
3. start
4. aren't allowed
5. be used

UNIT 034

A

2. were sent
3. hit
4. was grown
5. found

B

2. was told
3. 's kept *OR* is kept
4. was repaired
5. are used
6. were worn

C

2. will deliver → will be delivered
3. were enjoyed → enjoyed

4. must cook → must be cooked
5. stole → were stolen
6. ✓
7. Does food allow → Is food allowed
8. was broken → broke

D

2. I was invited by the Millers
3. Those buildings were designed by Mr. Lee
4. The book will be signed by the author
5. This place is visited by many tourists
6. The television was invented by John Baird
7. A traffic jam can be caused by an accident

UNIT 035

A

2. The cookies are
3. Has Ted done
4. Does Mitchell live
5. Was Julie sleeping
6. We should take
7. Have you found
8. can I ask you

B

2. Have
3. Does
4. Did
5. Are
6. Has
7. Were
8. Do

C

2. ✓
3. was → did
4. ✓
5. Who the girl is → Who is the girl
6. ✓
7. you bought → did you buy

D

2. When are you moving to Australia
3. Where will you meet him
4. Can you come to my office

UNIT 036

A

2. What did John send
3. Who did they visit
4. What did he eat

B

2. What sports do you play
3. Who are you inviting
4. What fruit does that store sell
5. Who should I contact
6. What is the problem

C

2. Which book
3. Which car
4. Which shirt

D

2. Which
3. What
4. Who
5. Which
6. What
7. Which
8. What

UNIT 037

A

2. Why
3. When
4. Where
5. Why
6. Where

B

2. When will your parents be
3. Where do you live
4. Why should I wear
5. Why are you bringing
6. Where is she from
7. When is Sharon leaving

C

2. When did Ivan leave the office
3. When does the bus come
4. Why is the mall closed
5. Where can I find the elevator

D

2. Where
3. When
4. Where
5. why

UNIT 038

A

2. How did you come
3. How can I turn off
4. How do your kids get to
5. How should we prepare

B

2. How was the concert
3. How is the food
4. How are your parents
5. How was your holiday

C

2. How old
3. How much
4. How often
5. How far
6. How long
7. How much
8. How tall
9. How many

D

2. How is the scent
3. How much is it
4. How long will it take

UNIT 039

A

2. didn't you
3. don't they
4. hasn't she
5. can't you
6. isn't it

B

2. have you
3. am I
4. can he
5. are you
6. do we

C

2. wasn't it
3. can you
4. is it
5. haven't you
6. does she
7. aren't they

D

2. No
3. Yes
4. No
5. No
6. Yes

E

2. isn't it
3. didn't you
4. haven't you

UNIT 040

A

2. why Emily was late
3. where I parked my car
4. what I should write in the report
5. when John will be back
6. why the manager called me
7. how you can answer this question

B

2. Do you know where they lived before
3. Do you know what Tony does
4. Do you know how many children they have
5. Do you know what their hobbies are

C

2. if (*OR* whether) many people came to the party

3. if (*OR* whether) Annie is going to visit us tomorrow
4. if (*OR* whether) you've seen my brother *OR* if (*OR* whether) you have seen my brother
5. if (*OR* whether) Joey can play the violin
6. if (*OR* whether) Hannah has gone home

D

2. where the station is
3. how I can buy a ticket
4. if I'll arrive at the airport
   OR if I will arrive at the airport

UNIT 041

A

2. Losing
3. making
4. Wearing
5. watching
6. Swimming
7. Planting

B

2. reading that book
3. talking about her
4. Eating too much food
5. Running with these old shoes

C

2. Riding a roller coaster is exciting
   OR Riding a roller coaster is scary
3. Taking a taxi is cheap
   OR Taking a taxi is expensive
4. Traveling alone is safe
   OR Traveling alone is dangerous
5. Playing chess is fun
   OR Playing chess is boring

D

2. promises to be home by 6
3. needs to finish the report by Monday
4. plans to visit her grandparents tomorrow
5. hopes to win a Nobel Prize

6. expects to get the job

UNIT 042

A

2. hiring
3. to do
4. to help
5. singing
6. to believe

B

2. opening the door
3. cleaning the bathroom
4. to buy this house
5. to play the flute
6. looking at me

C

2. choose to become
3. avoids driving
4. expect to spend
5. gave up smoking

D

2. enjoy going
3. hope to have
4. mind working

UNIT 043

A

2. going
3. feeling *OR* to feel
4. to join
5. writing *OR* to write
6. driving *OR* to drive
7. learning

B

2. stop laughing
3. stop to ask
4. Stop worrying
5. stop to buy
6. stop to take

C

2. to finish
3. going

4. taking
5. to call

D

2. to draw → drawing
3. ✓
4. moving → to move
5. to paint → painting
6. ✓

UNIT 044

A

2. want us to have
3. want me to move
4. want you to call

B

2. allowed Ben to use the camera
3. told Brian to answer the phone
4. expected David to call back soon
5. wanted Nick to speak louder
6. advised Nancy to go to bed

C

2. me run
3. him buy
4. me drive
5. us stay
6. them pay

D

2. help you find *OR* help you to find
3. help you carry
   OR help you to carry
4. help you answer
   OR help you to answer
5. help you wash
   OR help you to wash

UNIT 045

A

2. post office to send a package
3. hospital to visit his friend
4. library to return a book
5. zoo to see the pandas

B

2. to get some fresh air
3. to help him
4. to buy some ice cream
5. to stay healthy
6. to make an appointment

C

2. time to visit
3. questions to ask
4. games to play
5. book to read
6. snacks to share

D

2. things to do
3. work to finish
4. meetings to attend
5. time to talk

UNIT 046

A

2. feet
3. days
4. ladies
5. children
6. benches
7. parties
8. wives
9. knives
10. kilos
11. loaves
12. friends

B

2. a book
3. babies
4. tomatoes

C

2. loaf → loaves
3. child → children
4. ✓
5. peach → peaches
6. boy → boys
7. womans → women
8. ✓
9. photoes → photos

10. ✓

D

2. knife
3. knives
4. people
5. jacket

UNIT 047

A

2. air
3. rain
4. an umbrella
5. a taxi
6. salt
7. a man
8. an orange

B

2. apples
3. snow
4. a bicycle
5. sugar
6. a baby
7. a dog
8. music
9. water
10. flowers

C

2. ✓
3. egg → eggs
4. an information → information
5. teacher → a teacher
6. ✓
7. times → time

UNIT 048

A

2. pants
3. fish
4. a key
5. glasses
6. sheep
7. An apple

B

2. two cartons of milk
3. a piece of cake
4. three cans of soda
5. a loaf of bread

C

2. two box of cereals
   → two boxes of cereal
3. ✓
4. sock → socks *OR* a pair of socks
5. deers → deer
6. ✓
7. ✓
8. snows → snow
9. papers → paper

D

2. slices of pizza
3. cup of coffee; cans of soda
4. bottle of water

UNIT 049

A

2. an apple
3. a ticket
4. the office
5. the bill
6. a car

B

2. an accident
3. the cake
4. a funny joke
5. the window
6. the phone
7. a heater
8. an exam

C

2. a question
3. The water
4. an umbrella
5. the key
6. the book
7. a problem
8. a mountain
9. the suit

10. an orange

UNIT 050

A

2. the radio
3. golf
4. the moon
5. math

B

2. the ocean
3. history
4. the Internet
5. The government
6. baseball
7. breakfast
8. the world

C

2. go home
3. go to the airport
4. go to the movies
5. go to work
6. go to the bank

D

2. police → the police
3. ✓
4. sun → the sun
5. at the home → at home
6. ✓
7. the politics → politics

UNIT 051

A

2. it
3. He
4. me
5. They
6. us

B

2. her; She
3. He; him
4. you; you
5. We; us
6. They; them

C

2. It
3. him
4. us
5. They
6. We

D

2. Us → We
3. ✓
4. I → me
5. ✓
6. Them → They

A

2. It's 12:30 *OR* It is 12:30
3. It's warm *OR* It is warm
4. it's close *OR* it is close
5. It's summer *OR* It is summer
7. It's Tuesday *OR* It is Tuesday
8. It's 15 miles *OR* It is 15 miles
9. It's December 25th
   OR It is December 25th
10. It's 8 o'clock *OR* It is 8 o'clock

B

2. It
3. they
4. you
5. It
6. We
7. It
8. It

C

2. Is it midnight
3. It's 2 p.m. *OR* It is 2 p.m.
4. It's summer *OR* It is summer;
   it's very warm *OR* it is very warm

A

2. my bag
3. your key
4. our dog
5. his ball

B

2. his
3. hers
4. yours
5. theirs

C

2. its
3. your
4. Our
5. hers
6. theirs

D

2. Whose glasses; his
3. Whose wallet; yours
4. Whose scarf; hers

E

2. mine
3. yours
4. his
5. his

A

2. Laura's husband
3. our kids' presents
4. your brother's boat
5. Richard's voice
6. her friends' problems

B

2. Scott's
3. The Andersons'
4. Lucy's
5. Kevin's

C

2. the price of this chair
3. the title of the book
4. the number of your hotel room
5. the top of the mountain
6. the start of the year

D

2. ✓
3. parents's → parents'

4. the page's top
   → the top of the page
5. Rose' → Rose's
6. ✓
7. Mr. Cowan → Mr. Cowan's
8. ✓
9. The best friend of Mia
   → Mia's best friend
10. ✓

A

2. yourself
3. ourselves
4. myself
5. himself

B

2. herself
3. him
4. her
5. himself
6. himself

C

2. I made dinner by myself
3. He went to the park by himself
4. I was shopping by myself
5. She was playing games by herself
6. We're traveling by ourselves
   OR We are traveling by ourselves

D

2. me
3. yourself
4. yourself
5. them
6. myself

A

2. that book
3. that painting
4. this ring

B

2. that

3. Those
4. this
5. that
6. This
7. those
8. These

C

2. How much are those socks
3. How much is that cake
4. How much are these spoons
5. How much is this perfume
6. How much are those sunglasses

D

2. that
3. these
4. those
5. Those

A

2. one
3. ones
4. one
5. one
6. ones

B

2. a new one
3. some cheap ones
4. an important one
5. some chocolate ones
6. a bigger one
7. an exciting one

C

2. Which ones
3. Which one
4. Which one
5. Which ones

D

2. big one
3. green ones
4. red ones

A

2. any snow
3. some paper
4. any sports
5. any trains
6. some friends
7. some rest
8. any money

B

2. any
3. some
4. any
5. any
6. some

C

2. something
3. Someone OR Somebody
4. somewhere

D

2. somewhere
3. someone OR somebody
4. anything
5. something
6. anywhere
7. Something
8. anyone OR anybody

A

2. no bread
3. no money
4. no tickets
5. no choice
6. No children
7. no rain
8. no windows

B

2. any; No
3. none
4. any
5. no
6. any
7. None

C

2. nowhere
3. nothing
4. nothing
5. nowhere
6. no one OR nobody

D

2. no
3. any
4. none

A

2. There isn't much space
3. There isn't much money
4. There are many kids
5. There isn't much bread

B

2. much interest
3. much furniture
4. many cups
5. many dogs
6. much information
7. much time

C

2. a lot of coffee
3. a lot of vegetables
4. a lot of fun
5. a lot of noise

D

2. much OR a lot of
3. a lot
4. a lot
5. much OR a lot of
6. a lot
7. a lot of
8. A lot
9. a lot of
10. much OR a lot of

A

2. a little water

3. a few roses
4. a few tickets

B

2. little information
3. Few cars
4. little sugar
5. little space
6. few letters

C

2. little
3. a little
4. a few
5. few
6. little
7. A little
8. few

D

2. few
3. a few
4. little
5. a few

UNIT 062

A

2. all
3. Every
4. All
5. every
6. All

B

2. All students
3. Every flower
4. Every seat
5. All men

C

2. All languages have
3. Every story has
4. All children need
5. All rain comes
6. Every table is

D

2. every weekend

3. every month
4. all week
5. all day
6. every morning

E

2. everywhere
3. everything
4. everyone OR everybody
5. everywhere

UNIT 063

A

2. Both women
3. Neither seat
4. Both cars
5. Neither store
6. Both babies

B

2. Both
3. either
4. Neither
5. both
6. either

C

2. Both novels
3. Both houses
4. Either month
5. Neither kind

D

2. Either
3. both
4. either
5. both

UNIT 064

A

2. Some of them
3. Most of them
4. None of them
5. Most of them
6. Some of them
7. None of them
8. All of them

B

2. Did you catch all of those fish
3. None of us liked it
4. I often visit some of my cousins
5. Most of the shops are expensive
6. None of these buildings were here
7. I put most of mine

C

2. Some animals
3. Most of the work
4. all animals
5. Most trees
6. some of these muffins
7. all of them
8. none of my friends

D

2. Both of our cars
3. Neither of his parents
4. either of the restaurants
5. neither of us
6. both of you

UNIT 065

A

2. long hair
3. old car
4. blue eyes

B

2. cold weather
3. pink roses
4. empty seats
5. medical school

C

2. smells delicious
3. feel scared
4. sounds good
5. tastes great
6. look happy OR feel happy

D

2. black
3. tall
4. kind

UNIT 066

A
2. quickly
3. nervously
4. comfortably
5. brightly

B
2. heavily
3. simply
4. perfectly
5. noisily
6. well
7. automatically

C
2. speak loudly
3. walk; angrily
4. drive safely
5. solve; quickly

D
2. well → good
3. ✓
4. quiet → quietly
5. beautifully → beautiful
6. ✓
7. terrible → terribly
8. ✓

UNIT 067

A
2. interesting
3. seriously
4. smart
5. completely
6. heavily
7. strange
8. regularly

B
2. fast
3. beautifully
4. hard
5. late
6. safely

C
2. easily → easy
3. frequent → frequently
4. ✓
5. sudden → suddenly
6. ✓
7. newly → new
8. noisy → noisily

D
2. quickly
3. nervous
4. long
5. late

UNIT 068

A
2. often
3. sometimes
4. never
5. rarely
6. always
7. usually

B
Sample answers:
2. I sometimes exercise
   OR I rarely exercise
3. I often watch movies
   OR I sometimes watch movies
4. I always read books
   OR I never read books
5. I often clean my room
   OR I rarely clean my room
6. I often listen to music
   OR I sometimes listen to music

C
2. She's always smiling
   OR She is always smiling
3. Nick often plays
4. We'll never move
   OR We will never move
5. You should never leave
6. Danny sometimes meets
7. You can always talk
8. We rarely finish
9. I'm usually free
   OR I am usually free

D
2. 's rarely been *OR* has rarely been
3. 've always wanted
   OR have always wanted
4. 's never ridden
   OR has never ridden
5. 've sometimes felt
   OR have sometimes felt

UNIT 069

A
2. too fast
3. too dark
4. too long
5. too high

B
2. too expensive for us
3. too spicy for me
4. too hard for him
5. too early for them

C
2. too sick to go
3. too heavy to lift
4. too large to see
5. too busy to take

D
2. too much rain
3. too many words
4. too many cars
5. too much food
6. Too many tourists

UNIT 070

A
2. loud enough
3. large enough
4. tall enough
5. long enough

B
2. hungry enough
3. close enough
4. enough information
5. enough paper

6. hard enough
7. enough doctors
8. wide enough

C

2. big enough for two people
3. old enough to drink
4. comfortable enough for me
5. lucky enough to meet

D

2. enough books for the students
3. enough time to get to the station
4. enough exercise to stay healthy
5. enough toys for all of our cousins

UNIT 071

A

2. so tall
3. so heavy
4. so long
5. so small

B

2. so many passengers
3. so much food
4. so many questions

C

2. so many clothes
3. so many languages
4. so much gas
5. so much water
6. so much sugar
7. so many countries
8. so many sisters

D

2. so quiet
3. so many people
4. so high
5. so much time

UNIT 072

A

2. smaller
3. sweeter

4. colder
5. sooner
6. older

B

2. shorter than David
3. warmer than New York
4. longer than the Amazon

C

2. has lower grades than Theo
3. has darker hair than Beth
4. is weaker than steel
5. is noisier than the countryside

D

2. smarter than me
   OR smarter than I am
3. taller than us OR taller than we are
4. faster than her
   OR faster than she is
5. deeper than me
   OR deeper than I can
6. harder than them
   OR harder than they do

UNIT 073

A

2. thinner
3. easier
4. more interesting
5. worse
6. lower
7. earlier
8. bigger
9. more serious
10. farther
11. wider
12. closer
13. better
14. stronger
15. more important

B

2. more expensive than the brown
   cap
3. farther than Seattle
4. faster than the man

5. heavier than the white box

C

2. more carefully
3. hotter
4. more useful
5. larger
6. cheaper
7. happier

D

2. ✓
3. more easy → easier
4. ✓
5. dangerous → more dangerous
6. good → better

UNIT 074

A

2. more beautiful; the most beautiful
3. better; the best
4. cleaner; the cleanest
5. hotter; the hottest
6. happier; the happiest
7. larger; the largest
8. worse; the worst

B

2. the most creative person
3. the strongest animals
4. the busiest man
5. the most delicious dish
6. the freshest vegetables

C

2. more expensive than;
   the most expensive
3. the youngest; younger than
4. higher than; the highest

D

2. is the oldest
3. is the best
4. is the heaviest
5. is the shortest

UNIT 075

A

2. as fast as
3. as cheap as
4. as tall as
5. as heavy as
6. as new as

B

2. can't eat as much as Jim
   OR cannot eat as much as Jim
3. isn't as far as the mall
   OR is not as far as the mall
4. doesn't go to work as early as Ian
   OR does not go to work as early as Ian
5. isn't as high as that tower
   OR is not as high as that tower
6. isn't as cold as Beijing
   OR is not as cold as Beijing

C

2. can eat much more than me
3. is farther than the park
4. goes to work earlier than Sally
5. is higher than this tower
6. is colder than Tokyo

D

2. as carefully as possible
3. as often as possible
4. as loud as possible
5. as quickly as possible

UNIT 076

A

2. on
3. on
4. in
5. at
6. at
7. in
8. in
9. on
10. at

B

2. in
3. At
4. on
5. on
6. At
7. on
8. in

C

2. at his desk
3. in the living room
4. at the mall
5. on the table

UNIT 077

A

2. on 2nd Avenue
3. at a birthday party
4. in the sky
5. on the bus

B

2. at
3. on
4. at
5. on
6. in

C

2. at the concert
3. on the train
4. at Ann's house
5. In a book
6. in prison
7. on the first floor

D

2. in bed
3. at the doctor's office
4. on Main Street
5. at home

UNIT 078

A

2. by *OR* next to
3. behind
4. in front of
5. behind

B

2. over
3. among
4. under
5. between

C

2. in front of
3. next to
4. behind
5. among
6. by
7. over
8. under

D

2. behind
3. next to
4. between

UNIT 079

A

2. is going over
3. 're getting out of
   OR are getting out of
4. is driving along
5. 's walking up *OR* is walking up
6. is passing through
7. is going past
8. 's falling off *OR* is falling off
9. 's walking across
   OR is walking across
10. is driving around

B

2. down
3. under
4. over
5. to
6. into
7. from
8. toward
9. on
10. off
11. through

12. out of

UNIT 080

A

2. at 7:18 p.m. *OR* at 7:18
3. in 1879
4. at night
5. on April 10

B

2. on
3. at
4. On
5. in
6. in
7. at
8. on

C

2. in February
3. at lunch
4. at 10 a.m.
5. on our anniversary
6. in the 20th century
7. in the evening
8. on Saturday night

D

2. on the weekend
3. at 11 o'clock
4. in the morning
5. in the afternoon; at night

UNIT 081

A

2. during
3. during
4. for
5. for
6. during

B

2. During the weekend
3. For eight years
4. During our meeting
5. During the winter
6. For five minutes

7. For about four months

C

2. in
3. during
4. for
5. during
6. within
7. in

D

2. for → during
3. within → in
4. during → for
5. ✓
6. in → within
7. ✓

UNIT 082

A

2. from June to July
3. from 10 a.m. to 7 p.m
4. from Monday to Friday
5. from April 20 to May 5

B

2. 's known Jason since high school
   OR has known Jason since high school
3. hasn't smoked since last year
   OR has not smoked since last year
4. 's been married since July
   OR has been married since July
5. 's had a car since 2014
   OR has had a car since 2014

C

2. by
3. until
4. by
5. by
6. until

D

2. from; to *OR* until
3. by
4. until

UNIT 083

A

2. without his glasses
3. with a swimming pool
4. without a helmet

B

2. by subway
3. with brown hair
4. without a ticket
5. by plane
6. of this pair of jeans
7. on foot
8. without my wallet
9. about the meeting
10. like a fish

C

2. without stopping
3. by turning off the lights
4. at skating
5. about getting a promotion
6. for joining our book club

UNIT 084

A

2. at
3. about
4. of
5. to
6. in
7. for
8. of

B

2. different from
3. proud of
4. full of
5. sure about

C

2. similar to Italian food
3. short of money
4. married to Julia
5. familiar with this city

D

2. busy with

3. sure about
4. mad at

UNIT 085

A

2. 're looking at *OR* are looking at
3. 's asking for *OR* is asking for
4. 's writing to *OR* is writing to

B

2. apply for
3. answer
4. depends on
5. belongs to
6. reach
7. worry about
8. discuss

C

2. ✓
3. called to → called
4. waiting → waiting for
5. ✓
6. reached to → reached

D

2. apply for
3. looking for
4. talk to
5. depends on

UNIT 086

A

2. work on
3. go out
4. slow down
5. get up
6. hold on
7. come back
8. get on
9. eat out
10. get out of
11. hand out
12. take off

B

2. hand in this report
   OR hand this report in
3. take them away
4. clean it up
5. turn on the oven
   OR turn the oven on
6. write it down
7. took out our trash
   OR took our trash out
8. switch on the light
   OR switch the light on
9. call her back
10. turned up the volume
    OR turned the volume up

C

2. drop me off
3. tried it on
4. Turn off the TV *OR* Turn the TV off

UNIT 087

A

2. or do you need more time
3. and it hurt a lot
4. but he couldn't attend
5. but it tasted terrible
6. or do you want to drive yours

B

3. so she bought a new one
4. She bought a new TV because her TV wasn't working
5. so he was very tired
6. He was very tired because he ran for an hour
7. so she took some medicine
8. She took some medicine because she had a headache

C

2. because of
3. because
4. because
5. because of
6. because of

UNIT 088

A

2. When he sat on the chair
3. when they arrived at the theater
4. when it started to rain
5. when he woke up

B

2. Do not use your cell phone while you're driving
3. Can you set the table while I make dinner
4. While I was taking a shower, Tom called me
5. I'll get a shopping cart while you find a parking space
6. While Matt was playing soccer, he got injured

C

2. 'll meet *OR* will meet
3. go
4. 'll wait *OR* will wait
5. cooks
6. come
7. 'll see *OR* will see
8. saves

UNIT 089

A

2. after I took a shower
3. before I ordered a cup of coffee
4. Before I left home
5. After Diane entered the room
6. before the police arrived
7. after he eats breakfast in the morning
8. After the visitors checked out of the hotel

B

2. after reading
3. before the exam
4. before driving
5. after the show
6. after our wedding

284

C

2. Before baking the muffins
3. After pouring the muffin mix
4. before putting the mixture
5. after 25 minutes

A

2. since
3. until
4. since
5. since
6. until

B

2. hasn't called me
   OR has not called me
3. opened last month
4. broke my leg
5. haven't traveled anywhere
   OR have not traveled anywhere
6. 've lost 10 pounds
   OR have lost 10 pounds

C

2. until we arrived at the theater
3. until she showed them the proof
4. until it turns brown
5. until she returned from vacation
6. until the paint dries

D

2. since he lost his camera
3. until he moved to Taiwan
4. since he moved to Taiwan
5. until she bought a car
6. since she bought a car
7. until she got married
8. since she got married

A

2. If the traffic is bad
3. If we are in the same class
4. If I get this job
5. If the guests arrive
6. If the supermarket isn't closed

B

2. I'll become a famous designer
3. I'll make a lot of money if I
   become a famous designer
4. I'll help poor children if I make a
   lot of money
5. I'll feel happy if I help poor
   children

C

2. Holly forgets our appointment
3. You'll feel better
   OR You will feel better
4. Brandon will get it
5. your sister comes to Toronto
6. you're with me
   OR you are with me

D

2. it rains
3. I'll visit *OR* I will visit
4. you want

A

2. If it were sunny *OR* If it was sunny
3. If I were in Paris *OR* If I was in Paris
4. If I had more free time

B

2. It wouldn't be *OR* It would not be
3. she got up
4. Ryan would become
5. I won
6. we wouldn't wear
   OR we would not wear

C

2. If I were you, I wouldn't drive
3. If I were you, I'd say sorry to her
4. If I were you, I wouldn't drink it

D

2. If Ted didn't work in the
   afternoons, he'd get up early
3. If Brenna were busy, she couldn't
   meet us *OR* If Brenna was busy,
   she couldn't meet us

4. If Dan didn't have a knee injury,
   he could play soccer

A

2. If the mall were open
   OR If the mall was open
3. If I find it
4. If Ashley weren't so tired
   OR If Ashley wasn't so tired
5. If the restaurant weren't full
   OR If the restaurant wasn't full
6. If we took 4th Avenue
7. If I see him
8. If she doesn't sleep late

B

2. were fresh
3. 'd attend *OR* would attend
4. 'll pick you up
   OR will pick you up
5. had a car
6. doesn't like coffee
   OR does not like coffee
7. 'd be healthier
   OR would be healthier
8. don't take an umbrella
   OR do not take an umbrella

C

2. rains
3. performed
4. will come

A

2. who has six children
3. who plays the violin
4. who are very famous
5. who fixes cars
6. who is 99 years old

B

2. who
3. which
4. who
5. which

6. who
7. which
8. which

C

2. I bought a new sofa which (*OR* that) was on sale
3. The store which (*OR* that) is around the corner sells magazines
4. The people who (*OR* that) live downstairs are very nice
5. I found a suitcase which (*OR* that) belongs to Mr. Harris
6. Sarah taught the students who (*OR* that) graduated last year
7. A man who (*OR* that) is standing across the street just waved to us
8. We're excited about the festival which (*OR* that) will begin next week

A

2. The dress which I wore
3. the cake which you're baking
4. The show which you were watching
5. The book which Brian Smith wrote

B

2. used to have a friend I trusted
3. know a neighbor that has many pets
4. that drove us to school isn't my sister *OR* that drove us to school is not my sister
5. ate all of the chocolate he bought in Belgium
6. I saw last night is open until next week
7. went to a restaurant that's famous for its dessert *OR* went to a restaurant that is famous for its dessert
8. the boss introduced to us today is going to attend the next meeting

C

2. was sold → which (*OR* that) was sold
3. ✓
4. exercise → who (*OR* that) exercise
5. was → which (*OR* that) was
6. ✓

D

2. which opened
3. who studied
4. you visited

A

2. There are some people
3. There are some fish
4. There is a lake

B

2. There was
3. there aren't *OR* there are not
4. There wasn't *OR* There was not
5. There are
6. there isn't *OR* there is not
7. Are there

C

2. Have there been any visitors
3. There have been a lot of accidents
4. Has there been a change
5. There haven't been many tourists *OR* There have not been many tourists
6. There hasn't been any rain *OR* There has not been any rain

D

2. There weren't many people *OR* There were not many people
3. There isn't a cloud *OR* There is not a cloud
4. Is there a rental shop
5. There was one

A

2. bought Jen a doll
3. showed Kim his room
4. made Jake some coffee

B

2. bought an apartment for him
3. taught music to students
4. show my new car to you
5. made breakfast for me
6. send Christmas cards to his friends

C

2. Did Tim send you those gifts
3. Money can't buy us happiness
4. Laura teaches yoga to students
5. Can you show your passport to me
6. My mother made a sweater for me

D

2. gave a ring to me
3. send your friends invitations
4. make a cake for you

A

2. Slow
3. Wake
4. Do
5. Be

B

2. Don't take
3. Don't swim
4. don't smoke

C

2. Let's listen
3. Let's not watch
4. Let's start
5. Let's not go
6. Let's ask

D

2. How expensive

3. How exciting
4. What a nice car
5. What lovely flowers
6. What a great view

UNIT 099

A

2. They said (that) they were getting married
3. She said (that) she was on vacation
4. They said (that) they were going out
5. He said (that) he would call (Betty *OR* her) later
6. She said (that) she couldn't find her dog

B

2. They told me (that) they were getting married
3. She told me (that) she was on vacation
4. They told me (that) they were going out
5. He told Betty (*OR* her) (that) he would call (her) later
6. She told Mark (*OR* him) (that) she couldn't find her dog

C

2. told
3. said
4. said
5. told
6. told
7. said
8. told

UNIT 100

A

2. too
3. either
4. too
5. either
6. too
7. either

8. either

B

2. Neither have I
3. So can Brian
4. Neither is Maria
5. So are we
6. Neither does mine
7. Neither was the salad
8. So do Jim and Emily

C

2. either
3. So
4. too
5. So
6. either
7. Neither
8. too
9. Neither
10. So

REVIEW TEST Answers

TEST 1

2. works; 's listening *OR* is listening
3. is reading; teaches
4. is shopping; helps
6. Is Mom making pancakes
7. We don't use it *OR* We do not use it
8. Do you know him
9. Lisa and Anton aren't from England
   OR Lisa and Anton are not from England
10. Julia doesn't wear glasses
    OR Julia does not wear glasses
12. Do you practice
13. Do birds eat
14. Is it raining
15. Does Brian take
16. Are you watching
17. Does she work
18. Are you ready

20. b)	21. b)
22. a)	23. b)
24. c)	25. b)
26. c)	27. a)
28. b)	29. a)
30. a)	31. a)
32. c)	33. a)

TEST 2

2. walked
3. visited
4. saw
5. took
6. bought
8. I didn't see *OR* I did not see
9. Was Susie
10. I have
11. Did you go
12. Is he
13. I don't know *OR* I do not know
15. Lucy didn't go *OR* Lucy did not go
16. Did Ben clean
17. Were you studying
18. We were waiting

20. a)	21. a)
22. b)	23. a)
24. c)	25. a)

26. a)	27. a)
28. c)	29. c)
30. b)	31. a)
32. b)	33. a)

TEST 3

2. We haven't eaten dinner yet
   OR We have not eaten dinner yet
3. Mark has been to many concerts
4. Has the snow just stopped
5. Aaron and Nick have made some muffins
6. Mandy hasn't ridden a roller coaster
   OR Mandy has not ridden a roller coaster
8. 've known each other *OR* have known each other
9. hasn't rained *OR* has not rained
10. 's been sick *OR* has been sick
12. called
13. 've watched *OR* have watched
14. came
15. got
16. 's grown *OR* has grown
17. broke
18. 's worked *OR* has worked

20. b)	21. a)
22. c)	23. c)
24. a)	25. b)
26. b)	27. b)
28. a)	29. a)
30. b)	31. c)
32. b)	33. a)

TEST 4

2. He's going to marry her *OR* He is going to marry her
3. Are you speaking
4. Are you going to watch the fireworks
5. I won't forget it *OR* I will not forget it
6. Alex and I aren't playing soccer
   OR Alex and I are not playing soccer
8. 's going to drink some wine
   OR is going to drink some wine
9. is going to stop at the light
10. 're going to get on the train
    OR are going to get on the train
12. 'll write *OR* will write

13. won't stay *OR* will not stay

14. 'll turn on *OR* will turn on

15. won't touch *OR* will not touch

16. won't tell *OR* will not tell

17. 'll cook *OR* will cook

18. 'll meet *OR* will meet

20. c)	21. c)
22. b)	23. b)
24. a)	25. c)
26. b)	27. c)
28. a)	29. a)
30. b)	31. a)
32. c)	33. a)

TEST 5

2. He might not come

3. I think he should get

4. Would you like to dance

5. I don't have to go

7. can't use the car *OR* cannot use the car

8. have to call the police

9. might fall down the stairs

10. don't have to be scared *OR* do not have to be scared

11. must fix the roof

13. could

14. didn't have to *OR* did not have to

15. shouldn't *OR* should not

16. must not

17. had to

18. couldn't *OR* could not

20. a)	21. a)
22. a)	23. c)
24. b)	25. a)
26. b)	27. c)
28. c)	29. b)
30. b)	31. a)
32. a)	33. a)

TEST 6

2. were made

3. was written

4. were taken

5. was stolen

7. pets aren't allowed *OR* pets are not allowed

8. The house wasn't sold *OR* The house was not sold

9. The Mona Lisa was painted by Leonardo da Vinci

10. These dishes can't be used
    OR These dishes cannot be used

12. was canceled

13. had

14. was broken

15. didn't finish *OR* did not finish

16. was invented

17. watched

18. wasn't washed *OR* was not washed

20. a)	21. b)
22. a)	23. c)
24. a)	25. b)
26. a)	27. c)
28. a)	29. c)
30. c)	31. b)
32. b)	33. a)

TEST 7

2. What

3. Who

4. Where

5. When

6. Who

7. When

8. What

10. where I can put this

11. why you bought this hat

12. when Erica will get here

14. How much does this necklace cost

15. How many people work here

16. whether you'll be busy *OR* whether you will be busy

17. When did Cindy go

18. Where is this wine from

20. a)	21. b)
22. c)	23. a)
24. a)	25. b)
26. b)	27. a)
28. a)	29. c)
30. c)	31. a)
32. c)	33. b)

TEST 8

2. waiting in line *OR* to wait in line

3. singing

4. cooking

5. to go to the museum

6. reading books *OR* to read books

8. to send

9. make *OR* to make

10. eating

11. stay

12. moving

13. to learn

15. Aaron let me use his

16. Does Kim need to buy

17. Nicole taught me to dance

18. Swimming is good

20. c)	21. a)
22. b)	23. a)
24. b)	25. c)
26. b)	27. c)
28. b)	29. c)
30. c)	31. c)
32. b)	33. a)

7. few

8. many

9. every

10. a little

11. much

12. all

13. little

15. Both of them are

16. Most of my cousins live

17. he has none

18. Neither of them is mine

20. c)	21. a)
22. a)	23. b)
24. a)	25. c)
26. b)	27. c)
28. a)	29. c)
30. b)	31. b)
32. c)	33. a)

TEST 9

2. many students attend the concert

3. some snow on the road

4. get a glass of orange juice

5. buy new ones

7. principal's office

8. David's seat

9. Andersons' house

10. Sam's suitcases

12. an umbrella

13. salt

14. a taxi

15. the drums

16. the airport

17. money

18. information

20. c)	21. b)
22. c)	23. a)
24. a)	25. c)
26. b)	27. b)
28. a)	29. c)
30. c)	31. c)
32. a)	33. b)

TEST 11

2. 's sitting uncomfortably

3. 's thinking hard

4. 're shouting angrily

6. is rarely crowded

7. not tall enough to ride

8. too tired to go

9. enough for everyone

10. can always use my car

12. good

13. larger

14. more beautiful

15. highest

16. hottest

17. faster

18. strong

20. c)	21. b)
22. a)	23. b)
24. c)	25. c)
26. a)	27. a)
28. a)	29. b)
30. b)	31. b)
32. b)	33. c)

TEST 10

2. any

3. some

4. any

5. no

TEST 12

2. at work

3. on the 4th floor

4. at home

5. in the bathroom
7. by this Friday
8. For five years
9. in 10 minutes
10. from Korea
11. to Germany
12. behind the curtains
13. down the stairs
15. turn on the air conditioner
     OR turn the air conditioner on
16. excited about the trip
17. spends money on unnecessary things
18. clean up the trash *OR* clean the trash up

20. a)	21. b)
22. c)	23. b)
24. c)	25. a)
26. c)	27. c)
28. c)	29. b)
30. b)	31. c)
32. b)	33. a)

7. told me he wanted
8. Let's not cook dinner
9. said that she was sleeping
10. What a delicious lunch
12. either
13. So
14. either
15. So
16. Neither
17. Neither
18. too

20. c)	21. a)
22. a)	23. c)
24. b)	25. c)
26. a)	27. b)
28. c)	29. b)
30. b)	31. a)
32. b)	33. c)

TEST 13

2. or should we take a bus
3. because I drank too much wine last night
4. but she couldn't come
5. so she took some medicine
7. if I finish work
8. if I were you *OR* if I was you
9. since she left the company
10. when Martin opened it
11. while she's on vacation *OR* while she is on vacation
13. who was on TV last night
14. (who) she met during the trip
15. (which) Ted's dad built

17. b)	18. c)
19. c)	20. b)
21. c)	22. c)
23. a)	24. b)
25. b)	26. c)
27. c)	28. a)
29. b)	30. a)

TEST 14

2. There is a bird
3. There is a table
4. There are three glasses
5. There are four boys

GRAMMAR GATEWAY
BASIC

INDEX

INDEX

The numbers in the index are unit and section numbers.

HACKERS

Grammar
Gateway
Basic

Hackers Language Research Institute
23, Gangnam-daero 61-gil, Seocho-gu, Seoul, Korea
Inquiries publishing@hackers.com

ISBN 978-89-6542-318-8 (13740)

Printed in South Korea

4 5 6 7 8 9 10   26 25 24 23 22

Strengthen your English skills!
HackersIngang (HackersIngang.com)

• MP3 files for use with this book
• Video lectures on basic-level grammar
• Free English content and online forums